The Art and Business of Songwriting

The Art and Business of Songwriting

LARRY D. BATISTE

Oxford University Press is a department of the University of Oxford. It furthers
the University's objective of excellence in research, scholarship, and education
by publishing worldwide. Oxford is a registered trade mark of Oxford University
Press in the UK and certain other countries.

Published in the United States of America by Oxford University Press
198 Madison Avenue, New York, NY 10016, United States of America.

© Oxford University Press 2024

All rights reserved. No part of this publication may be reproduced, stored in
a retrieval system, or transmitted, in any form or by any means, without the
prior permission in writing of Oxford University Press, or as expressly permitted
by law, by license, or under terms agreed with the appropriate reproduction
rights organization. Inquiries concerning reproduction outside the scope of the
above should be sent to the Rights Department, Oxford University Press, at the
address above.

You must not circulate this work in any other form
and you must impose this same condition on any acquirer.

Library of Congress Cataloging-in-Publication Data
Names: Batiste, Larry D., author.
Title: The art and business of songwriting / Larry D. Batiste.
Description: [1.] | New York : Oxford University Press, 2024. |
Includes bibliographical references and index. |
Identifiers: LCCN 2023045532 (print) | LCCN 2023045533 (ebook) |
ISBN 9780199893126 (paperback) | ISBN 9780199893102 (hardback) |
ISBN 9780190651046 (epub) | ISBN 9780197751350
Subjects: LCSH: Popular music—Writing and publishing. |
Popular music—Vocational guidance.
Classification: LCC MT67 .B27 2024 (print) | LCC MT67 (ebook) |
DDC 782.42/13—dc23/eng/20230928
LC record available at https://lccn.loc.gov/2023045532
LC ebook record available at https://lccn.loc.gov/2023045533

DOI: 10.1093/oso/9780199893102.001.0001

Paperback printed by Marquis Book Printing, Canada
Hardback printed by Bridgeport National Bindery, Inc., United States of America

Table of Contents

A Note from the Author — ix
Acknowledgments — xi
Introduction — xiii

PART I: THE ART

1. Ready, Set, Go! — 3
  Self-Inventory: Preliminary Reflections — 3
  Self-Inventory Exercise: Art — 6
  Self-Inventory Exercise: Business — 8
  Taking Action — 12

  Songwriter Spotlight: Salaam Remi — 16

2. Writing Songs That Connect — 20
  A Catchy Title — 21
  How to Find a Title — 21
  Develop the Concept — 25

  Songwriter Spotlight: Ivan Barias — 30

3. Building a Song — 34
  The Driver — 34
  Song Sections — 35
  Song Structure — 37
  Summary — 43

  Songwriter Spotlight: Lamont Dozier — 44

4. Let the Music Play — 47
  Music Theory and Songwriting — 47
  Notes, Intervals, Scales — 48
  Know Your Chords — 55
  Creating a Sound — 58
  Chord Progressions — 61
  Bring in the Rhythm — 63
  Creating Contrast — 65
  Understanding Music Genres — 68
  Summary — 71

  Songwriter Spotlight: Donald Lawrence — 73

Table of Contents

5. Writing Unique and Memorable Melodies — 75
Elements of a Memorable and Unique Melody — 75
Other Considerations — 79

Songwriter Spotlight: Narada Michael Walden — 83

6. Finding the Right Words to Say — 89
Lyric Toolbox — 90
The Story — 91
Improper Grammar — 92
First, Second, Third Person — 92
Creative and Easy to Follow — 93
Song Sections and Their Functions — 93
Lyric Structure — 95
Writing Lyrics to Existing Music or Melodies — 99

Songwriter Spotlight: DJ Toomp — 103

7. Rewriting — 105
Flexibility — 106
Momentum — 107
Rhythm — 107
Tempo — 108
Music — 108
Lyrics — 108
Melody — 109
Less Is More — 110
When Is the Song Finished? — 110

Songwriter Spotlight: Bonnie Hayes — 112

PART II: THE BUSINESS

8. Building a Songwriting Career — 121
Phase One: Business Housekeeping — 122
Royalties — 123
Establishing a Publishing Company — 127
Getting Things Started — 129
Phase Two: Personal Housekeeping — 130
Collaborations — 131
A Way of Life — 132
Your Network Is Your Net Worth — 133
Phase Three: Getting Your Song Out There — 135

Songwriter Spotlight: Andre Pessis — 147

9. The Business of Digital Music — 150
Why Digital? — 150
Music Streaming — 150
Getting Paid for Digital Sales and Performances — 151
Digital Music Distribution — 153

Online Marketing and Promotion	154
Time for Release	158
Livestreaming	160
Playlists	161
Songwriter Spotlight: Peter Asher	163
10. Building a Fanbase	166
Image	167
Audience and Message	169
Streaming Music and Promotion Platforms	170
Promotional Tools	171
Live Performances	176
Additional Streams of Income	181
Summary: Building Your Fanbase	183
Songwriter Spotlight: James McKinney	185
11. Internet Radio	187
Benefits for the Independent Artist	188
How Internet Radio Makes Money	189
Getting Your Music Played	190
Starting Your Own Internet Radio Station	193
Songwriter Spotlight: Preston Glass	197
12. D.I.Y. Masters—Finding Success Without a Major Record Label	199
Fantastic Negrito	202
Meklit Hadero	205
Cornell "CC" Carter	211
Kev Choice	215
Index	221

A Note from the Author

While creating the outline for this book, it occurred to me that my approach to songwriting is just one of many methods used by successful songwriters. Songwriters generally select a method or method that best fits their style and overall goals. The joy is in knowing various factors influence one's approach and mastery. No two writers' songwriting methods are the same. You must consider the writer's culture, environment, genre, personality, access, and choice of tools, skills, and experiences. For this reason, it's not surprising to receive such a wide range of different responses along the "What is the best approach to writing a song" spectrum when asking the same questions to several people. For example, producer Narada Michael Walden cites the most important part of the song as the chorus, while producer Saleem Remi says the lyrics or story are the most critical aspect of a hit song. Although many successful songwriters' destination is similar, their journeys are quite uniquely their own.

After many years of writing, analyzing songs, collaborating, and interviewing songwriters, I've concluded there are three main approaches to songwriting:

Spontaneous—This writer experiences the unconstrained, instinctive vibe and revelation of ideas first before organizing the song's structure. An advantage to this method is that the writer provides a much greater platform for unique ideas to enter the process. The flip side is that so much content is generated that it becomes time-consuming trying to select the ideas that are cohesive and consistent with the chosen topic or concept.

Linear—This writer has a structured approach to songwriting. The writer may prefer to write the chorus first or determine the sections (verse, B section, etc.) in advance to know exactly how much time is needed lyrically to arrive at the chorus. This works well for the writer who is confronted with time restrictions. Some find that it's more efficient to work from a blueprint. If you're not an experienced writer, you may have trouble creating fresh ideas using this method.

Combination of Spontaneous and Linear—This writer leaves the door open for creativity while compartmentalizing the activity as it occurs. In other words, the right and left-brain are working simultaneously. What a concept!

The commonality among these great songwriters and producers is their great understanding of their strengths, weaknesses, tools, and natural and learned abilities. With this understanding and knowledge of who they are, they can create a productive working environment where they can comfortably generate great songs.

I am honored to have had the opportunity to sit with some of the most prolific songwriters and producers in the music industry and talk about their philosophy and approach to the craft and art of songwriting. I was quite eager and curious to talk with them, and fascinated to learn how similar and/or different my approach was to theirs. I had the opportunity to catch up with Peter Asher, Ivan Barias, Lamont Dozier, Preston Glass, Bonnie Hayes, Donald Lawrence, James McKinney, Andre Pessis, Saleem Remi, DJ Toomp, and Narada Michael Walden to chat about their methods and approach to writing hit songs. I'd like to share some of these conversations with you in the Songwriter Spotlights throughout the book.

Acknowledgments

First and foremost, I would like to thank God, who has granted me the gift of music, knowledge, blessings, and the opportunity to share my gift. Thank you to Oxford University Press and to the ever-so-patient and talented Norman Hirschy, Academic and Trade Executive Editor, for your confidence in me and this project. Special thanks to project managers Rachel Ruisard at OUP and Jacqueline Pavlovic at Newgen KnowledgeWorks, and copy-editor, Elizabeth Bortka for tying up the loose ends. Thanks to Tom Kenny, for your invaluable contribution as reader and editor during the writing process. Thanks to all the reviewers for your valuable comments. I would like to extend my sincere thanks to my family: mother and father, Roy Adrian and Evola Christine Batiste for laying the foundation and being my biggest cheerleaders at an early age; my mother-in-law, Christinea Beaty Morton, for influencing me to do great things; my wife, Dr. Lynda Batiste Beaty, for her love, inspiration, and willingness to assist me throughout the entire writing process; my daughters, Adrianne, Simone, and Camille Batiste; my brother Roy Batiste and my uncle Bob White at CRW Photos for their unconditional support and inspiration. I also thank my mentors, William "Bill" Bell, Phillip Reeder, Jeffrey L. Graubart, Dr. Steven Savage, Hillel Resner, Quincy Jones, and Amy Tan. I appreciate my mentors for showing me where to look, but not what to see. Thanks to the participants, Peter Asher, Ivan Barias, Cornell C.C. Carter, Kev Choice, Aldrian "DJ Toomp" Davis, Lamont Dozier, Preston Glass, Meklit Hadero, Bonnie Hayes, Donald Lawrence, James McKinney, Fantastic Negrito, Andre Pessis, Salaam Remi, and Narada Michael Walden for sharing your expertise and experiences in the music industry. Thank you to Tony Lufrano for contributing illustrations, and Warren Foster Sr. and Brett Watson at Anointed Media for videoing the interviews. I would also like to extend my gratitude to my music business partner, Claytoven Richardson, and professional organizations: the Recording Academy, West Coast Songwriters, the Arhoolie Foundation, the National Association of Music Merchants, and Music In Schools Today. I'd like to acknowledge Steve Ashman, Dick Bright, Anthony Paule, Christine Vitale, Michael Anthony Quinn Sr., Michael Ashburne, Jefferi Beaty, Donald Washington, Michael Aczon, Jeff "Skunk" Baxter, David Porter, John Lee Hooker Jr., Michael Rogers, and Sheila E. Escovedo for their aide at one point or another. Lastly, I wish to thank my family, friends, and supporters for their love and encouragement throughout my writing journey.

This book is dedicated to songwriters, producers, artists, teachers, and all who advocate for improving the livelihood of music creators.

Introduction

The song is the beginning and the end of everything in the music world. Without the song, the artist has nothing to sing. Without the song, the producer has nothing to produce. Without the song, there's no connection for the listener. The song is the foundation on which the artist and producer build and create the final product for the public's listening pleasure. Great music production on a bad song is like building a mansion on a foundation of quicksand. A bad song sinks immediately. Conversely, a great song plays on forever.

I define a songwriter as someone who writes the music, lyrics, and melody of a song. This book offers an opportunity for the reader to learn and apply the craft of professional songwriting including song structure, lyric and melody writing, and integration of essential elements found in hit songs. In addition, the book discusses critical business aspects of songwriting, such as publishing, networking, and media income.

The book includes interviews from iconic songwriters and producers such as Peter Asher, Lamont Dozier, and Narada Michael Walden, among others; plus, independent recording artists, including Meklit Hadero and multiple Grammy Award winner Fantastic Negrito. Possessing knowledge in both artistic and business aspects of songwriting is essential for a successful career in the music industry. The information in this book applies to every genre of popular music and is written in a manner that is user-friendly to music professionals, as well as music enthusiasts.

One of the most common traits of songwriters and artists before, during, and even at times after success is overcoming the fear of nonacceptance. No matter how confident you are as a songwriter, the fact that music is very subjective constantly puts you in a vulnerable position. Vulnerability will always exist, so we must accept it as a part of a songwriter's DNA. *The Art and Business of Songwriting* is written to provide songwriters with knowledge and confidence that will convert feelings of vulnerability into authenticity. The book is designed for you to discover and develop your authentic voice by helping you to identify your personality traits, skills, passions, and goals while providing information, techniques, and strategies that will help you navigate a successful songwriting career.

There are endless pros and cons to a career in the music industry. The pros are that there are limitless amounts of evolving opportunities and possibilities to explore as technology continuously offers new business models. There is also the satisfaction of earning an income by doing what you love to do, in addition to having the opportunity to travel, collaborate with other artists, engage with fans, and constantly explore new experiences. The obvious con is there is no guarantee of success. Other disadvantages that occur for many up-and-coming songwriters include an unsteady income or having a job that doesn't allow you the time to put into developing a music career, a nontraditional family life, and nonexistent health care benefits and retirement income. In reading this book, my wish is for you to acquire as much information as you can so that you can make intelligent decisions in charting your path.

The Art and Business of Songwriting is a "one-stop shop" resource guide for songwriters who are interested in improving their songwriting skills, developing a fanbase, or writing songs for other artists who already have a fanbase. After reading this book, the reader will be able to identify and use songwriting tools that will generate an artistic and commercial hit. I hope this reading will serve as a good companion for you as you navigate your way through building a songwriting career.

Well, the key to success is getting started. So here we go!

PART I
THE ART

1
Ready, Set, Go!

Developing songwriting skills is an ongoing and evolving process. Many people have good song ideas or can create musical phrases here and there. You may have heard people say that some songwriters are "naturals" or born with "God-given talent." I'm one of those people who say these things, and I truly believe them to be true. Although it's helpful to have natural musical instincts, these attributes are only the beginning of what it takes to advance the art of songwriting.

Becoming a talented and successful songwriter is a learned skill. We see and hear things differently than others. We take mundane conversations and life experiences to new levels; we take sparks and turn them into blazing fires. As we journey through the life of a songwriter on the road to success, we encounter the dynamics of establishing a career. I wish I could tell you the course is a straight shot without any stumbling blocks or obstacles. However, the art and business of songwriting just doesn't work like that.

Self-Inventory: Preliminary Reflections

Although everyone's journey is different, there are some common principles that, if followed, will lead you in the right direction. Getting started is as simple as putting one foot in front of the other. Whether you realize it or not, once you've made up your mind that you're ready to become a songwriter, you've already completed the first hurdle. However, there are still a few questions to answer.

What do I need to get started?

To get started writing songs, you need to be open, honest, dedicated, disciplined, and present—always. Commit to developing your skills. Dedicate time every day to work on songwriting and some related aspect of the music business.

Why is it important to listen to other music?

Like building a masterpiece in any type of structure, it is beneficial to have a wide assortment of tools to work with. Learning several types of music is like adding a variety of tools to your toolbox. Listening to and learning music that is both domestic and global, and in varied musical genres, is a great advantage for any songwriter. Ask yourself: "Why do I like this music?" "Why does this music appeal to other people?" If your goal is to make music that people can relate to, it would be wise to incorporate elements that you and others find appealing into your compositions.

If one of your goals is to write songs for other artists, there's a good possibility that songwriting could lead to producing for other artists, as well. If producing opportunities begin to occur, it is important to dig deeper into more critical aspects of recording, including instrument choices, arrangements, textures, technology, recording techniques, and mixing. Developing these areas is essential in terms of creating your sound and understanding how to achieve desired outcomes for those who may employ you. We are a product of our environment, experiences, and influences. As these elements are incorporated into our system, we can express them in a way that is unique and critical to the development of our style.

Do I need to know how to play an instrument?

Knowing how to play an instrument is certainly helpful, but not mandatory, when setting out to write songs. However, there are several advantages to knowing how to play an instrument. An instrument provides a reference point and accompaniment to lyrics and melodies. It certainly makes arriving at your destination easier, especially when you're ready to make a demonstration recording of your song or teach it to other performers for a live presentation.

Also, the more skilled you are on your instrument or vocals, the more competent and confident you are, and the sharper the tool you will have to work with when developing songs. The better you know how to handle your tool, the more benefits you will receive from it. Thus, the act of songwriting and playing your instrument would become like connecting with an old familiar friend to escape the pressures of the day. I strongly recommend that you learn how to play at least one chordal instrument for songwriting.

I play by ear. Do I need to know music theory?

Playing and creating music by instinct or by ear is a talent that typically comes naturally but can be developed. Music theory is the study and understanding of principles of music and its notation, ranging from basic to complex. Music theory and playing by ear are vital ways to learn about creating music. Each entity can live separately from the other. However, the more integrated, the better.

Understanding music theory and notation is crucial in communicating with musicians or vocalists who read music. Having the ability to communicate and express your ideas to a larger demographic increases the number of possible opportunities for work. Understanding harmonies, chord structures, and progressions, which is a part of music theory, also plays a major role in song arrangements and production. Although this book will not include a section on music theory in its entirety, it will discuss its basic principles—such as understanding chords and progressions as they relate to songwriting—in Chapter 4.

I sometimes hear people say, "I play by ear," as if that is a shortcoming. They feel somehow as if they're not quite adequate as a musician if they do not read music. Many great musicians have never learned to read music. Stevie Wonder and José Feliciano are perfect examples of that.

One advantage to playing by ear is the incredible ear training one develops. Your memorization and retention skills are highly sharpened by this practice. Even though you may not formally learn music theory, all music creators and performers learn some degree of music theory through familiarization and memorization. Possessing great ear training skills allows you the freedom to express and incorporate whatever thoughts, feelings, emotion, or genre sensibility comes to mind.

It's not necessary to know how to notate and read symbols for songwriting once you have committed to memorize patterns, chords, voicing, rhythms, melodies, accents, and sound. However, most songwriters who regularly work with musicians slowly but surely over time learn basic musical languages, such as names of chords, symbols, and time signatures.

Do I have what it takes to be a successful songwriter?

Most people, when thinking of songwriting as an occupation, tend to only consider the creative side of the profession. A great song is a foundation for both the artist and the songwriter's success. However, it is only a part of the tools needed to craft a great career. It is pretty much expected that when presented with an opportunity, this tool will be sharpened and ready to go. Let's touch on a few of the other areas and considerations needed to master the profession of songwriting.

You must commit and be willing to take responsibility for building your career. Think of yourself as a company and apply the principles associated with running a successful operation. You are a songwriting business that consists of both creative and business entities. Educate yourself on how the songwriting business operates so that you'll know how to be most effective. You must be able to use your creativity to generate a product that appeals to a target audience. Can you be both creative and think like a consumer?

You need to know who you are and what you consider to be a success in the music industry. Conduct a self-inventory of your personality and character traits. A self-inventory will help you to identify what success is to you and measure your level of achievement according to personal goals and personality. What are your interests, passions, likes and dislikes, strengths, and weaknesses? Are you self-motivated, shy, outgoing, disciplined? Knowing your personality traits and skills will help you with your artistic development in terms of authenticity, as well as help you to determine what part of your business you're good at and where you will need assistance. After completing the self-inventory, formulate a plan to develop areas where you are strong and strengthen areas where you are weak.

Self-Inventory Exercise: Art

This Self-Inventory exercise is divided into six sections: **Personality Traits; Preferred Working Conditions; Passions; Skills (Art & Business); Goals;** and **Transferable Skills.** Answering these questions will provide valuable insights into your interests, talents, abilities, and values. You will master talents that are strong and identify and develop areas that are weak. You must know where you are to know where you're going.

Personality Traits

How do I feel about myself in general?
Attractive—Above-average; Average; Unattractive
Confident—Comfortable in public; Start conversations; Outgoing; Spontaneous
Shy—Don't like to talk a lot or draw attention to myself; Moderately sociable
Intelligent—Average; Very knowledgeable; Brilliant

What are my professional characteristics?
 Prepared; Perfectionist; Complete tasks immediately; Respect others' time; Organized; Disciplined; Helpful; Punctual; Original; Moral and ethical behavior; Own up to mistakes

Character traits
Am I disciplined?
Am I responsible/dependable?
Am I proactive?
Am I a self-starter?
Am I a creative person?
Am I a private person?
Am I approachable, cordial, forthcoming, enthusiastic?
Do I like to be the leader or visionary; or do I prefer supervision?
Do I like dealing with administrative duties?
Do I like dealing with people?
Do I like working with people who are musically or culturally different than I am?

Do I like creative input when working on other's projects?
Do I prefer to work on projects with people I admire and respect?

What are my negative traits?
Am I abrupt, arrogant, fearful, indecisive, insecure, insensitive, irritable, negative, presumptuous, procrastinating, reactionary, suspicious, tense, unapproachable, uncooperative, shy?

Preferred Working Conditions

Do I like working alone?
Do I like collaborating with a team?
Do I like working in a quiet space?
Do I like working in a shared space?
Do I like working on various projects at once?
Do I like my workplace to be neat?
Do I like my workplace to visually appeal to others?
Do I like working in a mobile environment?
Do I like working outdoors?
Do I like work that is challenging?
Do I work better with strict deadlines?

Passions

Do I like being creative?
Do I like discovering new technology?
Do I like using music technology and computers when creating?
Do I prefer acoustic or traditional instrumentation when recording?
Do I prefer multitracking and layering music parts when recording?
Do I like exploring uncharted territories?
Do I like helping people?
Do I like learning?
Do I like reading?
Do I like working behind the scenes?
Do I like receiving recognition publicly?
Do I enjoy interacting with people?
Do I enjoy dancing?
Do I like working in various fields within the entertainment industry?

Skills

What Music Skills Do I Have?

Answer question and rate your skill level ranging from 1 to 4:
1 = beginner; 2 = average; 3 = proficient; 4 = expert

How would I rate my primary musical talent?
How would I rate my secondary musical talents?
How would I rate my music education background (either formal education or time on task)?
How would I rate my ability to identify and write a commercially successful song?

Self-Inventory Exercise: Business

Managing your songwriting career is like operating a business. Determine the areas of expertise needed to run your company. Setting up your songwriting publishing company and the business of songwriting is discussed in greater detail in Chapter 9. For now, let's examine your innate skills for business. I've identified the following skill areas for you to consider:

Do I have leadership skills?

Visionary and overseer of the team and operations: A leader has a general knowledge of all aspects of the company and how they function.

Do I have the talent and patience to oversee logistics?

Overseer of operations: The person who answers the Who, What, When, Where, and Why by identifying and designating the right person or entity to implement plans.

Do I have postproduction skills?

Creative and artistic skills in post-production are essential. Proficiency in image, graphics, brand/logo, product concept and design, website design, and content development such as print, photography, graphics, and videos is a must to promote products and events. You must have the ability to think like an artist and consumer.

Do I have literary skills?

Basic reading and writing abilities are definite necessities to both the art and business of songwriting. Reading improves your knowledge base, which enables you to write about places and situations that you may not have personally experienced, which also enhances your imagination as well as the ability to discover new business trends. The other side of literary skill is practical: writing effective press releases, newsletters, and other communication tasks.

Am I a good communicator?

Strong communication skills help to develop and strengthen professional relationships between yourself and musicians, organizations, and fans. Proper protocols such as keeping your associates informed and appropriately thanked are key to nurturing relationships with artists and people with whom you conduct business.

Can I oversee the completion of a song production?

The skills required to complete a song production include the ability to identify a hit song, oversee the song arrangement, pre-production, recording, studio, hiring music talent, producing, engineering, mixing, mastering, choose manufacturing options for physical distribution, and/or online distributor.

Do I know how to make my audience aware of my product?

Sales, marketing, promotion, social media, blogs, commercial/noncommercial radio, internet/satellite radio, video, and TV outlets, print media, booking, distribution, merchandise, licensing, and a network of various personal and business resources.

Am I good at networking?

Developing your network is an essential skill used to gain resources and opportunities. Your *network* is your *net worth*. This job requires great communication skills and a confident personality.

Do I like researching?

Discovering and understanding evolving trends, business practices, and tools are essential to your success. Full knowledge of all options is needed to make strategic business decisions, and to seek and take advantage of job opportunities (potential clients, projects, promoters, festivals, showcases, licensing, trends, contacts).

How are my administrative skills?

Understanding and implementation of performance booking, publishing, accounting, legal, registrations, negotiating, budgeting, newsletters, posters/flyers, bar codes, database, and overall operations are needed.

Goals

What are my short-term and long-term goals? Identify your short-term and long-term goals and research the Who, What, When, Where, and Why.

- Recording my own songs
- Having others record my songs
- Developing a fanbase
- Performing my songs in coffee houses, festivals, touring
- Mentoring
- Philanthropy

Transferable Skills

The skills that are used as a professional songwriter are transferable and can be implemented in songwriting, business, and across multiple disciplines.

Below is a list of everyday skills that you may currently use as a songwriter, vocalist, performer, producer, and recording artist.

> Budgeting
> Analysis
> Delegating
> Adapting
> Communication
> Computer software
> Critical Thinking

Finance
Leadership
Listening
Time Management
Organization
Negotiating
Planning
Presentation
Research
Resourcefulness
Social Media
Public Relations
Marketing
Team Building
Networking
Mediation
Strategic Planning
Technology
Positive Attitude

Now that you've looked at yourself and decided that you have what it takes to be a songwriter, it's time to dive into what songwriting actually is.

There are no right or wrong answers to the previous exercises. The self-inventory is simply meant to make you aware of things about yourself that you may like or may want to change. Completing these exercises gives you more clarity and vision of your unique path to a songwriting career that is authentically based on your personality, passions, and skills. Once you've identified your strengths and weaknesses you can begin to develop in areas that need improvement.

Identifying your audience, researching the best ways to connect with them musically and physically, and finding key business contacts are also crucial initial steps in building the core of your company. From understanding the principles of supply and demand, budgets, marketing, social media, relationship building, and trends, to assembling the best team to implement your goals and strategies, to financing, developing an evaluation process, balancing your career with family and relationship commitments—there is a lot to consider in building a career as a songwriter!

Along with the daily details and demands of your business, be prepared to exercise a great deal of patience and flexibility. Overall, operating your business is engaging because you're passionate about what you do. Most of the time, the stumbling blocks will be the various personalities you encounter along the way. Flexibility is a key skill to have in the music industry and life. If you remember that there's more than one way to accomplish a goal, you will be all right.

Always be prepared for spontaneous event networking or impromptu one-on-one business-related conversations. Although you must be willing and ready to go, when necessary, you must become an expert at evaluating propositions so that you spend your time wisely. In general, if there is a possibility of meeting professionals related to your business, you must show up. You never know where or when unexpected opportunities will occur.

Taking Action

Motivation

Anxiety about the outcome of your song or personal issues, fear and insecurity, and the inability to focus are the most predominant motivation killers. These are common conditions that are not exclusive to songwriters but are in fact, a part of life. Unfortunately, these are lifetime conditions that are often arrested but tend to rear their ugly heads from time to time.

Combat these negative thoughts by knowing what triggers your emotions in a good or bad way and figure out how to neutralize them. Use visualization, acknowledgment of your strengths, and success of past and current events in your life as your tools for motivating yourself.

Belief in oneself is both empowering and encouraging. Therefore, making a self-evaluation and having knowledge of your strengths and weaknesses can give you a great sense of direction and motivation. Other ways to get motivated include:

- Remind yourself that this song or project cannot begin without you. It will not happen unless you get it started.
- Remove distractions—social media and your cell phone are on the top of the list of offenders. If you work from home, try to stay away from household distractions such as noticeable repairs, bills, incomplete paperwork, or other obligations.
- Set a designated time and place each day and commit to it.
- Exercise—Being active will boost your mood and energy. It helps to wake up your creativity and gets the juices flowing.
- Remind yourself of the value of time.
- Set deadlines.
- Keep writing in your mind. Collect titles, phrases, situations, and ideas throughout the day.
- Remember your passion for writing music and allow it to fuel your will.

Exercising repetition and development of your skills on your instrument or voice is another way to relieve anxiety, fear, and induce your passion and incentive to write.

Other great motivators are to have gratitude and appreciation for the talent that you have, as well as generate a positive outlook on life. Name it and claim it by setting your goal of writing into action. My theory is that if we remove anxiety and insecurity issues that affect us during the writing process, the inability to focus and create will resolve itself.

Inspiration

There are times when ideas are slow to unfold, and you find yourself searching for inspiration. It can be frustrating. There are also times when ideas are coming so fast that they're overwhelming. What do you do with a bunch of bits and pieces of ideas, some of which may not even fit the original idea you began with, but they're still great ideas?

Don't worry if your ideas are not relevant to the song you're currently writing. Always keep a recording device handy, collect your ideas, and organize later. I think we can all agree that a rapid stream of ideas is the less common of the two issues surrounding inspiration.

It is normal for initial ideas for a song to flow spontaneously, then slow down as you work toward completing the composition. As you learn various steps to take during this process, the journey will become less frustrating and more of a compelling proposition.

Sources of inspiration vary from songwriter to songwriter. Some prefer to count on spontaneous intuition as their approach to songwriting. They initially rely solely on a vibe and feeling to get them started. Once the ideas are flowing, they develop and organize the song from there. Other writers prefer a more structured approach, such as identifying the title, then using the title to inspire the story. Both approaches are a productive way to achieve great results. If you have time restrictions such as a deadline, you may want to use the structured approach.

Finding inspiration lyrically can certainly benefit from using a structured approach. Titles are a great logical source of lyrical inspiration. It makes sense to write the story once the title is in place, as the title is usually the foundation and the inspiration for the story.

A great title can pique a listener's interest before the song is even heard. The title is where every word and aspect of the story usually leads. Finding the inspiration for the title is easier than one might think. Conversations are probably my number one source of inspiration for song titles. Everyday dialogue about real-life situations that truly interest and affect the average person is where I find titles that have the best connection with people. Talking with a friend, family member, or business associate can bring out heartfelt convictions, emotions, topics, a different way of looking at things, or the discovery of a new place.

It's amazing how a location or an object can be the inspiration for a song title. Songs like "Hotel California" by the Eagles, "Made in America" by Toby Keith, "Trampoline" by Shaed, and "Photograph" by Ed Sheeran are a few songs that come to mind. People and fictional characters are also great inspirations. "Steve McQueen" by Sheryl Crow and "Werewolves of London" by Warren Zevon are examples of such songs. At times it may not be the title, but a catchy phrase that will birth a song.

Inspiration for music is derived from just as many sources as inspiration for lyrics. Experimenting with a chord progression, melody idea, or a phrase that excites you is a good way to develop music inspiration for a song. Great chord progressions and melodies that work together are sometimes discovered by simply playing around on your instrument until an idea comes that makes you want to hear it repeatedly.

Most of the time, the drums or percussive rhythm will derive from the music pattern that you establish. If you create the drum pattern first, begin experimenting with chords, melody, and music accents, while going with your instincts, to create a solid music foundation or pattern. I often get rhythm ideas from sounds I hear as I walk past construction sites, or hear street noises, traffic, or a combination of beats or patterns from existing music.

For me, it's easier to develop a song structure based on sections of chords and melody, or music phrases that work together. Once I have established what feels like a verse and chorus, it is easier for me to find a title and write lyrics.

Reading is great because it allows you to know people, cultures, and places you haven't been. Researching topics, networking with bloggers, and looking at headlines from newspapers and magazine articles are great sources of inspiration as well. Success stories about the challenges and victories of up-and-coming songwriters along their road to success can also be a valued source of inspiration.

If I've been at it for a while and am still lost for ideas, I sometimes stop writing and start another activity. Taking a walk, exercising, cooking, shopping, watching TV, or listening to the radio can inspire good songwriting ideas. It's amazing how many ideas come to mind when you're not trying to find them.

Many people are inspired by the act of collaborating with others. Ideas that you may not have ever come up with on your own may be sparked by a word, phrase, title, or the other person's experience, or a shared situation with your collaborative partner.

Listening to and learning song structures of hit songs is an incredible source of inspiration. If you're like me, you believe that you have impeccable taste in music. I'm inspired when I hear songs that make me feel great! What makes the song appealing to you? Is it the beat, memorable melody, the story, the catchy chorus, the emotion, the sound of an instrument or sound of the recording, the chord progression, an unexpected musical section or break, the way the artist performs the composition, or all the above?

Imagination

As previously stated, songwriters hear, see, and understand things differently from other people. The ultimate act of creativity is having the ability to be open to new ideas, concepts, and images inspired by a person, place, thing, event, memory, or resourceful thinking. The ability to express original ideas and concepts in your own unique way is the most important tool in the songwriter's toolbox. Originality and creativity in expressing your ideas make your songs stand out from others' and greatly increase your chances of success.

Don't be afraid to ask yourself "What if?" when creating a new song idea. When you explore all possibilities and go beyond what is present and already stated, you will find new characters, situations, topics, and uncharted territories to write about.

You have gathered by now that the art and business of songwriting is all about your talent, awareness of who you are, confidence, and willingness to take control of your destiny. It's about bringing together your creative side and your organizational side. Ready? Now it's time to act with intent.

Songwriter Spotlight

Salaam Remi

Salaam Remi. Photo by Riccardo Savi/WireImage/Getty Images

Salaam Remi is a record producer, songwriter, and musician who has written and produced recordings such as "All I Want Is You" and "Come Through and Chill" by Miguel, *The United States vs. Billie Holiday* motion picture soundtrack, the *Rush Hour* movie theme, "Here Comes the Hotstepper" by Ini Kamoze, "Lie to Me" by KEM, as well as Nas, Amy Winehouse, Jazmine Sullivan, Fergie, the Fugees, Alicia Keys, Ne-Yo, Whitney Houston, Leona Lewis, Ludacris, James Arthur, Tamia, Ledisi, Toni Braxton, Nelly Furtado, and many other artists, including himself as a solo artist.

Batiste: One of the most exciting things about writing this book is having an opportunity to talk to some of the most famous and important people in the music industry, yet who are often unknown to the public: record producers. Who are some of the people you've worked with?

Remi: I have been working a long time. Over the years, I have worked with the Fugees, Amy Winehouse, Nas, Alicia Keys, Miguel, Jasmine Sullivan, and many others. I am a producer, songwriter, arranger, and musician, and pretty much at this point . . . responsible as an executive at Sony Music, helping to sign and develop new talent.

Batiste: What instruments do you prefer to work with?

Remi: I pretty much play the basic rhythm section, the drums, the bass, the guitar, and the keyboards . . . you know, all types of instruments. But most of all, I play the imagination.

Batiste: Okay, "imagination," that is nicely put. You work with a variety of diverse artists. What do you look forward to when starting a new project?

Remi: It is usually a new voice with a new story. I feel like every day you meet a new person; or if you already know someone . . . they have a story to tell. I love the fact that when I wake up in the morning, I might not know what story I may be laying out by the time I go to sleep. So, it gives me a reason to get up the next day and try it again. I am looking for adventure.

Batiste: Tell me a little bit about the beginning. Was there a particular song or artist that you heard when you were growing up, that made you say, "This is what I want to do"?

Remi: I can't say there was one thing. My dad was in the business. And he did everything for the musicians, from executive to manager. So, I think that I saw it as a potential profession even though I was still going to school for business management and other things that were more scholastic: electronics, business management, you know, anything that sounds good that keeps your parents out of your hair. But at the end of the day, . . . me being a musician and being from a musician family allowed me to excel at this.

Batiste: Right, right. What key elements are necessary for a hit song?

Remi: For me, I am all about lyrics. I have done many years where I focused on music, the beat, and how hot the beat could be. What type of sound, the arrangement, and everything else. But I focus on the lyrics and voice. Once I have a lyrical space and a voice, I feel like a story is being told. Then I can be more creative with the arrangement because I know that the lyrics and the vocals are strong.

Batiste: And what about collaboration? Do you like collaborating? If so, why, and how often?

Remi: Yeah, for me, for the most part, I usually work with the artist. I have not had [as] much . . . success working with the songwriter who is just a songwriter and then giving [the song] to the artist, who is just an artist or a singer. I usually help a singer become an artist by having their lyrical voice also be found so that they can just do what they want to do. And within that, I help them unlock the space where they can take everyday experiences and find a way to articulate them. You know, when we are on our go time, breakfast brings one experience and lunch has another one.

Batiste: Right, I can see how collaborating with an artist as opposed to bringing him or her a completed song from the outside would allow the artist to tell their own story. It personalizes the song and enables him or her to deliver a more authentic performance.

Remi: Totally. It is about telling their story.

Batiste: Do you find it hard to maintain that sense of musical integrity when trying to deliver a hit record?

Remi: Not really. For me, my career has been based on a balance of art and commerce. My most commercial records have been my most artistic ones. So, whether it was the Fugees or Amy Winehouse, none of that stuff was cookie-cutter pop at the time. But it surpassed the pop of the moment. So, for me, it is about staying artistic and then crystallizing whatever that intent is. . . .

Batiste: Right, I can imagine you rely a lot on your creativity. No matter what the genre is, you're able to have all the ingredients that make a hit record.

Remi: It usually is all the lyrics, and everything else from there is what I put around it. The lyrics are the key and for me, then I just come up with something interesting. I listen to a lot of music. Most of the music I make is based on gospel, jazz, blues, and reggae. I like to leave the skin on my chicken, something that has a real continuity. For me, it is always about coming up with something strong and sturdy and then finding the right story to tell over it. If the story is good, then I don't have to ask the question.

Batiste: Speaking of story, do you have any story you could share how a particular song came about, or a writing experience?

Remi: I guess I can say Miguel's single that came out in 2013, "How Many Drinks?" The first day he came to meet me, he had completed pretty much of his album. He came to meet me and I played him some tracks that eventually became "How Many Drinks?" I played the track, and he was like, "Wow, this is great." I said, do you want to write something? So, he wrote basically what sounds like the first verse and the chorus of the song. I was like "Okay, interesting." Then he says "I don't want to be too R&B flavor. I want something with some guitars on it." So, then I was going through some tracks, and I found some tracks that became his first big single "All I Want Is You." When I played it for him, he said, "Okay, that's guitars; it doesn't have any R&B flavor." To him, he just heard something that sounded sort of sinister. I had made it for Ceelo. He was singing all these melodies. He was mainly freestyling for about fifteen minutes. I was like "Okay, there you go." He was like, "But what do I say?" I just looked at him and said, "Why don't you just tell the truth?" And he looked at me like he was a bit hesitant. Then he said "Okay, can you leave the room?" [Laughing] Okay, so I left the room. We were working in my house, so I just went downstairs, and I could hear everything he was doing. But he went on and told the truth and I guess he found his truth in saying, "Regrets gets exhaustin', all I want is you." He told his truth, talking about whoever he was with at the time, something that just stuck at the time. So, I helped unlocked his writing process. Now when I listen to his songs, all I hear is him telling truth. I am sure that is something he incorporates into his writing style. That's all it was: I wanted him to unlock his truth and as you unlock your truth you never run out of good things to say.

Batiste: Yes. The buying public is smart, and they sense an honest record. If you could create a unique pairing of artists to create a great production of music art, what would that combination of artists be?

Remi: That's a good question. I guess I want to hear Dennis Brown, the reggae singer, singing some Marvin Gaye songs. Somewhere in that pocket. Somewhere in there; that's warm and would hit me right. Dennis Brown covering some Marvin Gaye songs. That's my energy.

Batiste: That's a good one. I can dig that. What advice would you give to an upcoming producer-songwriter?

Remi: I think the biggest thing is you must be serious about what you are doing. I was up at 5 am being serious about what I had to do today. At a point where most people would be thinking, "You have achieved it all." I think if there is an effort to be given, give your thousand percent effort. A hundred is not enough. A thousand percent effort; just push all the way with it. And if you are focused on what you want to do and where you are headed with it, eventually you will reach what you want to do.

Batiste: Okay, thank you, I appreciate you.

Remi: No problem, I got your back.

2
Writing Songs That Connect

The composer of a song cannot compose it wrong. I have always held this philosophy because the songwriter has the artistic freedom and responsibility to deliver his or her ideas as moved to do so. A songwriter's only obligation is to be creative and find satisfaction in expressing his or her writing talent.

You must ask yourself, "What do I want to accomplish from my songwriting efforts?" Your writing efforts are motivated by your desired outcome. You may be writing for your enjoyment and not concerned about commercial success or building an audience for your material. If this is the case, you may wish to gloss over this chapter. However, if your goal is just the opposite, and you are trying to build a successful songwriting career, read on.

Most songwriters desire to write songs that are heard and enjoyed by the entire world. However, there are many factors involved in achieving this goal that are beyond the control of the songwriter, such as marketing, press, radio, playlist pluggers, and financial support. Many great songs don't see the light of day. It truly takes a great team working in the business of creating awareness of the song to make it a commercial success.

Therefore, I'm using the term "hit song" to include a song that has every element it takes to become a commercial hit record whether it has the team behind it or not. A great song will always be a great song, no matter if you're able to find a successful placement for it immediately, years from now, or never. The root of success starts with a phenomenal product. Although there are no guarantees of commercial success, you put yourself in a good position by delivering the best product possible.

Hit songs, no matter what genre, must have an appeal that resonates immediately with the listener. The song must have an indefinable likability that touches the heart and soul of the listener. The listener gravitates to the song because there are certain appealing elements—the way the vocals are performed, along with a great storyline; a memorable melody; an irresistible sing-along chorus; the flow of the rhythmic beats; the prominence of an instrument; or keywords in a track.

Regardless of the style of music, these elements enhance the likelihood of the song surviving production trends throughout the years, regardless of personal partiality for the instrumentation or the arrangements.

How do you get started? The simple answer is that a hit song starts with a great musical and/or lyrical idea. The inspired idea may be derived from a guitar riff, bass line, a rhythm, chord progression, memorable melody, or a catchy word or phrase. Or it may be a past or current event that sparks the initial idea. Once the idea is conceived, this inspiration must be shaped and organized into a form that can easily be understood by the listener.

Lyrically, one can start with a relatable idea, whether it be a catchy phrase, a word, or a set of words that evokes emotion, that could fit in any part of a song like a verse, pre-chorus, or chorus. Usually, I like to start the lyric part of the songwriting process by creating a great title and developing the story around the title's topic.

A Catchy Title

The title is one of the most important elements of any song. It clues the listener in on what the song is about. Also, the title helps the writer to develop the blueprint for the composition. No matter what element drives the initial idea, all roads lead to the heart of the song, the title. It takes a clever writer to create a title that conveys the maximum message while using the fewest words possible.

One word song titles that come to mind include "Paparazzi" by Lady Gaga, "Respect" by Otis Redding and remade by Aretha Franklin, "Focus" by H.E.R.; "Butter" by BTS; and "Irreplaceable" by Beyonce. These titles are far more appealing than titles such as "I Love You Because You're Good to Me" or "I Need You Every Day."

Even if your subject matter is one that people are familiar with, try to select the words or phrases that will seize the listener's instant attention. If the subject matter is relatively unknown or has to do with the future, decide if your viewpoint is pessimistic or optimistic. In 1984, Prince released the song entitled "1999" which is one of the most popular party songs and one of the most futuristic titles of all time. It maintained regular airplay and increased sales as the date drew nearer to the year 1999. Most songs that reference the future are optimistic in that they inspire hope. Some other examples include, "Don't Stop Believin'" by Journey, "Best Day of My Life" by American Authors, and "Happy" by Pharrell.

How to Find a Title

A resourceful songwriter learns to pay attention to things going on in everyday life, from the simplest sound to the most complex thoughts, from the sounds of inner-city traffic to imagining the sounds of fleeting love. Songwriters should always be equipped with a notebook and/or recording device, because you never know where or when the next title is going to emerge.

For most people, the preferred device to capture an initial idea is a cell phone. Titles are found in bits and pieces of conversations, images, and situations that surround you daily. Pick key phrases and thoughts that may hit home with listeners. After settling on a title, explore unique ways to express the idea. Search for words that create moods, emotions, and imagery. Once you arrange the words in coordination with the melody and rhythm in a catchy phrase, you are on your way to writing your song.

Creating song titles is a learned talent that is developed with discovery and practice. Some years ago, I ran into an old high school buddy, and we started talking about our experiences as teenagers. My friend made the comment, "Boy, if I only knew then, what I know now." We both laughed at the time and went on to another topic. Reminiscing with my friend brought up fond memories and sparked impressive thoughts. Later that day, I went home and wrote a song entitled "If I Knew Then (What I Know Now)."

A songwriter must make use of metaphors, euphemisms, innuendo, and other devices to capture the interest of the listener. Some of my favorite titles using metaphors and figures of speech include: "OMG (Oh My God)" by Usher featuring Bruno Mars; "Hey Look Ma, I Made It" by Panic! At the Disco; "Still Crazy After All These Years" by Paul Simon; "Practice What You Preach" by Barry White; "With a Little Help from My Friends" by the Beatles; "Leave the Door Open" by Bruno Mars and Anderson Paak; and "High Horse" by Kacey Musgraves.

In most situations, the title is revisited in the chorus. However, there are some cases where the title is not mentioned in the chorus of the song, sometimes not at all. In those cases, the author still uses all the elements associated with a great song. The artist may choose to make the title of the song a word or phrase that expresses the meaning rather than include the actual words in the body of the song. Some examples of songs that do not mention the title in them are: "Pulling Teeth" and "Governator" by Green Day; "On Love, in Sadness" by Jason Mraz; "Drew Barrymore" by SZA; "American Gigolo" by Weezer; and "Dilemma" by Nelly featuring Kelly Rowland.

No matter how creative you are, there are times when you may be dealing with a time constraint, or you may be a victim of brain freeze—what authors call "writer's block." Whatever the reason, there is a remedy. The following song title exercises may be used to jump-start your efforts.

Exercise I: Adjectives and Nouns

A method used to find unique titles is to pair unlikely words together, like adjective and nouns. This exercise is simply called "Adjectives and Nouns." Here is an example of how the exercise works:

1. Make a list of 10 adjectives. This list should be made at random without thinking about the actual choices.
   - Fearless
   - Juicy
   - Happy
   - Sad
   - Reliable
   - Soft
   - Hard

- Generous
- Exceptional
- Healthy

2. Make a list of 10 nouns. This list should be made at random without thinking about the actual choices.
   - Car
   - House
   - Dog
   - Street
   - Ocean
   - Store
   - Cake
   - Concrete
   - Nail
   - Wallet

3. Take a word from the list of adjectives and randomly place it in front of a word from the list of nouns.

Fearless	Car
Juicy	House
Happy	Dog
Sad	Street
Reliable	Ocean
Soft	Store
Hard	Cake
Generous	Concrete
Exceptional	Nail
Healthy	Wallet

Like a hand in a glove, some of these pairings will naturally combine to form a unique title, while other pairings may simply spark great ideas. My favorite combinations from this batch of words are "Hard Cake" and "Exceptional Ocean." I can imagine the story's concepts to accompany these titles! For "Hard Cake," one scenario (and probably the most obvious) could be of a sweet, naive girl desiring to live on the edge.

Exercise II: Single-Word Titles Using Nouns, Adjectives, and Verbs

Another way to generate ideas for song titles is to create "Single Word Titles." Single nouns, adjectives, and verbs make awesome titles. This exercise can initiate some unique ideas for the subject matter. Some examples of hits with single-word *noun* song titles are "Umbrella" by Rihanna; "Airplanes" by B.o.B. featuring Eminem and

Haley Williams; "Shallow" by Lady Gaga and Bradley Cooper; "Money" by Pink Floyd; and "Alright" by Kendrick Lamar.

Adjectives are used to describe or modify a noun. They have a special character and expression of their own, which can be an easy trigger for song ideas. Examples of single-word song titles using *adjectives* include "Speechless" by Dan and Shay; "Beautiful" by Christina Aguilera; "Bulletproof" by LaRoux; "Crazy" by Patsy Cline; and "Levitating" by Dua Lipa featuring DaBaby. Each of these titles opens a Pandora's box of storylines.

As far as creating imagery, there is nothing like the use of an action word to motivate a writer to develop an idea for a story. The word can be taken literally for what it is, or it may inspire a writer to think of words that are opposites of that action word. For example, the word "Go" used in the title "Go Away" could inspire the opening line of "Feel free to stop by anytime." The concept of using opposites, in this case, may lead to the chorus having a great impact when it occurs.

The use of *verbs* may also stimulate you to think of other keywords or phrases that are associated with them in some way. Some well-known examples of verbs as single-word titles include "Burn" by Usher/Nine Inch Nails; "Listen" by Beyonce; "Imagine" by John Lennon; "Dreamin'" by Young Jeezy featuring Keyshia Cole; "Slide" by Goo Goo Dolls and H.E.R.; and "Talk" by Khalid. Each of these titles presents a clear action picture.

Exercise III: Objects in the Room

One of my favorite song title exercises is called "Objects in the Room." In this situation, you simply look around wherever you are and find an object in the room to inspire a title. This may be the only time when an overly furnished room can be used to one's advantage. For example, I was in a lecture room that the previous evening had doubled as a recording lab. This room was loaded with items that projected song titles.

Rug = "You Lie Like a Rug"
Window = "I Can See Right Through You"
Pencil (with broken lead) = "Pointless"
Cords lying on the floor = "My Hands Are Tied" or "I'm Twisted about You"
Speakers = "Speak to Me"

Nonsense Song Titles

For generations, music audiences have enjoyed songs containing words that are entirely made up. Some have meaning, and others have no meaning at all. These nonsense word inventions are usually inspired by a good rhythm, catchy melody, a trend in pop culture, or a phrase. The title may just sound good when it's delivered or repeated. Songs like "La La La" by LMAO; "Blah Blah Blah" by Ke$ha featuring 30H!3;

"Whoop, There It Is" by Tag Team; and "Imma Be" by the Black Eyed Peas fall into this category.

Develop the Concept

Now that you have an interesting title, the next step in connecting to your audience is to develop a captivating concept for the song. Besides a great melody and lyric, people want to be engaged in the subject matter. Create a scenario that listeners can relate to. Being able to identify with the story's character or situation makes the listener feel as if they are a part of the action. Once the concept and the scenario of the story are decided, it is easier to navigate the lyrics to their destination.

Be sure to keep the lyrics conversational, with each line continuing the thought from the previous line while making sure that all lines support the concept of the song. If writing for a particular artist, you should consider the artist you are presenting the song to. Make sure the concept and story are believable and match the character of the artist and his or her fanbase. Whether writing songs for yourself or others, think of yourself as a storyteller. Your job is to encourage the active imagination of the listeners.

Songs incorporate the same characteristics as mini movies, including emotion, mood, suspense, and drama. Things rarely go as intended, so it is important to include twists and subplots in the story. Be creative and make the set of circumstances in your story as true to life as possible. After you have an appealing concept that many people can relate to, write lyrics and melodies that are unambiguous, straightforward, and memorable.

Most importantly, the concept of the music and lyric must be a compatible match.

Popular Concept Ideas

Love
Without a doubt, love is the most universal topic that people want to hear songs about. At some point, in one way or another, love has affected everyone, so it makes sense that the topic resonates with listeners. Love as a subject has limitless territory available to cover. Here are some of the emotions and situations surrounding the topic of love:

- New love
- Seasoned love (better with time)
- Lost love
- Love vs. Lust
- Cheating love
- Toxic love

- Missing love
- Saying goodbye to love
- Looking for love
- Love triangle
- In love with someone who's not in love with you
- Someone in love with you, but you're not in love with them
- Unavailable love
- The fear of falling in love or losing love
- Needing to be loved in a different way
- Run away from love
- Self-love
- Brotherly/sisterly love (family)
- Never been loved
- Too many loves
- Non-committed love
- Out of control love
- Pre-arranged love
- Unexpected love
- Online love
- Older/younger relationship (Fall/Summer)
- Stalking love
- Imaginary love
- Puppy love
- Shy love
- Making love/romance

Friendship and Bonding

Relationships with people in general, whether business associates or neighbors, can be rewarding, disappointing, predictable, and unpredictable. However, it is your friends that you count on to share the good and bad times. The dynamics between friends vary. At times, a friendship can demand the same amount of energy that would be given to a loved one. Close friends may eventually bond into a brotherhood or sisterhood that blood family cannot match.

Most people care for friends in a strong and deeply emotional manner. Therefore, friendships and bonding are in second place when it comes to the most popular topics for songwriting. Personal conversations and unique situations that you care about are the sources of inspiration for many song concepts. Here is a list of some of my favorite friendship and bonding songs:

- "You've Got a Friend" by James Taylor
- "Humble and Kind" by Tim McGraw
- "Famous Friends" by Chris Young and Kane Brown
- "Lean on Me" by Bill Withers

- "I Won't Let Go" by Rascal Flatts
- "With a Little Help from My Friends" by the Beatles
- "Best Friend" by Saweetie featuring Doja Cat
- "Count on Me" by Whitney Houston and CeCe Winans
- "That's What Friends Are For" by Dionne Warwick and Friends

Having a Good Time
Today people are plagued with multiple responsibilities and complex problems relating to the economy, pressures of work, personal schedules, management of relationships, pandemic fallout, and tasks that can drain emotional energy. During these times, it can be therapeutic and relaxing to hear uncomplicated songs that encourage us to put our cares aside and simply have a good time.

For example, the song "I Got a Feeling" by the Black Eyed Peas was one of the biggest songs of summer a decade or so ago. Although the song had the benefit of having a major label and huge marketing behind it, the product was an easy sell. The simplicity of the concept along with great lyrics and easy sing-along melody increased the song's attractiveness. In addition, the sentiment of the song expresses the fun task of enjoying one's friends. This song is built on a strong foundation of a contagious beat, repetitious synthesizer chord progression, and the very catchy lyric phrase of "I got a feeling that tonight's gonna be a good night." This repeated, chanted phrase drives the concept of letting go of your worries and getting on with celebrating life.

Shock Therapy: Controversial or Thought-Provoking Titles
Throughout the history of music, thought-provoking and controversial song titles and topics have proven a huge factor in their success. Songs dealing with politics, gender identity, racism, religion, sexual harassment, domestic violence, environment, incarceration, and gun violence are easy triggers for controversy, both good and bad. People, in general, are attracted to songs, artists, and contentious topics.

Childish Gambino's song "This Is America" in 2018 brought attention to the ongoing issue of police brutality toward innocent black citizens and mass shootings in the United States. The song and music video went viral due to the content and shock of the images. It topped the charts in various countries and received multiple Grammy Awards in 2019.

In 2008, the song "I Kissed a Girl," by Katy Perry, had a huge impact on music consumers and the record industry. Today, a song about kissing a girl sung by a female artist would be as common as wearing a favorite pair of shoes. However, back in 2008, this topic caused many eyebrows to rise, and its success raged like a wildfire. The song topped the Billboard Hot 100 chart in the United States and held top chart positions in more than 30 countries.

The title and its controversial subject matter are unique because the concept captures your attention while provoking contentious thoughts. The theme of this song is a heterosexual girl being attracted to another female who takes the relationship a step further with an experimental kiss. When a kiss occurs between same-sex individuals several scenarios exist. Whether the interpretation is that the girls are gay or straight, the girl in the song is characterized by an assertive streak but with an innocent sentiment to the story. The person is likable, regardless of the listener's sexual preference. This topic was obviously on the minds of many people based on the record's success. Males and females alike were fascinated by this tale of an experimental bliss.

Along with Perry, other hit songwriters for this song include Max Martin, Dr. Luke, and Cathy Dennis. Awesome lyrics accompanied by a great, driving beat and a simple sing-along melody combined with an infectious hook guarantee a hit record.

I kissed a girl and I liked it
The taste of her cherry Chapstick
I kissed a girl just to try it
I hope my boyfriend don't mind
It felt so wrong it felt so right
Don't mean I'm in love tonight
I kissed a girl and I liked it . . . I liked it

"I Kissed a Girl" © 2008
Songwriters: Katy Perry, Max Martin, Dr. Luke, and Cathy Dennis
Publishers: When I'm Rich You'll Be My Bitch, EMI Music Publishing Ltd.

On the other hand, controversy can become the artist's enemy when it is linked to the negativity that is deemed unforgivable in the court of public opinion. Most career-ending controversies are a result of a song's content or an artist's behavior that directly targets a group of people. For example, in 2003 the Dixie Chicks, one of the most successful country groups in the world, essentially had their career ended after being boycotted for their anti–George W. Bush comment regarding the invasion of Iraq. Although some fans stood behind them, radio stopped playing their music, and they have never recovered.

Other song concept ideas include:

Family
Social Issues
Politics
Loss
Victory
Religion
Music
Conflict
Travel
Protest
Past/Future/Present

As you can see, once you find the song's title and concept, you are well on your way to creating a well-crafted song.

Phrases and Keywords

After the initial inspiration for the song is solidified, I tend to start writing the story based on the title. I've found that once I have discovered the subject matter, it is much easier to write the concept and develop the story for the song. To help further the story development, you may want to make a list of phrases and keywords that are associated with the title. For example, if your song title is "Smells Fishy to Me," you may think of phrases and keywords like:

Phrases
Hooked on your love
Falling deep or Fell so deep
Once a breath of fresh air
In over my head

Keywords
Suspicious
Honest
Sincere
Trust

Exercise IV: Keep a Journal

Create an ongoing Brainstorming Chart that includes song titles, concepts, keywords, and phrases. The songwriting chart should include the following:

- A collection of titles
- Story scenario based on the title
- Interesting angle or twist in your story
- A list of keywords and phrases related to the title and topic
- Keyword organization (opposites, similarities, etc.)
- Phrases, words, rhythms, or melodies that jump out at you

Song Referred to in Chapter 2

"I Kissed a Girl" © 2008
Songwriters: Katy Perry, Max Martin, Dr. Luke, and Cathy Dennis
Publishers: When I'm Rich You'll Be My Bitch, EMI Music Publishing Ltd.

Songwriter Spotlight

Ivan Barias

Ivan Barias. Photo by Jesse Grant/Stringer.

Ivan Barias is one-half of the Philadelphia production team duo Carvin & Ivan. He has 19 Grammy nominations and counting. He has written and produced songs for Jazmine Sullivan, Jill Scott, Musiq Soulchild, Justin Timberlake, Mario, Chris Brown, Ledisi, Raheem DeVaughn, Keyshia Cole, Jaheim, Estelle, Floetry, Skillz, Ace Hood, Faith Evans, Rick Ross, and others.

Batiste: How did your songwriting and producing career get started?

Barias: I've always been musically inclined. I remember listening to Michael Jackson and when I first saw the video for "Billie Jean." He was walking on the street and the pavement lighting up—something pulled me; something drew me to it. It made me feel like I wanted to make music. I dabbled back then, but my turning point came when I started discovering hip-hop. I became an MC. I used to rap. I started listening to a lot of groups like A Tribe Called Quest and people like that. Something about it created a sense of musicality for me, and it made me want to explore creating music just to create tracks for me to rap to. The thing about A Tribe Called Quest that stood out was that they were probably one of the most musical groups out there doing hip-hop at that time. They were incorporating complex jazz loops from people like Freddie Hubbard, and prominent stuff like Bob James, Grover Washington Jr., and things of that nature. When I started buying records is when I learned about diverse genres and that led me to become the person that was more inclined to creating music as opposed to consuming it.

I'm inspired by life around me. Although I'm in the music industry, I try to associate myself with a lot of people who are carrying on outside of the music industry, take on their energy, stories, then create around them. I'm inspired by everything I see around me. Life . . . and it comes out through our records. The music that Carvin and I create is soundtrack music from people's daily lives. So that energy we take on is something that we tend to add back into our music.

Batiste: What is your creative process and what equipment do you use to achieve the result?

Barias: The creative process varies all the time. Sometimes I will come up with a melody and build off it. I would sit at the piano and mess around with a sound, a synth, or string patch, and just build an idea off it. Sometimes it's chordal or sometimes I just sit there and play around with some chords. Other times, I think about the story. For example, when Carvin called me when he had an idea for the song "Don't Change" for Musiq Soulchild, He said, "Hey, I got a concept." He only had two or three lyrics, "I'll love you when your hair turns gray, I'll still want you if you gain a little weight." That's all he had, and he started describing the concept. Just having that, I went into the studio and created something to fit what he was hearing. I brought in a couple of musicians, and we sketched it out. It was a similar scenario with another song we did with Musiq Soulchild called, "Teach Me." Carvin had a concept, and it was mainly more of a vocal thing that he had, and we went into the studio and created around it. So, it varies, sometimes it will be tracked from scratch and sometimes it will be lyrics that inspire the track.

I write songs on the keyboard. I use Pro Tools to record and mix a lot of the sessions. To produce songs, write, and compose, I use Logic and Ableton Live. I use a variety of DOS music software and the Native Instruments Maschine.

Batiste: How do you present completed songs to artists, or partially finished songs for the possibility of collaboration?

Barias: It depends. Sometimes we just give the artist songs from top to bottom—for instance, "Finding My Way Back," that we did for Jaheim. We wrote that with the Grammy-winning artist Miguel in the studio. It was a song that we had that we were going to pitch to another artist. Somebody heard it and they wanted it for Jaheim. Other times, like when we work with Faith Evans or Ledisi, we'll go into the studio and if it's a track already made, then we'll write to it; Or sometimes they'll have an idea, and we'll build a track for them.

Batiste: How much do you think about sales, record label demands, and the audience during the creative process?

Barias: The keyword is balance. You must maintain that balance when you create music. Was it Bill Parcels who said this? "If you listen to the fans, you'll be sitting in the stands next to them." So, you can't listen to the public too much. You must go with your gut feeling, your convictions, and create what's inside of you, and do the best that you can. But at some point, you must understand that this is commerce. Once you burn or you bounce that product, you put it on a disc and it leaves your studio, and you're expecting some type of currency in return. So, you've got to think about the fans. When you create music, you still have to make sure that creatively, it's challenging and it's different, and it's pushing the envelope, but, it's simple enough where the average person can hear it and be moved and captivated by the lyrics. So, I always say it's a delicate balance. Professionals understand that balance.

Batiste: How do you go about creating a memorable melody?

Barias: I would like to say that there's a formula, but there isn't. Certain familiar things happen in the musical composition that people have heard throughout history that you can still build on. There's a certain familiarity that the ear expects. When you're playing a certain chord change or progression, people expect the song to resolve in a certain degree of that scale. If you understand a little bit of music theory, you can anticipate where you can go with a melody and build something that even though people might think it's formula or predictable, I don't call it that; I just call it playing on people's sense of familiarity, just like if they were to go to a fast-food restaurant, people know how they like their fries. They like their fries hot with a little bit of salt. You're not going to give them cold, stale fries. You must give them something that they expect so that you can create something that will be memorable.

Batiste: Advice?

Barias: Know the difference between being objective and subjective. When you're objective, that gets you in the door. Learn how to be a team player, learn how to take constructive criticism, learn how to sacrifice your personal feelings for the good of the team. That gets you in the door. Being subjective is what keeps you there. That's your conviction. That's your taste. That's what you get paid for. Don't become a butthead. Understand that what got you there was your great attitude and your work ethic. Don't lose yourself in a situation where you lose all your convictions, . . . lose all your intent when you create music, because that will be the beginning of your end. Stay authentic, be genuine, be you, and stay convicted, and you'll have a long, fruitful career.

3
Building a Song

A great song begins with an outstanding idea. Whether it's a predominant bass line such as in the song "(I Can't Get No) Satisfaction" by the Rolling Stones, a musical or lyrical hook phrase like in "Shut Up and Dance" by Walk the Moon, or the imagery of a title such as "Your Body Is a Wonderland" by John Mayer, an exceptional idea lies at the root of an extraordinary song.

Regardless of how you start a song, the mission is the same: to make a connection and complete the journey, while maintaining or even building the interest of the listener through the entire excursion. The listener must be engaged to the point where they feel compelled to listen to your song repeatedly. You want the song to continue to occupy their minds, even when it is not playing. To achieve this, you must create an engaging chord structure or riff, or a lyric topic and story, that mirrors real-life experiences (past, present, or future) and resonates with listeners.

Keep in mind, the melody and lyrics are typically the most memorable elements of a song. However, the music accompanying the vocal presentation, whether created first or last in the process, serves as the foundation, and its role is equally important in creating the emotion of the song. In some cases, the music riff and vocal melodies are the same; this combination, along with a strong lyric, may be the exceptional idea your song is based on.

At the same time, always remember that the lyrics written for the musical riff must be a natural fit regarding the feel, vowel sounds, syllables, and message. For example, in the song "Tell Me Something Good," written by Stevie Wonder and recorded by Rufus featuring Chaka Khan, the words are sung perfectly in sync with the riff, which adds tremendously to the impact of the chorus.

The Driver

So, you have a great idea for a song, and you want to start building it out. Before you do, you need to ask yourself: What is driving this song home? What is the song's core element? It could be the melody, rhythm, lyrics, or all the above, but let's say that you have an idea or concept you feel is so exceptional that, once heard, no one will be able to resist. Now, you must ask yourself if your idea alone is enough to drive the song to its desired destination. Perhaps the initial idea is in concert with another element, and they are *both* the drivers of the song.

Most songs rely on a combination of drivers to arrive at their destination. A catchy chorus along with a driving bass line has proven to be a winning combination and a recipe for creating irresistible, hypnotic frenzies. Think about the bass line and subject matter of the song "Billie Jean" by Michael Jackson. In this case, the driver is the bass line. The repetitive four note bass pattern loops over the duration of one bar. The repetitiveness of the bass notes creates an intense rhythmic marching feel, which gives the listener a sense of urgency and movement. Other sections of the song such as the B section or pre-chorus are developed in support of the driver. For example, after the driving bass line is played in support of the verse, the bass pattern changes for the next section, which is the pre-chorus, also known as the B section. Here, the bass plays one single whole note per bar for eight bars, which slows the movement down considerably before returning to the driving bass pattern, which is now supports the chorus, "Billie Jean is not my lover. . . ." The chorus is the destination. It is usually the feel good or groove section and where the song title lives. On the songwriting journey all roads lead to the chorus. In other songs, the driver may be the vocal riff or melody, chant, or rhythm. Once the driver is identified, it's much easier to get where you're trying to go.

Your initial inspiration is likely expressed via your voice or a musical instrument, as you sing or play your ideas until they are well-developed phrases. A phrase is a group of consecutive melodic notes and chords that convey a complete thought. Songs consist of groups of melodic and chordal phrases. These phrases of independent complete ideas are called sections. All these terms will be explained further in the following chapters, but for now, it's enough to know that these are the building blocks of all songs.

Song Sections

Some songs might arrive in your brain in a flash, fully formed, but in the real world, most songs are built. Song sections are the parts that make up a song structure. A good way to start is to create a framework for the song.

First, identify what section feels like the main driving force. This section is where you will develop the central idea or topic of the song, also known as the chorus. You will also need to identify the section that will house the verse. The verse section's role is to support the transition musically and lyrically into the chorus. Write contrasting sections from the verse to the chorus so the listener can easily feel movement and transition from one section to another.

Contrasting sections does not necessarily mean that the music changes. There are many times when the same music is used in both the verse and chorus sections. In this case, varied rhythms and melodies can be used to create contrast and the feeling of movement toward a new destination. Also, it is common for instruments to drop out and reappear, as well as for new or varied melodies to be created in upcoming verses and choruses.

Songs are typically built on sections that repeat. These sections include the introduction, verse, pre-chorus, middle eight, bridge, vamp, and ending. Song sections and their functions are discussed in more detail in Chapter 6, but we need a few working definitions before we get there.

> **Introduction**—The intro section is an opening section at the beginning of the song that is commonly used to set the mood for the song. Sometimes a signature riff (a musical motive, lick, or melody that is identifiable only to this song) is featured. The percolating quarter-note synthesizer part in the introduction of the song "Work" by Rihanna featuring Drake, and the guitar riff in the introduction of the song "Adventure of a Lifetime" by the group Coldplay are clear examples. In other introduction styles, the verse chords may be played to get the listener in the mood for its melody if the rhythm is interesting, or the chorus chords with the instrumental melody are played to familiarize the listener with that section before it arrives later in the song. Your intro must be catchy enough rhythmically and/or melodically to pique the listener's interest in what's to come. Intros are usually four to eight bars in length.
>
> **Verse**—This section is typically the most musically sparse section, leaving space for the listener to follow on the lyric and its developing storylines leading up to the chorus. Musically, this section sets the vibe, tone, and chord progression, which will easily transition into the chorus as well. In each verse, the music remains identical to the previous one.
>
> **Pre-chorus, Climb, or B Section (optional)**—This section usually occurs just before the chorus as a build-up to make the chorus stand out. Not all songs need a pre-chorus. However, it is a device used to create a "tension and release" effect. The music in this section usually consists of unsettled chord movements or breaks. Sometimes the music will not change in this section and alterations will solely occur in the melody. The main function of this section is to be a tool to create tension so that the release of the chorus will have a maximum impact.

Note that "Tension and Release" is a very effective tool and can occur musically, melodically, lyrically, or by complete silence. One of my favorite examples of the use of silence to create tension and release is in Kelly Clarkson's song "Since You've Been Gone" where two beats of silence are utilized to create tension directly before the chorus begins. Wow, what a great impact it makes when the chorus comes in!

> **Chorus or Refrain**—The music in this section, also known as the **hook** is the catchiest of all the sections of the song. This section is called the hook because it provides a sense of release, repetitive rhythms that create a solid groove, and a feel-good music foundation that reels the listener in.
>
> **Bridge (optional)**—The bridge is a section that serves as a deviation from the regular pattern to change the pace and give the song some variation. In this

section, it is common for the progression of the chords, melody, and lyrics to differ from the verse and chorus sections. Some writers may choose a drum break or drums and vocals with no chords or music at all or a "breakdown" where instruments drop out to one or two, then build up again with the full instrumentation. This section can also be thought of as a second release.

Middle Eight Section (optional)—This section introduces new elements to the song and is created to keep the listener's interest. It usually occurs somewhere in the middle of the song and is most commonly eight bars in length. Some writers also refer to the middle eight as the "bridge," which is fine if it is the only section that is different from the verse and chorus. However, if this section is additional new music, it may be less confusing to call it the middle eight.

Vamp, Tag, or Coda—This is where the song has a repetitive pattern usually toward the end of the song, to fade out on. Sometimes this music is borrowed from the chorus or refrain sections. It can also be an entirely new section.

Ending—A definite musical arrangement that leads to a finish of the song.

The order of placement of the sections may be arranged according to what feels right to you in terms of movement, interest, and excitement, keeping in mind that all sections should transition to one another smoothly. This order is traditionally called the frame, or the song structure.

Song Structure

Most popular songs follow patterns that are easy for the listener to relate to. Music sections arranged in a particular order are called song structure or song form. A great song structure is crucial to the impact of a song. Without a structure, the listener may have difficulty following along, which can result in a loss of interest. Structure gives the song a sense of even distribution and stability. Not all songs have the same structure. Imagine if all cars were built alike, how boring that would be.

Although cars have a common or similar foundation, many have uniquely identifiable parts and features, which vary from vehicle to vehicle to distinguish one from another. Songwriters choose various types of musical parts and features as well. There is no wrong or right way to structure a song. Songs are works of art and the construction is left up to the writer's discretion. The writer must choose a structure that feels most natural and appropriate for the song. Depending on the type of song, it is important to place its sections in the order that will most effectively tell the story and keep the listener's attention.

The song structure chart template below contains the most used structures in popular songs. Notice the mixture of combinations and variations of single and double verses, choruses, and bridges.

Song Structure Chart Template

Example 1	Example 2	Example 3	Example 4	Example 5
A Verse	A Verse	A Chorus	A Verse	A Verse
B Chorus	B Chorus	B Verse	B Pre-chorus	A Verse
A Verse	A Verse	A Chorus	C Chorus	B Chorus
B Chorus	B Chorus	B Verse	A Verse	A Verse
C Bridge	A Verse	C Bridge	B Pre-chorus	B Chorus
B Chorus	B Chorus	A Chorus	C Chorus	B Chorus

Popular Songs and Their Structures

Assembling a song is like building a car. There are common features that all cars and songs have and then there are some that are built with special characteristics. Most hit songs are built on several basic formulas.

Example #1
Verse/Chorus/Verse/Chorus/Bridge/Chorus—"Bad Habits" by Ed Sheeran

Example #2
Verse/Chorus/Verse/Chorus/Verse/Chorus—"Watermelon Sugar" by Harry Styles

Example #3
Chorus/Verse/Chorus/Verse/Bridge/Chorus—"One More Time" by Daft Punk

Example #4
Verse/Pre-Chorus/Chorus/Verse/Pre-Chorus/Chorus—"Roll Some Mo" by Lucky Daye

Example #5
Verse/Verse/Chorus/Verse/Chorus/Chorus—"Somebody That I Used to Know" by Gotye featuring Kimbra

Although the examples above are the most used song structures, you want to arrange the sections in the order that best serves the song in keeping the listener's interest. For example, a songwriter may add a short tag of music, a vocal riff, or a middle eight section. Musical and/or vocal accents or breakdowns commonly serve as points of interest as well. Another way to keep interest in the song is to use melodic variation or vocals without instruments in repeating sections, such as muting the instruments for one or two bars of a verse or a chorus.

Common Varied Song Structures

Sometimes the way you want to express your song may not fall into one of the popular song structures. There are various reasons you may want to create an alternate structure. Most of the reasons are derived from a feeling that your song simply mandates something different to keep the listener engaged or simply for emotion or art's sake, such as restating the intro or adding a music section between verses, or perhaps the lyric phrasing may call for an extra bar.

Here are a few examples of varied song structures:

Intro/Verse/Verse/Chorus/Verse/Chorus/Bridge/Break/Chorus/Chorus
—"Wanted" by Hunter Hayes

Intro/Verse/Chorus/Verse/Chorus/Middle Eight/Verse/Chorus/Middle Eight/Chorus (Breakdown)
—"Hold On" by Alabama Shakes

Intro/Verse/Chorus/Verse/Chorus/Bridge/Chorus/Middle Eight/Chorus/Bridge 2/Chorus
—"Call It What You Want" by Bill Summers and Summer's Heat

Intro/Verse/Pre-Chorus/Chorus/Verse/Pre-Chorus/Chorus/Bridge (instrumental)/Verse/Verse/Pre-Chorus/Chorus/Chorus/Instrumental (over Verse/Pre-Chorus/Chorus progression)
—"We Take Care of Our Own" by Bruce Springsteen

Intro/Verse/Pre-Chorus/Chorus/Chorus/Verse/Pre-Chorus/Chorus/Chorus/Bridge/Break/Chorus/Chorus
—"Stronger" by Kelly Clarkson

Intro/Verse/Chorus/Verse/Chorus/Chorus/Middle Eight/Bridge/Chorus/Chorus
—"Adorn" by Miguel

Intro/Chorus/Verse/Chorus/Verse/Bridge (Instrumental)/Break (4 bars)/Verse/Instrumental Break (2 bars)/Chorus
—"If I Die Young" by the Band Perry

Restating the musical introduction is very common, as is incorporating music interludes. Here are some examples of this:

Intro/Verse/Pre-Chorus/Chorus/Intro2/Verse/Chorus/Verse/Pre-Chorus/Bridge (Instrumental & Vocal)/Chorus/Chorus
—"I Will Wait" by Mumford & Sons

Intro/Verse/Instrumental/Verse/Verse/Instrumental/Verse/Middle 8/Instrumental Break (over verse section)/Verse/Verse
—"Field of Gold" by Sting

Intro/Verse/Half Intro/Chorus/Half Intro/Verse/Half Intro/Chorus/Half Intro/Verse/Chorus/Chorus/Tag
—"Try" by Pink

> **Structures where the verse incorporates the title.** It is also very typical for titles to be written in the verse section. With this structure, the song title is incorporated at the beginning line, every other line, or the line at the end of the phrase. "Somewhere Over the Rainbow," made famous by Judy Garland, and "Hey There Delilah" recorded by Plain White T's are examples of titles used in the opening line of a song.
>
> Somewhere over the rainbow
> Way up high
> There's a land that I heard of
> Once in a lullaby
>
> "Somewhere over the Rainbow" © 1939
Songwriters: E.Y. Harburg and Harold Arlen
Published by: EMI FEIST CATALOG INC.
>
> Hey there, Delilah
> What's it like in New York City?
>
> "Hey There Delilah" by Plain White T's © 2008
Songwriter: Tom Higgenson
Published by: Warner Chappell Music, Inc.
>
> **Alternate Structures**
> Sometimes structures defy all logic on paper but are effective when the melody and lyrics are unique and catchy. An example of this would be the song entitled "Dearest" by the Black Keys.
>
> *Chorus/Intro (4 bars)/Verse/Music (4 bars)/Verse/Music/Vocal Breakdown (16 bars)*
>
> "Dearest" by the Black Keys © 2011
Songwriters: Barry Gibb and Robin Hugh Gibb
Publishers: Universal Music Publishing Group

Electronic Dance Music (EDM) Structures

The structure for Electronic Dance Music (EDM) is different than most common structures due to the context of its use. EDM is percussive electronic music, produced for a dance environment (i.e., nightclubs, festivals, raves). It is associated with techno, house, dubstep, trance, and their related subgenres. Whereas with most popular songs, the chorus is the peak of the song, EDM uses the "breakdown" or "drop" in the song as its high point. This breakdown is usually instrumental with fragments of vocal hooks being sung. The structure leading to the "drop" point is typically music with no more than one full verse and/or chorus. The songs usually have minimal vocals so that the disc jockey (DJ) can combine tracks from one song to another for smooth transitioning from song to song. Many popular music genres, including pop, R&B, and country are trending to EDM mixes of their songs to capitalize on a wider audience.

Harmony and Accents

Once you've established the foundation and structure of the song, add embellishments to give it more variety and dynamics. Two of the most common ways to accomplish this are to use harmony and accents. Harmony occurs when at least two notes are played simultaneously. In popular music, there are two main uses of harmony. One use of harmony is found in chords (three or more notes sounding simultaneously) that support and accompany the melody. The other use is when additional notes are played simultaneously with a melody. Vocal harmony, especially in the chorus section, is very effective in terms of adding variety and giving the song a sense of building. The lush and sultry blend of harmonious voices on the vamp of the song, "Close to You" by the Carpenters elevated the amount of heartwarming to another level of bliss. In the song "End of the Road" recorded by Boyz 2 Men, the harmony chorus gives the song a huge build and contributes greatly to its irresistible singalong feel. In some cases, harmonies are used to build and develop a song. For example, on the 2019 Grammy-award-winning song, "Never Alone" by Tori Kelly featuring Kirk Franklin, the harmony doesn't appear until the second chorus. This technique gives the vocalist an open space to set the tone and emotion of the song without any other vocals. Once the initial lyrical foundation is established, the background vocals are introduced and eventually transition from a supportive role into the foundation of the chorus, which allows the lead vocalist to add ad-libs in a call-and-response manner with the background vocals. An example of a powerful two-part harmony arrangement is the simple use of two voices on the song "Need You Now" by Lady Antebellum. This song won a Grammy award for both Song of the Year and Record of the Year in 2011. Lastly, the use of unison background vocals also serves as a powerful way to build a song's chorus. Doubling the melody with the same note and/or singing the same note octaves apart is a technique used on many hit records such as Ed Sheeran's "Shape of You" and his duet with Justin Bieber, "I Don't Care."

In popular music, additional instruments or voices performed simultaneously with an existing part are great techniques for reinforcement. These techniques are commonly used to create emphasis on certain parts and to add dynamics to the song. They are most effective when used as a gradual build-up at the point of the song of climax. Big accents are usually followed by a quieter section of music. When I first heard "Rosanna" by Toto I was moved by the excitement created by the dynamics of the song. In this song, accents and riffs are used to announce almost every new section. I found this use to be captivating and musically fulfilling. A simpler but just as effective use of accents is on the Katy Perry song, "Roar." The song builds by adding instruments, which play with an existing synthesizer long-tone melody. Instruments are continuously added and building upon this line. Eventually, this accented line provides a powerful infrastructure and wall of sound effects for the chorus.

I look at the harmony and accents as the icing on the cake. Their application to the composition is extra details that contribute significantly to the listening experience of a song.

Essential and Nonessential Materials and Ingredients

Now that you've built a frame, you must understand the use of essential and nonessential materials. If you were building a house, the essential items needed would include walls, a roof, windows, doors, plumbing, water, and electricity. Building a song requires essential materials or ingredients as well to make it sturdy and most effective. Let's look at the list of the essential ingredients below. These ingredients are discussed in detail in future chapters.

Essential ingredients
- a great idea
- a great chorus
- an incredible vibe and feel
- a strong memorable melody
- a solid structure: contrast between the sections
- a great story or topic
- lyrics that are conversational and could be understood by the general public
- an interesting and enjoyable rhythm
- tension and release
- a strong rhyme scheme
- great word choices
- a signature riff
- harmony
- an element of surprise

Nonessential items in a home would include furniture, wall hangings, high-tech electronics, and decor. Not all items are needed but are certainly nice to have if their use complements the essential ingredients. Warning: Be sure not to clutter your song with unnecessary ingredients that distract from the core idea. Such nonessential ingredients in a song include the following:

Nonessential ingredients
- string or horn arrangements
- instrumental solos
- elaborate instrumental and vocal arrangements
- sound effects

Originality

Probably one of the most challenging aspects of establishing a career in songwriting is discovering and developing your very own unique style. You want to incorporate relatable elements for the listener as well as create a personal and gratifying experience for yourself.

When it comes to common topics, uniqueness can be a challenge. Take a common topic such as love, for example. It's very easy to fall into the trap of presenting scenarios of falling out of love, falling into love, or cheating predictably or ordinarily. Although these situations may seem overused, without fail most people are affected by this topic, making these scenarios the most popular of all and well worth keeping. You are charged with making sure the story is compelling enough for the listener to want to hear the scenario again and again. This is achieved by presenting a unique or unexpected point of view or approach to the topic. Also, experiment by varying rhythms, melodies, instrumentation, sounds, and song structure.

Musically, you should always follow your instinct of what feels good and works best for the overall vibe and good of the song. Stay away from trends, as they usually have already passed before your idea will reach the public, thus killing all perceptions of uniqueness. Find the most interesting, honest, and sincere way to use instruments, melodies, words, and sound to express the idea. This takes many hours of experimenting, learning, and unlearning many principles of writing. The end must result in a creation that feels powerfully well stated and natural to you.

Remember that your core audience consists of everyday people from all walks of life. Do not write to impress other writers or musicians because they generally do not purchase music. Therefore, make your songs relatable, easy to understand, and singable.

Summary

Start with a great idea, one that will attract and keep the listener's interest for the entire length of the song. You must determine whether your idea or driver has enough gas to deliver the song to its full potential and destination. In other words, you must love this idea to the point where you just can't get enough of hearing it. Remember these key points:

- Build the frame; develop phrases into sections that are contrasting to one another.
- Create a structure for the song by putting the sections in an order that will have the most connection and impact on the listener's experience
- Use embellishments such as harmony and accents to build and help create dynamics and interests.
- Present the song most uniquely and creatively, yet simply and naturally enough for the listener to be able to connect and relate to it.

Songwriter Spotlight

Lamont Dozier

Lamont Dozier. Photo by Bob Berg/Getty Images.

A few years ago I had an opportunity to pull aside the late legendary musician, songwriter, and producer, Lamont Dozier, after an eight-hour Board of Trustees meeting with the Recording Academy. Although it had been a long day, he gracefully granted my wish! Dozier's work has included the Supremes, Marvin Gaye, Martha Reeves and the Vandellas, Mary Wells, the Marvelettes, and the Four Tops. Along with songwriting partners Brian and Eddie Holland, Dozier wrote 46 top-10 singles between 1963 and 1967, including producing and writing 13 consecutive number one hits for the Supremes as well as hits for Freda Payne and Chairmen of the Board. As a solo writer, he's written for artists such as Phil Collins, Boy George, Eric Clapton, and Simply Red. Lamont Dozier died in 2022 at the age of 81.

Batiste: How did you develop your gift for writing words and music?

Dozier: As a kid, I was influenced musically by my grandmother, who I lived with along with my grandfather. She was a music teacher and a choir director at the church. She taught me the importance of singing the right words and being able to express what the words meant to me in my delivery of them. I also listened to a lot of music. As early as elementary school I was encouraged to write poems and began to read up on lyric writing, listening to records, and studying writers like Rodgers and Hart and Rodgers and Hammerstein. I remember going to the theater to see "My Fair Lady" and being inspired to be a writer that wrote songs like that.

When writing songs on the piano, I always start with the bass line in my left hand first. This establishes a groove and some idea of a beat. Then I use my right hand to create the chord rhythm and/or melody and feel that works with the left hand.

Batiste: How do you come up with song titles and stories?

Dozier: Song titles mainly come from things I read or hear people say on television or in real life, for example, the song, "I Can't Help Myself (Sugar Pie, Honey Bunch)" by the Four Tops. When I lived with my grandparents growing up, I used to hear my grandfather greet female company with sayings like, "Hello sugar pie, honey bunch!" Things like that stick in my repertoire of memories. Also, when I was eleven years old, I started regularly sweeping the floor of my grandmother's beauty parlor and would overhear women's gossip. They would talk about everything under the sun. As a result, I gained great insight into how women thought and what their relationship issues were. This enabled me to write songs from a woman's point of view such as the Supremes hits like, "You Keep Me Hanging On," "Where Did Our Love Go?," "You Can't Hurry Love," "I Hear a Symphony," "Come See About Me," "Stop! In the Name of Love," and "Band Of Gold" for Freda Payne. I would think of a man's response to women's concerns and birth titles such as "Reach Out (I'll Be There)" recorded by the Four Tops and "How Sweet It Is (To Be Loved By You)" recorded by Marvin Gaye and James Taylor. I try to recall situations or scenarios people find themselves in and keep track of keywords or phrases that would either make a great title or a catchy phrase. If I have a good music idea and no title or words, I rely on the music to dictate the story. After playing the idea several times, eventually, a lyric concept develops. I collect and save all my ideas, which are in the tens of thousands.

Batiste:: What's in a typical day for Lamont Dozier?

Dozier:: I write every day, seven days a week. It's a discipline that I acquired due to my training at Motown Records. The Holland brothers and I (Holland, Dozier, Holland) were always engaged in a friendly competition with other very talented songwriters (Smokey Robinson, Norman Whitfield, Nicholas Ashford and Valerie Simpson, and William Mickey Stevenson) at Motown. Whoever came up with the best song, got the opportunity to have their song released by the artist. It required us to be at the top of our game. Therefore, we worked night and day, and never took anything for granted. You must be disciplined enough to work every day as though you have a deadline even if you're just adding new work to your song catalog. This way, you're always prepared to take advantage of an opportunity when the occasion arises. I wake up at 10 am every day and write for two to three hours. I take a one-hour lunch break, then I go right back to work until 6 or 7 pm.

4
Let the Music Play

The lyric of a song is absolutely a crucial element in forging a connection with the listener, as is a memorable melody played or sung. Although the listener will ultimately gravitate to the melodies and the scenario or characters in the story, it is the arrangement of sounds and beats that the listener immediately hears and responds to before the story begins.

In other words, it is the music—rhythm and chords—that creates an immediate appeal and sets the tone, the mood, and the most appropriate platform and setting from which the story will be conveyed. In some cases, the music is intricately arranged harmonically, while in other cases, the tone of the music may be set based on a melody, words, and/or a rhythm set to drums or a loop, without an emphasis on harmony or chords.

No matter what combination of approaches you take in building your song, remember: the goal is to create a connection to the listener.

Music Theory and Songwriting

Writing songs that easily connect with listeners is the goal of every successful songwriter. Although not mandatory, having music theory as part of your musical development certainly helps to make accomplishing this goal a more seamless journey for many.

Music theory is the understanding of fundamental concepts of four very important songwriting components: pitch, rhythm, chords/harmony, and melody. However, music theory is not a singular model. Various music theories include Middle Eastern, East Asian, and Western music. In popular music, Western common-practice tonal music theory, which uses functional harmonies based on the diatonic scales, is mainly applied.

The components of Western music theory include the understanding of pitch, measures/bars, music notation and note values, music staffs and clefs, time signatures, and syncopation. There are a multitude of books available on music theory, depending on how in-depth you plan to go with musical arrangements and instrumentation of your songs.

The purpose of learning music theory is not to guide your creativity, but to familiarize you with a working knowledge of how these essential elements of songwriting function and work together to enhance your creative experience. It is not necessary to learn music theory before beginning to write songs. With that being said, take time to gain knowledge of the areas of music theory that apply to the style of songs you write.

In modern popular music, there are many factors other than music theory that come into play, depending on the audience that you're trying to reach and your desire for innovation. For example, you may choose to write a song that doesn't rely on a harmonic structure but instead uses loops. One's focus might be on complex rhythms, syncopation, or percussive drum patterns and beats that fit well together as the song's foundation. This method of songwriting has created an opportunity for DJs and beatmakers to become very successful songwriters in popular music.

DJs and beatmakers typically collaborate with an artist by providing them with beats, loops, and/or samples (music taken from previously released works) to write lyrics and melodies to. Then the DJ or beatmaker will produce the record or hire a producer to ensure that the record has the structure, sound, textures, dynamics, hooks, and other elements needed to grab the attention of the listener. A good example is the song "Run the World (Girls)" by Beyonce. Musically, this song is based on rhythmic complexity and syncopation as opposed to harmonic complexity. The harmonies are found in the vocal performance. The music foundation is percussive and includes the use of synthesizers playing single-note syncopated rhythms as opposed to chords. The entire song is performed to a marching military drumbeat sample of the song, "Pon De Floor" by Major Lazer.

Notes, Intervals, Scales

It is difficult to discuss the development of chords, harmony, and melody without addressing a basic understanding of music pitches (also referred to as "notes") and how they are organized. So, let's get started with an overview of music notes and how they operate.

The music alphabet consists of only seven letters: A, B, C, D, E, F, and G. These seven letters repeat themselves in sequence. In other words, if our starting note is

FIGURE 4.1 Music Alphabet

A, then we continue to play through the cycle in the order of B, C, D, E, F, to reach the last alphabet G. After we reach the alphabet G, the next note letter name we play is A. This rule applies regardless of which letter in the cycle you choose to be your starting note. For example, a successive order of notes starting with the letter C would be C, D, E, F, G, A, and B.

Accidentals are symbols used to modify the pitch of a note by half-steps. If a note is raised in pitch by a half-step, we use the term "sharp," which is indicated by the symbol (♯). If a note is lowered in pitch by a half-step, it is called a "flat," which is indicated by the symbol (♭). A natural symbol (♮) cancels an accidental.

There are twelve distinct pitches (notes) to choose from in music. Each note is separated by a half-step distance between it and the next note. In Western music, the half-step is the smallest interval that can be played on most instruments. The only tones smaller than a half-step are quarter tones, which are used more commonly in Eastern music.

The distance, or number of half-steps, between each pair of notes is called an *interval*. For example, the interval between the notes C and C♯ is a half-step; and the interval between the notes C and D is one whole step, or two half-steps. Intervals provide the infrastructure for nearly every aspect of composition. Scales, chords, and melodies are all created by and based on an arrangement of intervals.

The letter names of the twelve music pitches are: C, C♯ or D♭, D, D♯ or E♭, E, F, F♯ or G♭, G, G♯ or A♭, A, A♯ or B♭, and B.

All twelve notes played in order are called a *chromatic scale*.

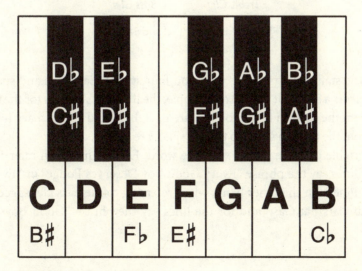

FIGURE 4.2 Chromatic Scale

Clefs and Notes

Music is the organization of melodies, chords, and sound based on scales. The main scale that forms the base of a song is referred to as the song's *key*. The key of a song is the tone center and has several compatible chords and scales that relate well to it. Many musicians learn to read music so that they can play songs. To create a common understanding for the name and duration of notes, they are placed on a *musical staff*. The music staff consists of five lines and four spaces.

Clef symbols are placed on the musical staff to indicate a higher or lower range of pitches. The note range varies from instrument to instrument—from high to mid-range to low notes.

The main clef symbols are *treble* and *bass*. The chosen clef sign correlates with the note middle C on the piano. The treble clef sign has a curl, which wraps around the note G and is used to indicate notes within the range of middle C and higher. The bass clef sign is shaped like a backward C followed by two dots positioned in the space of the F line—one above and one below the line. The bass clef indicates notes ranging from middle C and lower.

Treble Clef   *Bass Clef*

FIGURE 4.3 Treble Clef and Bass Clef

The music staff consists of five lines and four spaces. Each line and space of the staff represents a different pitch. For example, the line notes' names for the treble clef starting from the bottom to the top line are E, G, B, D, and F. The space note names starting from the bottom space to the top space are F, A, C, and E.

On the treble clef, the spaces spell the word, FACE, and when referring to the treble clef lines say the phrase "Every Good Boy Deserves Fudge" or "Every Good Boy Does Fine." On the other hand, when referring to the bass clef spaces, try the phrase "All Cars Eat Gas," and for the lines say the phrase "Good Boys Do Fine Always."

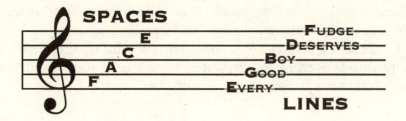

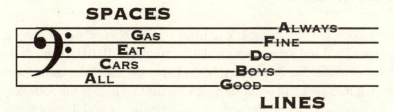

FIGURE 4.4 Spaces and Lines

Sometimes both the treble and bass staffs are joined together by a brace so the musician can see the full range of notes. This is called the *grand staff*.

FIGURE 4.5 Grand Staff

Octaves and Scales

Whether the notes you play in succession are ascending (moving higher in pitch) or descending (moving lower in pitch), you will eventually arrive at the point where the letter name repeats itself. The distance between the next highest or lowest repetition of the starting note is called an *octave*.

The word "octave" is derived from the Latin word "octavus," which means the number eight. There are various combinations of organized ascending groups of notes based on half-steps and whole steps, which occur within one octave. These set groups of notes are called *scales*. In Western music the main scales are major, minor, augmented, diminished, and pentatonic. There are more than 70 other scales derived from these main scales, but the most used are major and minor.

Most scales consist of seven notes. The eighth note is the repeated octave, which shares the same letter name as the first note of the scale. A scale's origin can start from any of the twelve pitches in the music alphabet.

Scales and Numbers

Scales are recognized by a number and letter system. Natural or counting numbers (for example 1, 2, 3) and Roman numerals (for example I, II, III) correspond with the letter alphabet names (for example A, B, C, etc.) in the scale. The counting numbers and Roman numerals are in order starting with the first note of the scale key. For example, in the key of C major, the corresponding counting and Roman numerals are as follows:

Letter:	C	D	E	F	G	A	B
Counting:	1	2	3	4	5	6	7
Roman numeral:	I	II	III	IV	V	VI	VII

The first note of the scale is referred to as the "root." The distance of each of the lettered and numbered notes in the scale are called *scale degrees*.

Often in rehearsal or recording situations, the arranger will simply assign notes of the chord on the spot by calling them out by numbers. Thus, if the song is in the key of C major and the arranger assigns you to play or sing the third, you should play or sing the note E, which corresponds to the third degree of the chord.

The Major Scale

The C major scale serves as a foundation for which all other scales are built upon. It is the center of all scales because all of the notes are natural (no sharps or flats).

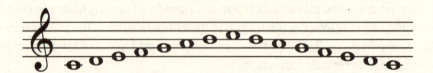

FIGURE 4.6 C Major Scale

The major scale is the most recognizable and most famous of all scales because it is represented in "Do, Re, Mi, Fa, So, La, Ti, Do." Below are the formulas for the major and minor scales. Remember, each scale formula has seven pitches.

FIGURE 4.7 C Major—On the Staff

Major Scale Formula = whole step–whole step–half step–whole step–whole step–whole step–half step

Major Scale Note Examples
C Major Scale:
C = C–D–E–F–G–A–B–C

FIGURE 4.8 C Major—On the Keyboard

The Minor Scale

The natural minor scale is a bit darker in sound because the third, sixth, and seventh intervals are lowered by a half-step as compared to the major scale. There are several minor scales based on the natural minor scale. The two main additional minor scales are the harmonic minor and the melodic minor scales.

Natural Minor Scale Formula = whole step–half step–whole step–whole step–half step–whole step–whole step

A Natural Minor Scale = A–B–C–D–E–F–G–A

FIGURE 4.9 Natural Minor Scale (Key of A minor—Relative to C major key signature)

Harmonic Minor Scale Formula (seventh degree of the natural minor scale is raised by one half step) = whole step–half-step–whole step–whole step–half step–whole + half step–half step. Notice the sixth degree of the scale is augmented by a half step.

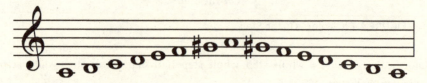

FIGURE 4.10 Harmonic Minor Scale

A Harmonic Minor Scale = A–B–C–D–E–F–G#–A

Melodic Minor Scale Formula (both the sixth and seventh degrees of the natural minor scale are raised by a half-step as it is ascending, however, the scale reverts back to the natural minor scale as it descends)

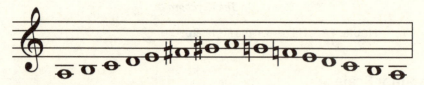

FIGURE 4.11 Melodic Minor Scale

A Melodic Minor Scale Ascending = A–B–C–D–E–F#–G#–A
A Melodic Minor Scale Descending = A–G–F–E–D–C–B–A

Key Signature

The *key signature* is a pattern of sharps and flats (accidentals) representing the key to the song. It tells you what accidentals coincide with the key. The key signature is based on a formula called the *circle of fifths* and appears on the music staff right after the clef.

Major and minor scales that have the same key signatures are called "relative keys." The relative major key for a minor scale is three half-steps above the root note of the scale. For example, the A minor scale's relative key is C major, which has no sharps or flats in its key signature. Below is a visual representation of major and minor key signature relationships among the twelve notes.

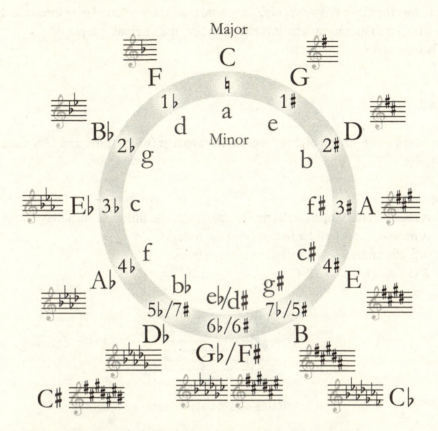

FIGURE 4.12 Circle of Fifths—Major and Minor Relative Key Signatures

Know Your Chords

Although the scope of music theory is large and you won't necessarily need to be fluent in its entire scope, chord theory is the most important area of music theory to know for popular songwriting. Having a clear understanding of how chords work helps you to:

- Identify the key of the song, which is helpful when working alone and with others.
- Understand *diatonic chords*: Chords that naturally exist within a key so that your chord progressions have cohesion.
- Create with inversions: The ability to vary chord tones for the purpose of coloring and dynamics.
- Communicate with other musicians by learning the chord Roman numeral system.

Before diving in, a quick refresher course: When two or more notes sound simultaneously, they become what is known as *harmony*. When a group of three or more notes sound together, they create a *chord*. Two-note chords are referred to as intervals. The way the chord's harmony sounds is based on how the intervals are placed.

Okay, now for the specifics.

Triad

A triad is a combination of three notes, such as a first (root), third, and fifth notes of the scale.

Major Triad
- A major triad comprises the first (root), third, and fifth notes of a major scale
- A major third is four half-steps from the root
- A perfect fifth is seven half steps from the root
- A C major triad is C-E-G

FIGURE 4.13 C Major Triad

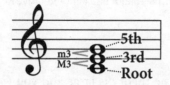

FIGURE 4.14 Major Triad Intervals

Minor Triad
- A minor triad comprises the first (root), third (lowered by a half step), and the fifth notes of a major scale.
- A minor third is three half-steps from the root
- A perfect fifth is seven half-steps from the root
- A C minor triad is C-E♭-G

FIGURE 4.15 C Minor Triad

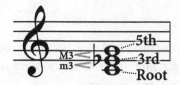

FIGURE 4.16 Minor Triad Intervals

Augmented Triad
- The notes in the augmented triad are the first (root), third, and a raised fifth. This means the fifth is moved up by a half-step, making it eight half-steps from the root.
- A C augmented triad is C-E-G♯.
- The augmented chord is represented by the "+" symbol. The letter name for the C augmented chord is C+.

FIGURE 4.17 C Augmented Triad

Diminished Triad
- A diminished triad is built with the first (root), lowered third (three half steps), and a lowered fifth, meaning the fifth is one half-step lower (six half-steps from the root) than a perfect fifth.
- The notes in a C diminished chord are C-E♭-G♭.
- A diminished chord is represented by the "°" symbol. The letter name for the C diminished chord is C°.
- The diminished chord is most typically used as a bridge or transition between two other chords.

FIGURE 4.18 C Diminished Triad

Creating a Sound

While playing around with basic chord structures, you can also start to determine how you want your song to *sound*. Is the tone you want to set happy, sad, amusing, energetic, mellow, dance-oriented, or other?

Usually, songs with a happy subject matter are based on major chords. The chords of the songs, "Beautiful Day" by U2 and "We've Only Just Begun" by the Carpenters use major chords and create the bright and energetic mood that the writer is trying to convey. On the other hand, sad or funk-driven songs are typically based around minor chords and are usually slow to mid-tempo. "Yeah" by Usher is an example of the use of minor chords to set the tone appropriate for the lyric.

Inversion

Having the flexibility to place notes of a chord in different positions offers the songwriter a choice of colors in the way the song sounds. This rearrangement of the note positions in a chord is called an *inversion*. Some of the purposes of inversion chords include assisting a melodic bass line to modulate to a new key, creating dynamics, and adding contrast and/or energy to a different part of the song.

> **Root Position**—The bottom note of a triad is called the "root note"; the middle note is the third; and the top note is the fifth.
>
> **First Position**—The third is at the bottom of the triad, the fifth is at the middle of the triad, and the root note becomes the top note of the triad.
>
> **Second Position**—The fifth is at the bottom, the root note is in the middle, and the third moves to the top of the triad.

Here are examples of a rearrangement of note position of the C major triad:

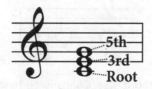

FIGURE 4.19 C Major, Root Position

Let the Music Play   59

FIGURE 4.20 C Major, First Inversion

FIGURE 4.21 C Major, Second Inversion

The Dominant Seventh Chord

- The dominant seventh chord is a major triad (1-3-5), plus a lowered seventh note.
- The symbol for the dominant seventh chord in G major is G7 (G-B-D-F).
- All the triad notes (1-3-5) don't need to be present along with the lowered seventh to create a dominant seventh chord. In other words, the dominant seventh chord can be 1, 5, and lowered 7, or 1, 3, and lowered 7.

The typical dominant seventh chord's function is to transition into the root, or tonic, chord. When the dominant seventh is played on the fifth interval of the key, the pronounced sound of the lower seventh in the chord strongly suggests resolving to the third on the root chord.

FIGURE 4.22 Dominant Seventh Resolving

Diatonic Chords

Diatonic chords are derived from the notes in major and minor scales. For example, a major scale consists of seven notes and has seven chords, each one built from a note or degree in the scale.

The key's diatonic chord can be thought of as related chords in a particular key family. The notes in the major and minor scales are numbered in scale degrees of 1 (root), 2, 3, 4, 5, 6, and 7. Diatonic chords are usually named with Roman numerals. Each one of the Roman numerals corresponds to the scale degree on the chord. For example, in a major key, the numerals would be, I, ii, iii, IV, V, vi, and vii. Capital letters represent major chords while lowercase is used for minor chords.

Diatonic Chord Formula for a Major Key (Roman Numerals)

I–ii–iii–IV–V–vi–vii°

The counting numbers and Roman numerals are in order starting with the first note of the scale key. For example, in the key of C major, the corresponding Roman numerals are as follows:

Letter: C   D   E   F   G   A   B   C

FIGURE 4.23 Major Key Diatonic Chords

Diatonic Chord Formula for a Minor Key (Roman Numerals)

i–ii°–III–iv–v–VI–VII–i

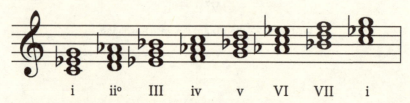

FIGURE 4.24 Minor Key Diatonic Chords

Chord Progressions

Understanding diatonic chords is extremely helpful when formulating *chord progressions*. A chord progression is the order of a succession of chords that occur in a functional pattern. This pattern of chords gives the song a sense of movement and lays the foundation that supports the melody.

Whether the combination of chords you choose is intended to create stability, tension, or simply to create the mood of your composition, your primary job as a songwriter is to find the chords and progressions that allow you to communicate what you want to express. You have the choice to build a song from just one chord or to create a series of diatonic chords to form a pattern to write a melody to.

One of the most common chord progressions is the first, fourth, and fifth chords (I–IV–V) of the major scale. These three chords are known as the *primary chords* and are the foundation of multiple music genres, including blues, gospel, country, and rock.

There is no set rule as to the order of chords you may use to express your creativity and originality. If you listen to "Kiss" by Prince, you will easily recognize the I–IV–V blues structure played in the style of R&B funk. In the song "I Still Haven't Found What I'm Looking For" by U2, the I–IV–I chord progression lays the foundation for the verse section. This progression seamlessly leads to the V chord at the chorus. The chord progression in the chorus is V–IV–I, as opposed to the reverse order of the traditional I–IV–V progression. The melody, lyric, and chord progression work so well together that it is hardly noticeable that the entire song is built on just three chords.

The second most common chord progression incorporates the sixth-degree chord (vi). There are a countless number of songs that have been written with this chord progression. Like the three-chord progression of I–IV–V, the four-chord progression I–IV–V–vi can start on any one of the chords. A few examples of chord progressions that implement the vi chord are the songs "Someone You Loved" by Lewis Capaldi, "Don't Stop Believin'" by Journey, and "Girls Like You" by Maroon 5 featuring Cardi B. (I–V–vi–IV); "Love the Way You Lie" by Eminem featuring Rihanna, "Despacito" by Luis Fonsi, and "Bad Liar" by Imagine Dragons (vi–IV–I–V).

After you've created your desired chord progression, create melodies that work well with the progression. Remember, there must be a good balance between the chords and melody. A complex chord progression best serves a less complicated melody. On the other hand, a more elaborate and complicated melody works best with a simpler and less complicated chord progression.

Spending time playing around with chords and learning songs written by others is a good way of expanding your chord library. It will eventually give you

Common Chord Progressions

Some chord progressions are used more than others simply because they sound better and are pleasing to listeners, and therefore are used in popular music. Here is a chart of traditional options using diatonic chords in a chord progression to segue from one chord to another.

Major and Minor Diatonic Chords, Progressions, and Segues

Number	Chord	Segue
I	C	Tonic/Root Chord *passage to anywhere*
ii	Dm	V or vii° chords
iii	Em	IV or vi chords
IV	F	ii, V or vii° chords
V	G	I or vi chords
vi	Am	ii, iii, IV or V chords
vii°	B°	I chord

FIGURE 4.25 Common Chord Progressions in Major Key (Diatonic Chords)

Numeral	Scale Chords	Segues To
i	Cm	Tonic/Root Chord *passage to anywhere*
ii° (ii)	D° (Dm)	V (v) or vii° (VII) chords
III (III+)	E♭ (E♭ aug)	iv (IV), VI (#vi°) or vii° (VII) chords
iv (IV)	Fm (F)	V (v) or vii° (VII) chords
v (V)	Gm (G)	VI (#vi°) chords
VI (#vi°)	A♭ (A°)	III (III+), iv (IV), V (v) or vii° (VII) chords
VII (vii°)	B♭ (B°)	i chord

FIGURE 4.26 Common Chord Progressions in Natural Minor Key (Diatonic Chords)

immeasurable tools to work with. There are endless ways music can be structured and I have found that analyzing chord progressions of others has helped me to discover chord patterns that I wouldn't have necessarily thought of on my own. The practice of learning various combinations of chord progressions and experimenting with chords that sound good together can be instrumental in developing your original sound.

Bring in the Rhythm

Rhythm is recurring notes and rests of longer and shorter durations that create patterns. It creates the sense of the beat and timing in a piece of music. Rhythm consists of the components *pulse, accents*, and *subdivision* performed within a determined measure of time. Meter represents strong and weak pulses that are a part of the rhythm. In other words, rhythm is where the notes fall, and meter is the element in the rhythm that represents how notes are emphasized and felt. Rhythm is the foundation that exists throughout almost all popular song genres. The rhythm creates a pulse, which is the heartbeat of songs. Add chords to the rhythm and you have two of the main components needed to create a solid music foundation to support the primary melody.

The patterns played by the drum kit instruments typically provide the foundation of the song's rhythm. The drum kit is a collection of drums played by one person and consists of the bass drum, snare drum, one or more tom drums, a hi-hat, and cymbals. Percussion instruments such as woodblock, cowbell, tambourine, congas, etc., are also a part of the drum family, typically played by an additional percussionist, and are used to enhance the rhythm.

Pulse is the heartbeat of the rhythm. The pulse is usually generated by the bass drum (or the cymbal in jazz music). The snare drum provides a backbeat that is usually a quarter note on the second and fourth beats of a $\frac{4}{4}$ tempo song. In some cases, there may be a note or pulse in a song that will create additional dynamics or lifts in the composition when emphasized. These prominent articulations performed by an instrument or voice are referred to as *accents*. The pulse and accents set the tone of the song by providing its feel, vibe, flow, mood, tension, and release.

Rhythm is mastered by understanding the technique of *subdivision*. Subdividing is the creation of chords, rhythm patterns, and/or melodies of various durations which all work well together on top of the pulse. In other words, the entire rhythm arrangement can be broken down into smaller parts.

The Groove

The groove is a series of rhythms played by instruments along with the drum kit that works well together. The groove is usually generated by the rhythm section (drums, bass, keyboards, and guitar). The rhythm section's primary role is to maintain a solid foundation consisting of a steady beat and subdivisions of musical parts playing simultaneously with each one complementing one another.

I like to think of the groove as a musical conversation. As with conversations between humans, communication is most effective when one person speaks or leads at a time. This is the same goal as in music. The melody is the person who has the floor. The role of the other instruments is to complement and support the melody. The groove works best when the low, mid-range and high music frequencies are present and balanced.

The groove is the foundation and heartbeat of the composition. Almost every style of music has its heartbeat, style, and accents that set it apart from other music genres. People, in general, want to feel "in the groove" of whatever is going on in their daily lives. Thus, the word groove and its offspring "groovy" are some of the most used words in the music universe! I suspect it is because the sentiment implies a feeling of things working well together.

Pulse

Let's first look at the pulse of the song. In the case of the song "Good As Hell," the pulse is generated by the drum pattern. Only three drums are notated on drum music charts, the bass drum, the snare drum, and the hi-hat.

Bass Drum—Sits on the bottom space
Snare Drum—Sits on the 2nd from the top line
Hi-Hat—Sits on top of the top line

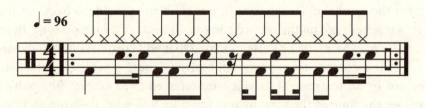

FIGURE 4.27 Drum Kit Pattern—"Good As Hell"

The combination of accents and subdivisions of the eighth and sixteenth note percussion pattern has a very important role in the groove and vibe of the song. This percussion pattern added to the drum pattern gives the groove its bounce. This could be heard clearly when the vocals are muted in the ninth bar from the beginning of the song.

FIGURE 4.28 Drum Kit Pattern + Percussion Pattern—"Good As Hell"

With the addition of the chordal pattern playing the same rhythm as the kick drum, the groove is set.

FIGURE 4.29 All Parts to The Groove—"Good As Hell"

Creating Contrast

A major component in keeping the listener's interest is to incorporate *contrasting sections*. Every great song starts with a terrific idea. However, a great idea can get old very quickly without variation. *Prosody* (change in rhythm and sound) along with the contrast in the melody are key elements in creating contrasting sections.

Imagine if you wore the same designer shirt every day. Your friends and colleagues would become bored and disinterested in your appearance. Your wardrobe would soon be thought of as predictable and unsurprising. The same analogy goes for how you structure your song. To help create prosody and contrasting sections, you must integrate varied rhythms, melodies, and harmonies between the song's sections.

Rhythm Contrast

The combination or pattern of rhythms that work well together gives the song its feel. Rhythm plays a crucial role in changing the mood and character of the song. Music rhythms are patterns of drums, chords, and notes played with various durations of length. A few ways to create a contrast in the rhythm from section to section are as follows:

- Change the drum pattern
- Change the rhythm of chords
- Vary rhythm from chord to single notes

- Vary the tempo (perhaps write an arrangement that starts with a slow introduction then leads to an energetic chorus)
- Add drum breaks that may feature percussion or a new instrument sound

A good example of rhythm contrast is displayed in the song, "Shut Up and Dance" by Walk the Moon. The verse and B sections of the song are sung over a syncopated rhythm pattern. The syncopated rhythm changes in the verse/B sections change in the chorus to legato notes in the bass, along with guitar power chords playing the length of each chord. The sections are held together by a hypnotic rhythm guitar throughout the song.

Melodic Contrast

The most memorable part of a song for the listener is the melody. Therefore, it is essential to have as much contrast in this area as possible without it being too complicated to follow. Here are a few simple ways to create a variance between the verse and chorus sections:

- If the verse melody consists of short melodic rhythms, make the chorus melody phrase simpler with notes that are longer in length and vice versa.
- Write a chorus melody with notes that are in a higher pitch than the verse. This gives the song a feeling of movement.
- Include a larger interval jump between notes in the phrase.
- Remember, the simpler the chorus, the easier it is for the listener to understand and enjoy!

A good example of melodic contrast can be found in "The Power of Love" by Celine Dion and written by Mary Susan Applegate, Gunther Mende-Kim, Candy de Rouge, and Jennifer Rush.

In this example, the verse melody starts in a low range and develops into higher notes leading into the next section, which is the chorus melody. This section is higher in range. The chorus section is followed by the second verse, which has a similar melody as the first verse but is embellished with higher alternate notes using the same rhythm as the melody in the first verse. The second verse leads back to the chorus melody, which resolves with the title of the song in the lyric.

The melody further builds in the bridge section before returning to the final chorus melody, again choosing alternative notes in an even higher register to evoke more emotion before landing on the final and highest note sung in the chorus, which in this case is the fifth of the chord. The song vamps in a sultry vocal ad lib in a lower register after the vocal melodies in the body of the song have been thoroughly massaged. The structuring of the vocal melody on this song truly takes the listener on a journey melodically.

Harmonic Contrast

Adding harmony to a song is a great way to enrich the melody and to make a section sound bigger. The recurrence of harmonies in music and vocals adds tremendously to the song's mood and dynamics.

There are several ways to build contrast harmonically. Some suggestions are:

- Set contrast between unison guitar or piano lead and accompanying lines and develop into harmonies and various chord textures as the song progresses.
- Add harmony to the prominent instrumental or lead vocal melody line.
- Affirm the lead melody's statement. Initiate call and response between vocals or between vocals and instruments, or two instruments.
- Add horn and string arrangements.
- Vary the volume and add dynamics between and within music sections
- Introduce a new instrument part and sound in the chorus to give the song a feeling of growth and movement.
- Add a string or keyboard pad (i.e., held chords) to give the chorus a fuller sound.

A good example of harmonic contrast can be found in "Uma Thurman" by Fall Out Boy. The magic of this song is its use of multiple rhythmic, harmonic, and unison parts in both the instrumental and vocal performances. The combination of these elements leaves no chance of losing the listener's interest.

Melody within the Chord Harmony

Sometimes countermelodies are played within the harmony of the chords. These are often arranged so that they interact in a call-and-response manner with the main vocal melody. When instruments, vocal harmonies, rhythms, and melodies interact and align with one another, a fantastic musical conversation is created, allowing the listener to make an easy and enjoyable connection with the song.

Musical Phrases and Countermelodies

Musical melodic phrases are combinations of notes, harmonies, and motifs, which provide tonal color that complement and accompany the main melody. The notes chosen to create the motifs are found within the scale that aligns with the chord used in the song. When a secondary melody is played simultaneously with the principal melody, the secondary melody is called a *countermelody*. Countermelodies help to facilitate a musical conversation between the main melody and accompanying instruments.

One way to effectively use a countermelody is to write a slower secondary melody if the principal melody has a faster movement, and vice versa. Another effective way to keep the listener's interest is to compose the secondary melody in a higher or lower register and to incorporate varied rhythms.

Examples where countermelodies play significant roles are found in songs like "Help" by the Beatles, where the verses are made up of two melodies (one moderate tempo and one slower) bearing the same lyric, and "Sailing" by Christopher Cross, where the repetitive arpeggio guitar melody gives the feeling of movement. Its hypnotic effect provides the perfect mood and setup for the slower-moving lyric melody.

Another example of two melodies that complement one another is found in the song "Stand Up," recorded by Cynthia Erivo for the motion picture *Harriet*. The lead vocal melody performed simultaneously with the unison chant-like vocal chorus melody at the beginning of the song fit like a hand in a glove. The song was nominated for an Academy Award in 2020, as well as earned Golden Globe Award and Critics' Choice Movie Award nominations.

The Signature Riff

One of the most common elements found in 99.9 percent of hit songs is the *signature riff*. The signature riff is a distinguishable lick, melody, pattern, or chord progression that is identifiable to a particular song and makes it recognizable right off the bat.

The lick is usually an instrumental hook that sets the tone of the song from the onset. It enables the listener to recognize your song instantaneously. Most times it incorporates melodic elements, which already exist in your song. It's not unusual for the signature riff to reoccur after you've established the core of the song. In many cases, it will reoccur after the first or second chorus, bridge, solo section, or outro of the song. It depends on when it feels like a natural time for the riff to reappear.

The signature riff should be uncomplicated and effortless to sing or hum along with. It's often thought of like a singalong refrain, so you want to apply the same principles used to write catchy hooks. Often, the notes of the signature riff are borrowed or alternate notes from the chorus, such as the guitar riff played at the beginning of "Start Me Up" by the Rolling Stones, or verse melody such as "Open Arms" by Journey. Sometimes a guitar riff, such as in the intro of "Makes Me Wonder" by Maroon 5, is just enough to do the trick. Another example is the isolated rhythmic piano on the introduction of the John Legend hit song, "All of Me."

There are many songs where the signature riff is the song's foundation. Songs like "Satisfaction" by the Rolling Stones; "Fancy" by Iggy Azalea featuring Charli XCX; and "I'll Take You There" by the Staple Singers are all distinct riffs that serve as the song's infrastructure.

Understanding Music Genres

As a songwriter, understanding various genres, the differences between them, and the culture that surrounds that style of music is key to knowing how to reach a targeted audience.

The term music genre refers to a style of music, such as pop, classical, country, gospel, rock, hip-hop, jazz, R&B, rap, and so forth. Although various styles of music have similar characteristics, many have characteristics that are unique to their genre. Five of the most common genres of popular music are pop, R&B, hip-hop, country, and rock.

> **Pop**—Verse/Chorus Structure. Pop music originated from the United Kingdom and the United States during the mid-1950s and is a term that is associated internationally with dance music, where the chorus (hook) is repetitive musically and lyrically and is written in a way that is singable and memorable. Pop derives from the word popular, meaning that it is liked, admired, or enjoyed by many people. Pop music reflects emerging trends and is meant to specifically appeal to a commercial audience. As would be expected, most regions around the world have their own variation of pop music.

Characteristics of sections of pop songs include intros, middle four- or eight-bar sections that serve as passages to the chorus, and sections where instruments drop out and re-enter. Repetitive riffs (a short repetitive collection of notes) serve as mini hooks that appear throughout the song to keep the listener's attention. The music is often repetitive, and the up-tempo songs are very danceable.

The common lyrical themes are about romantic relationships. Pop music uses elements of many other genres, such as R&B, rock, country, and Latin. Pop, by way of definition, can be considered in all the other music genres.

Subgenres of pop music: Christian, classical crossover, dance, electronic, Latin ballad, adult contemporary, Europop, pop/rap, pop/rock, soft rock, surf, teen, K-pop, traditional.

> **R&B**—Verse/Chorus Structure. Rhythm & blues is a term created in the 1930s used to delineate blues music for African American audiences from blues for mainstream audiences. Rhythm & blues music was often referred to as "Race Music." In the late 1940s, music producer Jerry Wexler officially coined the term *rhythm & blues* (R&B) for use on the Billboard charts after the term "Race Music" was deemed to be offensive. The new Billboard term "Rhythm & Blues" is used to describe new R&B rhythms rooted in blues.

Derivative terms for this form of music are soul, traditional (1950s–1960s) style, funk (1970s–1980s), hip-hop, and contemporary (includes elements of electronic/dance instrumentation and styles, and alternative and European influences).

The main R&B characteristic is soulful singing usually over a steady rhythmic groove rooted in blues. It may include syncopated rhythms and repetitious instrumental patterns accompanied by a strong backbeat played on the second and fourth beats on the snare drum. The drummer must play "in the pocket," meaning that they keep solid time with the kick and snare drums. The hi-hat and cymbal patterns must leave space for the instrumental ensemble parts to be supported and complemented.

70   The Art and Business of Songwriting

The bass guitar both supports and drives the groove with a repetitive pattern for other instruments to build upon and around. Another important characteristic in R&B music is the rhythm guitar. When the guitar plays rhythm, you may only need two or three notes of the chord to give the song a burst of energy. Space or rests also play an important role with rhythm guitar playing.

The keyboard's role is usually to provide either foundation rhythm or chords that serve as a pad or glue to the musical conversation. With the development of technology, electronic instruments with new sounds were incorporated into R&B, creating subgenres such as contemporary R&B, and combinations of pop, hip-hop, rap, and funk.

Subgenres of R&B music: Contemporary, hip-hop, neo-soul, adult contemporary, urban contemporary, disco, funk, Afro soul, blue-eyed soul, alternative, deep funk revival, doo-wop, smooth, boogaloo.

> **Hip-Hop**—Hip-hop music is a subculture and music movement that started in the 1970s. It was originally used to accompany rapping, MCing, DJing, beatboxing, and breakdancing. This music is associated with urban-inspired graffiti art, fashion, and a way for youth and rap artists to lyrically express personal and cultural experiences regarding injustices by legal institutions and discrimination in general. Hip-hop was developed in the United States by Latin and African Americans in the Bronx borough of New York City. Hip-hop is forever evolving and infuses rap vocals along with all forms of R&B, funk, electronic, pop, classical, and global music influences.

The main characteristics of hip-hop include prominent drum sampling (taking a portion of a pre-existing sound recording and reusing it to create a new work), percussion break sampling of another song, drum machines, turntables, scratching, loops, and breaks, using a DJ mixer, music sequencer, and keyboard. In this genre, the MC (storyteller/rap artist) is the star of the show. If the message isn't relevant, the entire piece is a no-go. The first hip-hop record to crack the Top 40 was "Rapper's Delight" by the Sugar Hill Gang, where the artist raps over an instrumental version of the hit song "Good Times" by Chic.

Hip-hop is probably the most stripped-down music form of all genres, instrumentation-wise, to ensure that the pulse and beat of the music serve in the role of supporting the vocal performance, as opposed to multiple instrumental parts arranged in a way that may compete with it.

Subgenres of Hip-Hop music: Gangsta, hyphy, jazz, ghetto house, g-funk, trap, rap rock/metal/Christian, crunk, mumble, alternative, hard-core, hip-hop, electro hop, emo, grime (UK)

> **Country**—Verse/Chorus Structure. Originated from the rural areas of the South and West in the early 20th century. The roots of country music are in folk songs, ballads, and a blend of blues, traditional Appalachian songs, and gospel. Instruments that are commonly used in country music are acoustic guitars, banjos, steel guitars, steel basses, and sometimes fiddle.

The songs of early country music were simple and easy to remember, with basic I–IV–V chord structure, such as in Charlie Pride's "Kiss an Angel Good Morning." As time went on, modern country music began to incorporate the vi chord in songs like "Come Over" by Kenny Chesney.

The subject matter of country songs typically centers around love, loss, cheating, drinking, redemption, killing, jail, and family. Nowadays, country music has incorporated characteristics of pop, R&B, and rap.

Subgenres of country music: Bluegrass, Appalachian folk, Ameripolitan, alternative, cowpunk, country/pop, country blues, polka, cowboy/Western, folk rock, Southern rock, rockabilly, Americana.

> Rock—Verse/chorus structure. Rock music is largely based on a repeated riff. The chordal structure in rock music is based on triads and driven by the electric guitar and drums, and occasionally incorporates a piano and/or organ. The beat is more driving and hard pounding. This music is energetic, and the overall sound is edgier than that of pop, country, and R&B music.

Blues musician Aaron Thibeaux "T-Bone" Walker was one of the first musicians to use the amplified guitar on a recording in 1942. In 1948, Leo Fender introduced the first mass-produced solid-body electric guitar. Shortly afterward, innovator Les Paul popularized the instrument with his recordings. However, it was Chuck Berry's style of playing the guitar that influenced rock music throughout the 1960s, up through today. Although influenced by blues, rhythm & blues, and country music, it is the raw and edgy tones that set it apart from other music genres. Rock has developed into various subgenres, including blues rock, folk rock, punk rock, and progressive rock, psychedelic rock, Southern rock, heavy metal, and many more.

Rock's typical chord progressions are I–IV–V triads. The order of these three chords also changes from time to time. Some of the variations include I–V–IV, IV–V–I, V–IV–I, IV–I–V, and V–I–IV. The authentic rock sound is intended to be raw. The foundation of rock music is based on simple un-syncopated rhythm with a solid two and four backbeat on the snare drum in a $\frac{4}{4}$ meter. The vocals are very much a part of the dynamics and tend to have as much edge as the guitar in the ensemble.

Subgenres of rock music: Rock & roll, blues rock, folk rock, country rock, jazz rock fusion, psychedelic rock, progressive rock, hard rock, heavy metal, punk, new wave, alternative rock, Brit pop, indie rock.

Summary

In closing, remember that music sets the mood and emotions of the listener usually before they hear the lyric and know the story. Although an extensive understanding of music theory is not necessary, a basic understanding of pitch, rhythm, chords/harmony, melody, and knowing various music genres is very helpful in connecting musically with your desired audience. Also, creating contrasting sections is a major component in keeping the listener's interest. Lyrics without music is simply poetry. So, create music that is imaginative, rhythmic, melodic, interesting, and supports the featured melody; and as usual, have fun!

Songs Referred to in Chapter 4

"Run the World (Girls)" © 2009 and © 2010
Songwriters: Beyonce Knowles, Terius Nash, Wesley Pentz, Adidja Palmer, David Taylor, and Nick "Afrojack" van de Wall
Publishers: Sony/ATV Music Publishing LLC, Warner Chappell Music, Inc., Kobalt Music Publishing Ltd., BMG Rights Management, New Royalty Consulting, LLC.

"Good As Hell" © 2016
Songwriters: Melissa Jefferson/Eric Frederic
Publishers: Lizzo Music Publishing, Songs From The Boardwalk, Frederic and Reed Music, Sony/ATV Music Publishing LLC

Songwriter Spotlight

Donald Lawrence

Donald Lawrence. Photo by DeWayne Rogers. Used with permission.

Gospel music is one of my favorite music genres! I was fortunate to catch up with the very busy Donald Lawrence, who took a few minutes to talk about his influences, role models, choirmaster expectations, approach to songwriting, artistry, inspiration, and advice for up-and-coming songwriters. He is known as a multiple-platinum-record-selling, Grammy and Stellar Award–winning gospel producer, choirmaster, songwriter, vocal coach/producer, and arranger. His projects include the Tri-City Singers, the Clark Sisters, Hezekiah Walker, BeBe Winans, and hundreds of collaborations.

Batiste: Who were some of your musical influences growing up?

Lawrence: Growing up anything overly creative was an instant magnet for me. As a songwriter, Andrae Crouch, Twinkie Clark, Walter, and Edwin Hawkins, Richard Smallwood, *and* musical theater legend Stephen Sondheim greatly influenced my songwriting. Their ability to create timeless melodies and their approach to storytelling is impeccable. I'm still a fan.

As a vocal arranger, Luther Vandross, Andrae Crouch, and Thomas Whitfield had a huge influence on me. The background vocal arrangement always supported and enhanced the story of the lead vocalist. The parts were delivered with such character. The background arrangement was always such a significant part of the groove and band arrangement.

Batiste: Where did you develop your production skills?

Lawrence: Production wasn't something I set out to do. It was mainly songwriting/vocal arranging until I heard Teddy Riley. He had a *huge* impact on me, and he inspired me to produce records. Teddy Riley was always on the cutting edge of production. He used a combination of diverse classic sound modules, outboard processors, and modern synthesizers, along with great vocal arrangements. Even to this day, I'm still star-struck. Brilliant!

Batiste: Your vocal production is stellar. What do you expect from the vocalist that works with you?

Lawrence: As a choirmaster and record producer, I expect the ears of the singers I work with to be on point. Them coming to rehearsal or the studio knowing . . . the parts is the basic. The nuances, the dynamics, the feel, and the heart of the song are where the work lies. . . .

Batiste: What is your approach to songwriting and what advice would you give to up-and-coming songwriters?

Lawrence: . . . In terms of approach, I usually hear lyrics, melody, and tempo all at the same time. I think because songs are visual for me, a scene . . . depicts the story [and] melody (happy or intense) as well as the tempo. At the end of the day, I'm more a musical theater songwriter with Gospel inference. . . .

The main thing about writing songs that connect with audiences is to be authentic. What comes from the heart reaches the heart. Go somewhere and come back with something. The moment writing a song takes you away is the moment it's truly inspired. We go *in*-spirit and we return *in*-spired. To be in spirit is to return with something that was inspired.

I feel we've gotten away from "Art." People write for chart positions as opposed to telling their story or sharing wisdom to help someone with a life. My advice to people who desire to have a long career in the music industry is: Don't be afraid to write from the heart and not just for "commerce." Don't be afraid of not fitting in. Let's get back to authentic individualized *art*. I love being able to distinguish Elton from Barry Manilow, Andrae Crouch from Walter and Edwin Hawkins, Sondheim from Lloyd-Weber. Let's birth new "Timeless Tunesmiths."

5

Writing Unique and Memorable Melodies

Elements of a Memorable and Unique Melody

Thank goodness for melodies. A song would not be a song if it did not have its melody as the main attraction. For certain, the most important element of a hit song is the melody. It is the focus and essence of every song in terms of what the listener remembers. Unless the song is driven by the bass line or a signature riff, it is very difficult to remember a song that does not have a strong melody. When all else fails, the melody can be hummed when the lyrics are forgotten.

The melody is the lead voice and has the floor in the musical conversation between the other instrumental or vocal parts in the song. The job of other vocal or instrumental parts is to support or accompany the melody. This goal can be achieved, especially if you buy into the philosophy that my elementary school teacher held. As I recall, his mode of operation was: "We can all talk, but not at the same time."

A melody consists of a series of single notes, a combination of scale fragments, note steps and leaps, and short and long phrase lengths and shapes. Melodies, which are repeated simple phrases that connect, are easiest to remember and sing. A good example is the opening-verse melody in the song "Grenade" by Bruno Mars.

- First, the short notes: Easy come–easy go–that's just how you live
- Followed by long notes: Oh, take–take–take it all
- Ending with short notes: But you never give

It almost feels like Morse code in its rhythm approach. This simple, mostly monotone melody is catchy and unchallenging for a non-singer, which enables the listener to focus on the words and meaning of the story with little effort.

One of the most frequent questions I am asked is, "What is a memorable melody?" The short answer is that a memorable melody is catchy, interesting, and easy to remember. Although creating a melody that's easy to remember is the goal, there are many characteristics and elements incorporated in writing a straightforward and undemanding melody. So, let's identify some of the effects and characteristics.

A memorable melody haunts your mind and captures your heart long after you've heard it. It is the melody you hum when in the grocery store, an elevator or somewhere unrelated to music. It's the tune you unconsciously sing while working, relaxing, or expressing an emotion. All these factors are the results of a memorable melody.

Memorable Melody Checklist

- Write melodic intervals that are close to one another stepwise
- Create phrases that are short and concise
- Use repetition and variation
- Write a melody with good contour and distinctive shape
- Use symmetrical phrases
- Work verse melody seamlessly into the chorus
- Keep range of the melody within 10 notes
- Create a vocal or instrumental countermelody

A great melody is distinctive enough to stand on its own without music. However, when the melody is not flying solo, it must work cohesively with other musical elements of the song. A melody is useless if it does not work well with the music chosen for its accompaniment. Although learning music theory is not required to write a great melody, it is helpful. The more you understand music and how it works, the easier it is to find the perfect marriage between the melody and its musical accompaniment.

Keep in mind when writing the melody to music, the melody should be as straightforward as possible. Build on a "motif"—a set of notes that are contoured into a complete musical idea—that is easy and simple to follow. A tune that is easy to follow, combined with subject matter that is relatable to a large general audience, is what makes a song a hit.

A unique melody is born when the melody incorporates an unusual or remarkable union between the chord progression, rhythm, and sequence of notes. Two of the most common requirements for developing a memorable melody are to write with a balance of repetition and variation.

Repetition

Repetition of rhythm and melodic patterns are key factors in making a song easy to remember. These key elements are why nursery rhymes and holiday songs are remembered effortlessly. See, for example, the nursery rhyme "Row, Row, Row Your Boat," written by Eliphalet Oram Lyte:

Row, row, row your boat
Gently down the stream
Merrily, merrily, merrily, merrily,
Life is but a dream

In this song, the repetition of the words "row" and "merrily" are presented three to four times. In addition, the notes of the melody have a bouncy rhythm and move stepwise in an ascending direction leading up to the word "stream," which happens to be the fifth note of the scale. The melody jumps up one octave from the beginning note to the word "Merrily."

In the second half of the phrase, each word is repeated four times in a catchy triplet rhythm of descending arpeggio notes (8, 5, 3, 1). The last line of the phrase, "Life Is But a Dream," ends with descending scale notes (5, 4, 3, 2, 1) on each word.

Variation

Variation stimulates curiosity, which makes one want to seek out more information on the subject. Therefore, deviation and contrast are crucial to keeping one's interest piqued.

There are several ways to vary melodies. I've found that the following seven variation styles should provide enough examples to get any budding songwriter up and going.

- *Short and long phrases, and interval jumps.* A common method of variation is a verse with a long phrase followed by one or two short phrases, or vice versa. Sometimes, one may insert an interval of a fifth to sixth higher or lower in the melody. This combination of variations can be done in any order. If you listen to one of the most memorable melodies of all time, "Somewhere over the Rainbow," written by Harold Arlen and Yip Harburg, you will notice that the interval jump occurs right at the beginning of the title followed by an asymmetrical second line. The verse section "Someday I'll wish upon a star and wake up where the clouds are far behind me" consists of short and long phrases.
- *Varied repetitive rhythms and sections.* Beyonce's "Single Ladies (Put a Ring on It)" is a great example of varying rhythm phrases in each section of a song. In this song, each section sounds like a chorus hook. The song repeats four different rhythm hook sections before it repeats a familiar section. After five sections, the song goes to the second verse, and even then, the second part of this new verse has an alternate rhythm leading to the chorus.

    Call & response: *All the Single Ladies*
    Verse: *Up in the club, we just broke up*
    Chorus: *Cause if you liked it, then you should have put a ring on it*
    Riff: *Oh oh oh oh oh oh oh oh oh oh oh oh*

- *Altering the range.* To create more drama or emphasis on a certain word or part in the melody, insert an interval of a fifth or sixth higher or lower than the rest of the melody, such as in one of the most memorable melodies of all time, "My

Bonnie Lies over the Ocean," where the interval between the word "My" and "Bonnie" is a sixth.

- *Insert pauses.* Sometimes a pause, or a "stop," directly preceding a chorus or new section gives the melody a chance to breathe a little. This space in the melody can bring more attention to what's coming, which may have a great impact on the new section. Songwriter Dianne Warren's chorus on "How Do I Live?" is a great example of this technique. The first beat is a quarter-note rest/pause. Then the chorus melody sung to the words "How do I live without you?" starts on the second beat. This song was a hit record for both Trisha Yearwood and LeAnn Rimes.

- *Make use of other notes in the scale.* Although melodies typically start and end with a triad interval of a chord in the key to a song, using other notes in the key signature within the phrase is an effective way to create an interesting melody. In the song "Under Pressure" by Queen and David Bowie (Classic Queen Mix), the first verse does what is typically expected in terms of the ending note being a part of the interval family. The second verse takes a total departure from the first verse. The ascending melody of the words "Chippin' around" starts on the third note in the scale of the key and lands on the sixth scale degree; then in the second half of the verse, the melody descends from the sixth note in the scale down to the sixth note of the scale below the starting point with the phrase "Kick my brains 'round the floor."

- *Transpose phrases, and with varied notes or two.* Sometimes phrases are transposed. When phrases are transposed, the same or similar notes and rhythm patterns are played or sung in a different key or with different chords within the key to a song. The rhythm pattern is the same with an alternate note in the middle or at the end. An example of a phrase being transposed is demonstrated in the chorus of "We Don't Talk Anymore" recorded by Charlie Puth featuring Selena Gomez. The line "We don't talk anymore" repeats three times. The notes in the first and third phrases are the same, but the last note in the second phrase is lowered by one half-step to fit with the chord being played at that moment. The listener sings the same or similar melody, yet it has the feeling of change.

- *Melodies that vary and build slightly from verse to verse.* Many songwriters choose the method of slightly varying the melody with each new verse. This method is opposed to the tradition of repeating the established first-verse melody on the second verse and beyond to tell its story. In most cases, the rhythm part of the phrase stays the same while alternate notes are used to help with dynamics and to emphasize the meaning and emotion of the words. This method of change with each new verse is effective because the melody builds and intensifies with the story. This method of melody writing is best illustrated in songs like, "Neither One of Us" and "I Don't Want to Do Wrong" by Gladys Knight & the Pips, as well as "Why I Love You" by Major.

Other Considerations

Range

It's very possible to intimidate a potential artist and lose a song placement if your melody isn't written in an appropriate range for a vocalist. The vocal range of most vocalists is within ten notes. In other words, they sing an octave plus a third without a struggle or strain. Once you write the melody beyond ten notes, the chances of getting someone to record it are slim due to the natural limitations of the voice. There are vocalists with four- to five-octave ranges including Stevie Wonder, Mariah Carey, Ledisi, Charlie Wilson, Celine Dion, and so forth, but they are few and far between. It's much safer to write in the appropriate range so that if someone likes your composition, they can simply change the key to fit their vocal range.

Remember, an interesting melody has a distinctive shape and contour. Along with repetition and variation, be sure to reserve enough of the higher notes to develop a climactic part of the melody that makes a seamless transition to the chorus (if you're not using a pre-chorus to make the connection).

Element of Surprise

Writing a melody that's unlike any other melody can be tricky if you do not allow yourself to break the rules. Take time to apply the "What If" principle. That's right, experiment with alternate notes, unexpected skips, jumps, patterns, and phrasing that are pleasing in sound, but may not be what the listener is expecting. The element of surprise will bring a unique quality to your melody.

A melodic element of surprise may be achieved by an unpredictable single note or a phrase. Using the single-note example, your phrase may consist of a series of ascending notes that would normally land on a certain, expected note. The most common ending to a melody phrase is for the series of notes to directly end on one of the chord's triad notes (1, 3, or 5). An alternative option may be to skip the predicted note and jump to an interval or two beyond the expected note then descend into the note. Some melodies may incorporate an entirely new rhythmic phrase within a section of the song.

Let's look at the surprise elements (note skips, jumps, and alternate melodic rhythms) in the verse of "Chasing Pavements" by Adele (songwriters: Adele Laurie Blue Adkins and Francis "Eg" White).

> *I've made up my mind, don't need to think it over*
> *If I'm wrong, I am right, don't need to look no further*
> *This ain't lust, I know this is love . . . But . . .*

Note that practically the entire first line, "I've made up my mind, don't need to think it . . ." is just two notes, The first word "I've" starts on the third of the chord, and the next few words, "made up my mind, don't need to think it," are sung on one note, the fifth; then the melody note jumps an interval of a fifth on the word "over," then descends stepwise. The next phrase repeats in another key. Then comes the unexpected melodic surprise on the words "I know" after the repetitive and symmetrical opening phrases. As a bonus surprise, the phrase ends with one last unpredictable interval jump on the word "But" to start the next verse.

Melodic Phrases

I consider it optimal to create melodic phrases to be like the conversational phrases we make while speaking. Can you imagine having a conversation with someone who speaks in a monotone voice? How boring would that be? When we talk, we use various rhythms, patterns, and inflections in our voices, which makes our conversations interesting. This is the same concept we use when we write melodic phrases.

At the end of a thought or statement, there is a natural break that signals the completion of the musical thought, just as there is at the end a phrase when speaking. This is important to understand when looking at the interaction between the melody and the notes of the chord that accompanies it. The first and last note of a melody phrase usually begins and ends on one of the triad intervals of the chord. For example, if your song starts or ends on the C major chord, the melody will typically start and end on the notes C, E, or G.

Melodic phrases vary in length. Popular music phrases are commonly four bars in length. However, phrases can be as short as one bar to as long as eight bars, as long as the final phrase feels like a complete thought.

Call and Response and Countermelodies

Countermelodies play simultaneously in other voices or instruments along with the prominent lead melody within a section of a song. The countermelody's role is to add a second and possibly third voice to the musical conversation.

There are many combinations one could use in creating countermelodies. Sometimes the main melody and countermelody may interact with one another, creating a secondary theme or a call-and-response type of melodic style such as in the chorus of "Rolling in the Deep" by Adele. The lead voice sings the line "We could have had it all," while the background vocals sing just as prominently, "You're gonna wish you never had met me . . . rolling in the deep."

At times, an instrumental melody's role may be just as prominent as the lead vocal in a song. A great example of an instrumental and vocal melody interacting with one another is found in the song "No One," performed and written by Alicia Keys. In this example, the piano plays a prominent arpeggio-style melody along with the vocal melody throughout the entire song. The other song that comes to mind is "Sailing," written and performed by Christopher Cross. I couldn't imagine hearing this song without the haunting arpeggiated melodic guitar accompanying the vocal melody. In both examples, the instrumental and vocal melodies are significant to the overall song to the point that it would be difficult to get the full emotion of the song without the two parts playing at the same time.

Another style of call-and-response melody writing is to have the call and response overlap with one another. If this overlap melodic style is written for vocals, it will require two or more people to sing it. A good example of this is the chorus of "She's Leaving Home" by the Beatles.

> *She (We gave her most of our lives)*
> *Is leaving (Sacrificed most of our lives)*
> *Home (We gave her everything money could buy)*

With the first melody, the note and word "She" overlaps the beat where the response begins, making it almost impossible for these two melodies to be performed vocally by a solo vocalist. However, both melodies are very important to the song.

At times the featured melody may switch or trade places between voices and instruments, such as in the Kool & the Gang classic dance song "Celebration." The keyboard and horn parts are a prominent part of the melody structure as they trade feature melody roles back and forth, while the background vocals sing the chorus "Celebrate good times, come on," leaving space for the lead vocalist to ad-lib.

Because the main goal of the songwriter is to make a connection with the listener, the author must create a user-friendly melodic theme that ensures the essence of the song is fully communicated and understood. Take into consideration all the elements discussed in this chapter and implement them as needed.

Songs Referred to in Chapter 5

"Chasing Pavements" © 2007
Songwriters: Adele Laurie Blue Adkins and Francis Anthony White
Publishers: Universal Music Publishing Group

"Single Ladies (Put a Ring on It) © 2008
Songwriters: Beyonce Knowles, Christopher "Tricky" Stewart, Terius "The Dream" Nash, and Thaddis Harrell
Publishers: EMI April Music, Inc., March Ninth Music Publishing, 2082 Music Publishing, B-Day Publishing, Songs Of Peer Ltd.

82 The Art and Business of Songwriting

"Row, Row, Row Your Boat" © 1852
Songwriter: Eliphalet Oram Lyte
Publisher: Public Domain

"She's Leaving Home" © 1967
Songwriters: John Lennon and Paul McCartney
Publishers: Universal Music Publishing Group, Sony/ATV Music Publishing LLC.

Songwriter Spotlight

Narada Michael Walden

Larry Batiste (left) and Narada Michael Walden (right). Photo by Bob White, used with permission.

Narada Michael Walden is a Grammy Award–winning producer, songwriter, drummer, multi-instrumentalist, arranger, and recording artist. His body of work includes "How Will I Know," "I Wanna Dance With Somebody," "I'm Every Woman," "So Emotional," "One Moment In Time" by Whitney Houston, the *Bodyguard* movie soundtrack, "Freeway Of Love," "Who's Zoomin' Who" by Aretha Franklin, "I Don't Wanna Cry" by Mariah Carey, "Nothing's Gonna Stop Us Now" by Starship, as well as legendary artists like Elton John, Diana Ross, Gladys Knight, the Temptations, Tevin Campbell, Al Jarreau, Al Green, Lisa Fischer, and Steve Winwood.

Batiste: What inspires you to write songs?

Walden: What inspires me is God and life! The simplest of things. I love music, so music is in my heart. So, it must come out. Quincy Jones told me a long time ago that people need helpers in making music. He said, "Narada, you should think about helping as an arranger and producer for other people because there are a lot of great singers, stars that need a helper, a producer in the studio." So, he was the one that pushed me more that way. To answer your question, music has always been inside of me. I have a guru; he's passed on. His name is Sri Chinmoy. Sri Chinmoy taught us that "Inspiration is here for us 24/7"—like birds flying in the sky and you reach your hand up, grab a bird, and bring it down any time of the night or day. Look at Paul McCartney, one of the greatest writers of the Beatles. Paul wrote "Let It Be" at three o'clock in the morning. Woke up out of a dead sleep. He made himself get up and grab the tape recorder and mumble "Let It Be" into that tape recorder. See, it's always there. It is just a matter of: are we receptive to get it? Anytime, God is there for us, anytime, anytime!

Batiste: Was there a songwriter or situation that made you say, "This is what I've got to do?"

Walden: Well yeah, When I was about four or five years old there was a record by Horace Silver called, "Senor Blues," from *Six Pieces of Silver* [Sings groove and melody]. So, I hear that groove and there's a little guy on drums named Louis Hayes, 18 years old from Detroit. So, I'm a little boy and I take my pie tin and my box thing and put it on my high chair to learn that piece. I've always been like that. Then Nina Simone. I had to learn her "Live at Town Hall."

Batiste: What instrument do you write with?

Walden: Drums! It's always been first, drums. Then I learned how to play the piano.

Batiste: What are the elements of a song that makes it a hit?

Walden: What you must have in a song to make it a hit is a great chorus, the hook. If anything is going to be strong, we must have that smash hook. Whatever the part we're going to have that stadium sing back with us, that audience sings back with us—when you go on any television show, no matter what show you go on, they're going to lock onto that song because of the chorus. Everything (verse, etc.) leads to the chorus. So how we get there, we can change up. Maybe we come from Mexico, maybe we come from Cincinnati, maybe we come from Hawaii or Alaska. I don't care how we get there if that punch line is powerful! [He starts singing "How Will I Know" by Whitney Houston.] Strong, got arms on it. you can grab a hold of someone and sing; or [he starts singing the chorus of "I Wanna Dance with Somebody" by Whitney Houston]. The whole world can sing that, see? So, I look for things that people can sing. Then I don't care how it goes. [He starts reciting the verse lyrics, "Clock strikes upon the hour," etc.] I don't care about any of that stuff. We can change it, keep it, or whatever, but as long as I got that hook.

Batiste: What about the melody? How do you create a memorable, hypnotic melody?

Walden: The way we make a hypnotic melody for the hook is two things: A crying melody that's simplistic, but rhythmic. See, you need both gears. I'm a drummer, so you don't want something that's just dot, dot, dot, dot (singing a straight quarter-note rhythm) so much so. You want it (He starts singing a combination of quarter notes and syncopated rhythm to end the phrase). You need rhythm on something. Then you can mess with the melody. But I'm about a strong rhythmic thing so I can jerk it. Keep it simple so they can lock on to it. Don't overproduce it so much so they (the listener) can hear it. But the rhythm is very critical. I'm going to go a step further. . . . A lot of people fall away as the artist. Why do they fall away, they're not hot anymore? It's because their rhythmic sensibility is not strong. And why are the hot ones are still hot? It's because their rhythmic genius is just that. People underestimate it, we never talk about it, but that rhythm thing is powerful. If James Brown was alive right now, if he wanted to have a hit right now, he would be dangerous right now at 90 years old because his rhythm is so hot! Why could Stevie Wonder be deadly right now? It's because his rhythm stank. Chaka Khan stank. Anybody bad . . . even Sade out of London could have a hit right now because her rhythm sensibility is such genius. The late Prince, same thing.

Batiste: What is your guilty music pleasure?

Walden: "Beat Detective." I like to play my drums as close to the meter as I can. And I like to become what I call "Beat Detective" and make my drums any quantification I like to my taste. So, it's perfect if I want, or it can be crooked (slightly off-center) if I want. I like to play with it, doctor it up. No one knows that, but I like to mess with it. The same regard as tunings for vocals. We never speak of it. It's like the Wizard of Oz behind the curtain. But, why our records sound good 20, 30, 40 years later is because we spent time with those vocals to make sure the artist is in tune. Whoever it is, they're always in tune or at least where we want them to be. It's all looked at, computed that way, thought about that way.

Batiste: Do you like to collaborate?

Walden: I love to collaborate!

Batiste: What do you like about it?

Walden: I like for someone to bring me something strong and let me doctor on it and make it even stronger. When someone brings me a strong chorus or an idea of a strong chorus, I'm excited. Then I can tear it up!

Batiste: After you have a strong chorus, how do you make all the other parts come together in terms of the verse melody and story?

Walden: If I have a strong chorus, all I'm doing is taking part of the music from the chorus and varying it; or if it is a major key chorus, then go to a minor key. Perhaps establish a minor key for the verse, so if it's sad, I can go a little deeper, because to me songwriting is like going deep in the ocean: Here's my story. I'm going down there. Come on with me. Then that bridge will come up in my heart zone. I'm going to say, "This is how I feel about things." Then here comes my chorus, BAM! Then go right back deep again to continue the story.

Batiste: In terms of vocal production, how do you get the emotion out of the artist to deliver the story?

Walden: If you give love to someone and explain to them what's happening where they can hear it and they can feel it; even if they can't always feel it because sometimes the artist doesn't like their hits. So, you got to get them to sing it because when they can hear their voice, they'll say, "Oh now I get it." If you can get them to sing one part of it, they can say, "Oh that sounds good."

Batiste: You're right because I heard that Chaka Khan didn't like her big hit, "I Feel for You."

Walden: That happens all the time. Dionne Warwick hated the song "Do You Know the Way to San Jose," Whitney had to be talked into "Where Do Broken Hearts Go." It happens a lot. You get them to sing a little piece of it and when they hear their voice, then they say, "Oh, okay"!

Batiste: How do you pick a hit?

Walden: I must imagine in my heart knowing that something's hit me strong. I also consider where we are in our timing. If dance is a hot thing, then I know the mood is a dance vibe. I know I can't go too wrong if I went in that direction. I'm also open to the universe, where we are, where the planet is, planet earth. Are we establishing this hit in America first or Europe first? If it's America, it's got to have some stank on it. Europe wants it too, but they aren't as critical of that from the giddy-up as we are in America. We are programmed in America. If we are traditional black people, we want to embrace our black radio stations first. That means we got to have something where black radio stations can go, "Oh, I love this." I'm aware of this as a producer. Even as a songwriter, I'm aware of that. Not that I must put it on everybody necessarily for all black people. You see, like Tracy Chapman and others, who are black artists, who are not trying to be that.

Batiste: When you produced and arranged the duet, "I Knew You Were Waiting" for Aretha Franklin and George Michael, what were you thinking there? Where are you thinking about the audience in terms of radio, crossover?

Walden: Same thing. [He starts tapping a funky kick drum pattern with his foot, clapping backbeat/snare drum sound with handclaps, making rhythmic sounds with voice; then singing the bass line—basically emulating the rhythm section groove.] See, the groove was already set up for the vocals to come in.

Batiste: How do you maintain your musical integrity while entertaining record labels' or executive producers' commerce concerns?

Walden: If you're working with Clive Davis as executive producer, he must be able to marry the song. He might want louder background vocals; he may want the first verse re-sung. Mainly he likes the vocals because that's his thing, the vocals. So, you give them these things. That's not a bad thing. If it means he's going to put that mack hand down and you hear the song on every radio station in the world, that's okay.

To answer the question about musical integrity, I don't worry about that. I am music integrity, period, like you are. That's my God gift. It's hard to have a hit, though. A hit is about, what can I do to ring that bell, loud, right? So, I'm always focused on what's going to ring that bell loud and jump on it. . . . I wear two hats. One is the songwriter that births the baby. But then, how are we going to take this baby out into the world? Well, right now the world's gotten tougher. They don't want to see pink booties. So now we've got to dress this baby a little tougher. See what I mean? Now that's the producer's hat. How do we arrange it? It's a good song, but how do we arrange it? Handclaps, no handclaps, big drums, no drums?

Whatever it may be, that's when you have the producer hat on. That's a whole other science. You've got to study Billboard's top 10 for that.

Batiste: What prepared you to wear all the hats you wear such as songwriter, producer, arranger, musician, and vocalist?

Walden: Well, I was born and raised in Kalamazoo, Michigan. Kalamazoo, Michigan, gets very cold. It's got beautiful seasons, springtime, . . . I was born in the springtime. It's so beautiful that the air would knock you out. You almost can't breathe. It's so powerful, you'll almost faint from the smell of flowers, the beauty of the robins, and the trees. It's incredible and beautiful. Then you have summertime, and it gets seriously hot. Then there's fall. It's a serious fall with all the leaves in every kind of brilliant color falling. Then you get an intense winter like 20 and 30 below zero. I mean snow as tall as you are, and you don't even blink. You learn to live a very serious life at a very early age. My parents were very serious as well. They were music lovers. They didn't play music; they were kids 18 and 19 years old. I'm the oldest of six kids. So, to be around them was always intense. My mom's dad was a floor cleaner and janitor, who worked in all the buildings in Kalamazoo. . . . He was a perfectionist. He cleaned everything properly. Washed the sinks, washed everything properly. My mom and dad were always like that. So, I understand perfection. That's my producer hat, but the artist in me is different. An artist must live and breathe where they are. So, I'm prepared for it because that's the way I was raised. It's what's in you, your work ethic. I want number one. I'm not afraid of number one records. I'm charmed by radio. I'm charmed by success. I'm charmed by someone that could have a big record that turns their life around. Look at Motown. The Temptations were ghetto boys. Smokey Robinson, one of our greatest songwriters of all time, one of the greatest angels, changed his life because he could write "Shop Around," "My Guy" for Mary Wells, "My Girl" for the Temptations, and produce it as well. See that's a monster. That man is a monster!! And with the help of his band member, Ron White discovered Stevie Wonder on a street corner impoverished. See what I'm saying? All that's in Detroit, Michigan, right next to me. Kalamazoo is close to Chicago, home of prolific songwriter Curtis Mayfield and his protégés the Five Stairsteps. I remember going to the Regal Theater in Chicago where I first saw Stevie Wonder. Oh, my God, I'm at the Regal Theater and it's packed with screaming girls. You see Stevie Wonder walk up on the stage and when he plays, he's so incredible. He's playing the song, "Fingertips," which was already a hit, but I had to see him with my own eyes. How could this kid that is two years older than me be as great as he was? I thought I was hot until I saw him. I could play drums, bongos, harmonica, but here he was, he could do all those things, brilliantly at twelve years old! And the audience is screaming for him. I just had to take it in. I couldn't believe it. . . .

Batiste: Is there a song that you've written or an artist you produced that has caused you to experience a light bulb moment?

Walden: I must refer to the beginning of my big success. My first platinum recording was with Aretha Franklin, the late Queen of Soul, on the song "Freeway of Love."

It was a song that lyricist Jeffrey Cohen and I wrote for myself which was supposed to go on my album. Frequent collaborator Preston Glass suggested that I record that song on Aretha's album. So, I re-cut it with Aretha in mind. To work with her was just spellbinding. You know it's one thing to hear about someone and their genius. It's another thing to have them look you in your eyes. When Aretha Franklin looked you in your eyes, you knew someone was looking at you. She was a very powerful woman! And could outsing anybody and could almost outplay anybody on the piano too. But she wants a smash, so we were both there to serve the same cause of having a smash song. That's what's so beautiful about music. You can be intimidated until you hit the play button and on comes your song, you hear the track, and everyone is digging it. Now the playing field is equal.

Batiste: How much time did you put into producing the track to get it to where you were confident that she would embrace it?

Walden: I cut the tracks at the Automat Studios in San Francisco, then had session vocalist Kitty Beethoven sing the demo. I sent it to Clive Davis at Arista Records. They liked it and sent it to Aretha for her approval. She had the song for about two months before we recorded the song, so she had plenty of time to learn it. So much time that I learned how she works during those months. There was no music or lyrics on the music stand for her. She had it all memorized. Every phrase, every breath, every catch line was well planned out. I had no idea she was that prepared.

Batiste: How long did that session take?

Walden: Aretha is like this. Aretha Franklin will come in and she'll sing what they call "down the octave" just to get warm, four or five times straight through the track. Then she'll say, "Okay, I'm ready." Now that first take she sings is a smash. Then you know you need more than one take, so you ask her to please do it again, right? She'll do it for you again. Then I may ask for one more good ending to choose from. What I've learned, maybe through working with her is that when the spirit starts circling and gets hot, get that heat before you start getting too technical. Before you bring the mind into it, let the soul do its thing. Work backward to frontwards. Get the ending and the soul you need first, then go through the song and get the technical thing. I've already made a demo of each song, so it's all laid out like a blueprint before the artist arrives. So, I know, that if they sing these parts right, it's going to fit like a puzzle. I leave room for the artist to go out of bounds a little bit. I know when and where to give them the leeway or not.

Batiste: That's awesome advice! Thanks, Narada!

Walden: My pleasure!

6
Finding the Right Words to Say

Writing lyrics requires you to use an additional set of skills, talents, and knowledge. A good writer can choose words that strengthen and clarify statements made in the telling of the story. Appropriate word selection is a learned process that with practice becomes a comfortable habit. When the words are coordinated with one another, they flow freely to develop authentic feelings and emotions within a song.

Successful lyricists write words that are in tune with the universe. They observe what is important to people, how they react to situations, and what makes them feel a certain way, such as what makes them happy or sad. Their lyrics are relatable and tangible. Words have a powerful impact, whether they are used to express an action or merely to paint the perfect imagery.

The word selection process requires critical listening and thinking skills to discover which words to choose and how to incorporate them into a phrase. Keep in mind that words have a visual, emotional, and/or symbolic significance. Your mission is to place the word or phrase where it creates the biggest bang and describes the truest intent of the message. I like to say, "Each word is a symphony within itself."

One needs to continually develop new ways to write about emotions that occur in daily life. To do this, you must become an expert at detecting and describing emotions, such as joy, fear, anger, sadness, and so on. Don't be afraid to use your thesaurus. You may find synonyms and antonyms that are even better than your initial word selection. And it's *not* cheating!

Words function to express clear and cohesive thoughts. The inclusion or omission of a word could distort or modify the entire meaning of the statement. For example, if Bill Withers omitted the words, "Ain't no" in his song entitled, "Ain't No Sunshine (When She's Gone)" and wrote the song title as "Sunshine (When She's Gone)," the song would have taken on an entirely new meaning. The mood of the song shifts from sad to happy. There are no throwaway words.

Word selection is also critical when you are tailoring your song for a particular artist for placement. A win-win situation for both the songwriter and the artist occurs when a song is both relatable to an audience in general and meaningful to the artist who records the song (along with his or her audience). The main concerns of the recording artist, manager, and record label are that the song is well crafted and true to the character of the artist, fans, and brand.

Lyric Toolbox

There are several tools you can use and activities you can practice to improve your lyrical vocabulary. Here are just a few:

Dictionary and thesaurus: The dictionary ensures that you are using the proper word to convey your intended meaning. The thesaurus helps you to find words with a similar (or opposite) meaning and provides choices that help you decide on the most descriptive word to best characterize a particular situation.

Read: One of the most important tools in your listening toolbox is your ability to keep your mind open and receptive to new and different ideas. A good way to start this venture is to constantly read information from a variety of sources. One of the huge attractions to writing lyrics is that you have the freedom to write from your own experience, from another person's experience, or the experience derived from your colorful imagination. Reading enables you to gain knowledge about situations and places that you have not directly encountered in your life. Through reading, a writer gains insight into diverse topics, including various cultures, myths, religions, trends, fashion, and technology. With much to select from, there is no limit on ideas for song topics.

Listen: Listen to all types of songs. As a song unfolds, pay particular attention to the way it is structured in regard to lyrics, music, instrumentation, arrangement, and emotion.

Collect Titles and Phrases: Always keep your eyes and ears open for interesting words, titles, and phrases. Take note of ordinary and frequently heard phrases such as "Still Crazy After All These Years" by Paul Simon, "None of Your Concern" by Jhene Aiko, "Water Under the Bridge" by Adele, and "One Too Many" by Keith Urban and Pink.

Save Keywords: Find and collect words that are pivotal or prominent in expressing your statement. Let's examine the opening lines in the song, "In My Life" by the Beatles.

> *There are <u>places</u> I'll remember*
> *All my life, though some have <u>changed</u>*
> *Some <u>forever</u>, not for better*
> *Some have <u>gone</u> and some <u>remain</u>*

The words "places," "changed," "forever," "gone" and "remain" are pivotal in helping the lines vividly express thoughts, which lead to the title, "In My Life."

Overuse of distinctive or memorable words will lessen their overall impact. For example, in the song, "Wind Beneath My Wings," recorded by Bette Midler, "wind," "beneath" and "wings" are the keywords used in the payoff line of the

> **Lyric Writing Aids**
>
> Thesaurus: Synonyms and Antonyms
> Rhyme dictionaries: Rhymezone or Rhymer
> Translation tools: Sanakirja or Google Translate
> Search Engine: DuckDuckGo (song titles, expressions, prepositions)
> TuneSmith
> MasterWriter
> Recording Devices
> Notebook/Journal
> Dictionary

chorus, "You are the wind beneath my wings." Therefore, if these words were used in the verses leading to the chorus, the impact of the payoff line in the chorus would be weakened, causing an anti-climactic effect.

Recording Devices: Your computer, notebook, phone, or other recording devices are essential for capturing ideas while they are fresh. Don't forget a notebook, too!

The Story

In Chapter 2 we discussed techniques for finding catchy song titles and developing concepts. We know that most hit songs are derived and driven by a great idea, whether it is a music riff, song title, or concept. However, a great idea must be accompanied by an awesome story.

In many cases, story concepts are inspired by conversations, news, trends, imagery, quotes, and things one might experience in daily life. Use the most effective words that express action, imagery, and emotion. Write from the heart about situations and circumstances that are true to life so that people can relate to them. Don't be afraid to be vulnerable.

Be careful not to present too many ideas. You do not want to complicate the message. To avoid this problem, I suggest that you create an outline for the story based on the title. Focus on words and lines that keep within the song's theme. Remember to present the storylines in a conversational and cohesive order. In other words, after the opening line, continue to develop the story by answering the question, "What happened next?" The following question to be answered is: "And then what happened?"

Choose words that illustrate pictures as the story goes along. Since the title of the song summarizes what the story is about, each storyline in the verse should lead your listener to the title of the song, which is usually in the chorus. The chorus lyric needs to be written to a catchy melody and/or rhythm that distinctly contrasts the verse section.

Because most popular songs are ones that connect with the listener, remember to write words and melodies that are unambiguous, straightforward, and memorable. The words must be naturally easy to sing and not crammed in to fit the melody. Finally, be sure that your story answers the five W's: Who, What, When, Where, and Why.

Improper Grammar

One of the most satisfying aspects of learning rules is the relief of knowing that it is okay to break them here and there. At times, a twist on a word is used in a phrase. This creates both an element of surprise and a new and fresh way to make a statement. For example, in Toni Braxton's song entitled "Un-break My Heart," written by Diane Warren, the title is more effective in grabbing the listener's attention as opposed to a title like "Don't Break My Heart."

A fabricated word or surprise word may be the best choice to use in a phrase to give the statement the effect the writer is seeking. For example, one of the lines in the first verse of Bonnie Raitt's mega-hit song "I Can't Make You Love Me," written by Michael Reid and Allen Shamblin, says, "Lay down with me, tell me no lies." The writer couldn't achieve the same emotional impact if the lyrics read "Lie down with me and don't tell me any lies." The phrase "Lay down with me, tell me no lies" accomplishes two things: avoiding having the word *lie* twice in the phrase, and delivering a statement that has a more heartfelt effect on the listener.

One of my favorite examples of an invented word is in the Justin Timberlake song "What Goes Around," where he says: "When you cheated girl, my heart <u>bleeded</u> girl." In this case, he chose to make up a word, based on the word *bled*. It feels right because his audience gets its meaning while he keeps the powerful image of bleeding and stays within the rhyme scheme.

First, Second, Third Person

Pronouns such as *I*, *me*, *you*, *he*, *she*, and *they* are important in clarifying who is being addressed in the story.

> 1st Person = This is the author or character's position, *I*
> 2nd Person = *You* is the focal point; refers directly to a second party
> 3rd Person = *He*, *she*, or *they*; refers to a third party

Depending on the nature of the song, choose which persona would make the song's connection more effective and meaningful. Experiment with writing in first, second, and third person to decide which gives the best intention of the song's sentiment. Let's experiment using the song "I Don't Wanna Live Forever" by Taylor Swift featuring Zayn Malik.

> I don't wanna live forever, 'cause I know I'll be living in vain
> And I don't wanna fit wherever
> I just wanna keep calling your name until you come back home

This song is written in first person. Imagine if the *I* was changed to *you* or *them*. The song's meaning would not have the same effect. When you exchange the word *I* with *he* or *they*, the story is weaker than when it's told from the character's point of view.

Creative and Easy to Follow

Variety in how words are used allows the writer to be unique. Since the composer is never wrong, he or she has the flexibility to write any combination of chords, notes, and words. Whether your music is complicated or simple, always choose words that will have the most impact and clarity. I prefer the less-is-more approach. Try to make the biggest impact with the least number of words. In this example, "I am so in love with you because…" changed to "I love you because…" the lyric is reduced from eight to four words.

Create melodies that are easy to follow. Listeners connect with melodies, words, and phrases that are easy to sing along with and music that evokes a certain emotion and is complementary to the story. For example, consider the song "Every Breath You Take," written by Sting and recorded by the Police. The song consists of a simple melody, a basic chord progression, and a seemingly uncomplicated story. Most people view the meaning of "Every Breathe I Take" as an expression of agape for the character of the song's love interest. However, upon further contemplation Sting realized that the song could be about an obsessive stalker. In many cases whether intentional or unintentional, ambiguity in lyric writing can give a song the ability to appeal to audiences on multiple levels.

> Every breath you take
> Every move you make
> Every bond you break, every step you take, I'll be watching you

Song Sections and Their Functions

Sections are parts that make up a song. Sections are developed and put in a particular order to form an arrangement also referred to as the song structure. Each section comes with a job description. Commonly used names of sections and their functions are as follows:

Introduction: This section may or may not have lyrics. Singing in this section usually consists of an ad-lib, a chorus or background part, or a written melody intended to accompany music as a setup or lead into the verse.

Verse 1: Lyrically, this section is where the story begins. Its function is to set the tone by introducing the situation, characters, and emotion of the song. Although there is no set rule, there are typically eight lines of lyrics in this section, of which the last few lines usually set up a transition into the chorus. Verses are usually 8 to 16 bars in length.

Pre-Chorus/B Section: This section is optional and is also known as a build, climb, channel, or setup. The section transitions the lyric and music from the verse to the chorus, usually feeling unsettled and serving as tension before the release in the chorus. For example, in the song "My Girl" recorded by the Temptations, the first verse starts by stating "I've got sunshine on a cloudy day . . . When it's cold outside, I've got the month of May"; then it uses a pre-chorus climb consisting of an unsettling melody (creating tension) lyrically, melodically, and musically by asking the question, "I guess you say . . . What can make me feel this way?", then transitions smoothly to the chorus (release) answering the question with "My girl, my girl, my girl."

Chorus: This section summarizes the story and acts as a release or solution; it's also typically where the title lives. This is a summary of what the song is about. I like to call it the feel-good section because the lyrics and music repeat and are usually the most fun and sing-along part of the song. The combination of a melodic and rhythmic line, along with an interesting title and topic for the lyrics are the essential ingredients for a catchy chorus.

This is the part of the song where the song topic lives, questions are answered, the bottom-line summary statement is made, and the solution is found. The lyric and melodic phrase is usually repeated each time this section appears. Be sure to keep the melody and lyric singable and conversational. Lyrically, I like to establish this section first. I use the title of the song as my blueprint that directs the development of the story. It sure helps to know where you're going before you start driving.

Chorus Payoff Line: The payoff line is the phrase that summarizes the thought or sentiment of the chorus. For example, in the Lady Gaga song "Million Reasons," in the verses she sets the tone of the song with the lyrics:

> *You're giving me a million reasons to let you go*
> *You're giving me a million reasons to quit the show*

In the chorus, she further expounds on the miserable situation with the opening line, "I bow down to pray . . . I try to make the worst seem better," before reaching the setup line, "I've got a hundred million reasons to walk away," which comes just before the *payoff* of the last line, "But baby, I just need one good one to stay."

Sometimes a chorus lyric, which consists of a single word, is powerful enough of a statement to serve as the entire chorus. Some examples are the songs "Hallelujah" by Leonard Cohen, "Still" by the Commodores, "Heathens" by Twenty One Pilots, and "Closer" by the Chainsmokers.

Verse 2: The function of the second verse is to move the story forward by adding new information. I call it the "And then what happened?" section. Each time this section returns, the story develops with more details. Many beginning songwriters make the mistake of reiterating the first verse by saying words that may be different from the first verse but bear the same sentiment without adding new information. Be sure that you are moving the story forward in the second verse.

Bridge: This section is optional. A bridge is used to create a deviation from a repetitive structure of the verse and chorus sections. Its function is to serve as a departure from what is presented and to give the song a breath of fresh air. It is typical for lyrics and music to be completely different in this section. New instruments and sometimes musical breakdowns (drums only or spare instrumentation) happen in this section.

Outline

After generating a title and concept for the song, it helps to construct an outline for the story. Outlining a strategy or plot in advance gives you a blueprint and enables you to shape the direction and order of details of the story. Songs have the same characteristics as movies: emotion, mood, suspense, and drama. As we know, life is full of surprises, so it is important to include twists, subplots, opposites, and tension and release in the story. Once the outline is complete, you have a view from the beginning to the end of the song. Now you can have a better sense of placement for the various parts of the story, such as the Verse, B Section, Chorus, or Bridge.

Lyric Structure

Most lyric structures follow the common song structures discussed in Chapter 3. However, lyricists can take more liberties with phrasing, patterns, and title placement within the song's structure.

For example, some writers may choose to write the title phrase at the end of the verse, such as in the case of Billy Joel's "She's Always a Woman to Me." Most songs written with the title phrase at the end of the verse have used the AABAABAA structure.

> She can kill with a smile; she can wound with her eyes
> She can ruin your faith with her casual lies
> And she only reveals what she wants you to see
> She hides like a child but <u>she's always a woman to me</u>

> **Song Outline: "Life Is Great"**
>
> In this example, the outline of this song sketches out a person's life that has been challenging but has lately completely turned around and is presently awesome.
>
> **Title:** "Life Is Great"
>
> **Verse 1:** Bad situation (negative)
>
> **Pre-Chorus:** Light is shed on the situation (hope)
>
> **Chorus:** Everything is wonderful now (positive)
>
> *The verse describes a particular situation or multiple situations that were negative. In the pre-chorus, something happens that gives the writer hope or optimism. This section transitions into the chorus. The chorus contrasts the verse with a positive outlook on life. We're now ready to move on to the second verse.*
>
> **Verse 2:** Things were not always this good/give example(s) (negative)
>
> *Further, develop the story. This is the "And then what happened" section. Tell a new part of the story. Perhaps present an example of a situation of a wrong that was committed.*
>
> **Pre-Chorus:** Hope leading to positive energy
>
> **Chorus 2:** Refrain—Everything is awesome/Life is great (positive)
>
> **Bridge:** New idea—Imagining the future (positive)
>
> *The bridge is a diversion from the verse and chorus, a new and fresh idea. Then it smoothly transitions to the next section (verse, chorus, or musical break).*
>
> **Chorus/Vamp:** Everything is awesome/Life is great (positive)

This verse is followed up with another verse before going to a new section.

Call and Response: The call and response can be between any combination of characters, such as the lead vocal and another vocalist, lead vocalist and background vocalist, lead or background vocals and instruments, or two different instruments. In this example of the song "Baby, It's Cold Outside," written Frank Loesser, the title is located at the end of every other bridge:

> *Female: I really can't stay*
> *Male: Baby, it's cold outside*
> *Female: I've got to go away*
> *Male: Baby, it's cold outside*

The Chorus-Verse Combination: The title and verse lyric are in that same section in a call-and-response style, such as in Katy Perry's "Wide Awake."

I'm wide awake [background vocals]
Yeah, I was in the dark I was falling apart with an open heart
I'm wide awake [background vocals]
How did I read the stars so wrong?

Altering Words in the Chorus: The chorus is also referred to as the "Refrain" because it consists of a repeated line or number of lines in a song. However, there are times when the author may choose to alter certain words so that the story continues to develop in the chorus along with the verses. This style is exercised in the song "7 Years," recorded by Lukas Graham. With each chorus, the character in the song gets older.

Chorus 1 (1st line): *"Once, I was seven years old..."*
Chorus 2 (1st line): *"Once, I was eleven years old..."*
Chorus 3 (1st line): *"Once, I was twenty years old..."*
Chorus 4 (1st line): *"Once, I was twenty years old..."*
Chorus 4 (4th line): *"Soon, we'll be thirty years old..."*
Chorus 5 (1st line): *"Soon, I'll be sixty years old..."*

Opening Lines

With all the things competing for one's time nowadays, attention spans have greatly diminished. Most people decide whether or not they like your song within the first 10 to 15 seconds. Therefore, the opening line of your song must be compelling enough to stimulate intrigue to hear the second line and the rest of the story. This task is accomplished by incorporating action, detail, and imagery.

Action: The process of doing something or something happening such as walking, talking, driving. Think verbs.

Detail: A specific feature or description such as a sound, light, smell, taste, time of day, day of the week, month, or location. The use of adjectives is effective here, as in, the *green* car or the *paisley-patterned* chair. You can also express emotions (i.e., frustrated, happy, sleepy, etc.).

Imagery: A visual description, which could include sound and weather terms such as a flowing river, a gentle breeze, flowers blooming, rain falling, or wind whistling.

A good example is an opening line like, *"Sitting on the edge of my brass bed, listening to the rain, thinking about what happened last night."* This opening line is certain to pique one's interest. The song asked the question, and the listeners want to know the answer. Much like the opening scene of a movie, the opening line of a song sets up the mood and emotion of the song.

Opposites and Twists on Words

The use of words with opposite meanings is one of the oldest and most effective devices in songwriting, as it is in literature. The contrast of opposites brings a more vivid image to the statement, making it a more powerful expression.

> **Song Titles with Opposites:** "I <u>Hate</u> Myself for <u>Loving</u> You" by Joan Jett; "If Loving You is <u>Wrong</u>, I Don't Want to Be <u>Right</u>" by Luther Ingram; "River <u>Deep</u>, Mountain <u>High</u>" by Ike & Tina Turner; "My <u>Strongest</u> <u>Weakness</u>" by Wynonna.
> **Song Titles with Twists:** "You Look Like I Need a Drink" by Justin Moore and "No Good in Goodbye" by the Script.

One of my favorite songs that enlists both a twist in the title, as well as opposites in the verse, is "Tears of a Clown" by the Smokey Robinson and the Miracles.

> *Now if I appear to be carefree*
> *It's only to camouflage my sadness*
> *And Honey, to shield my pride I try*
> *To cover this <u>hurt</u> with a show of <u>gladness</u>*

Notice the word choice of "camouflage" as opposed to choosing the word "hide" for the phrase "camouflage my sadness" jumps out, as opposed to merely saying "hide my sadness." The same thing goes for the word choice "shield my pride." The word "shield" most vividly describes the action that is the opposite of what clowns do; they are usually out front and showy.

Rhyming

Although rhymes are not necessary for songs to be successful, most phrases end with rhymes in contemporary popular music. I think it's simply because we've been taught and conditioned at an early age to hear phrases that end in rhyme. When you think about it, much of our initial learning during our school-age years was with the use of rhyme. An example of this is the famous French melody, "Ah! Vous dirai-je, maman," which was arranged by many composers, including Mozart, and became "The Alphabet Song (A, B, C, D, E, F, G . . .)," as well as the popular English lullaby "Twinkle, Twinkle, Little Star." The lyrics for "Twinkle" are taken from an early 19th-century poem by Jane Taylor. "Twinkle, twinkle, little star" ("A, B, C, D, E, F, G"), followed by "How I wonder what you are" ("H, I, J ,K, L, M, N, O, P").

> **Perfect Rhyme:** When two ending words from different phrases are exactly alike except for the beginning letter, as in joy/toy, play/day, not/hot. When using this

type of rhyme, the rhyme must add to the meaning of the song and not merely be placed there for the sake of rhyming.

False Rhyme: This rhyme has similar sounds but is not an exact rhyme. The vowel sounds are the same, but their consonants differ, such as *car/hard, came/gain*, and *time/mind*.

Semi-Rhyme: This rhyme has an extra syllable on one word, such as *ring/singing*.

Internal Rhyme: This is when two or more rhymes occur within a phrase. At times a word at the end of a line will have multiple rhymes within the phrase. For example: "Sitting in my <u>car</u> gazing at the <u>stars</u> on a warm summer's <u>night</u> with you by my <u>side</u>."

Masculine Rhyme: The masculine rhyme is a single-syllable rhyme such as *door/chore*. When the word is a long syllable, the final syllable is accented such as, *explain, domain,* and *complain*.

Feminine Rhyme: The feminine rhyme is a two-syllable word where the first part of the word is stressed or accented followed by an unstressed or unaccented ending such as *talking, baking, and hiking*.

Writing Lyrics to Existing Music or Melodies

Writing lyrics to a music track or existing melody requires a slightly different approach. My approach is to listen to the overall character, attitude, and feel of the music. Does it feel like the foundation for heartbreak or an exuberant love story? Is it passive or noncompliant? The best ideas are ones that are truly inspired while creativity, inventiveness, revelations, and imagination are at their peak.

However, while in that moment, there are a few questions you may want to consider: Who is the target audience and/or who is the artist you plan to pitch the song to? What style of writing would the audience/artist gravitate to? What is the intended artist's personality? Is the target audience young, old, male, female, fans of pop, jazz, rock, etc.?

Place yourself in the most inspiring environment to create your music. For me, I have a list of many places. The perfect writing environment is wherever my mind and spirit are still, free, and open to absorb incoming energy. Often, these places vary depending on the events of the day. I've written a ton of lyrics in my car. The car is probably the most frequently used environment for me because I can control my surroundings and express my ideas vocally without interruptions. Locations where I am most creative range from viewpoints throughout the city, to water locations, to woods, to busy or quiet parking lots.

Now that you've taken all of this into consideration, go back to the first sentence at the beginning of this section. Listen to the character, attitude, and feel of the music, place yourself in a creative environment, and start writing. Okay. Go!!

Rhyme Schemes

Rhymes generally have a repeating pattern or scheme. Here are some of the most common examples of rhyme schemes:

"If Only for One Night," written by Brenda Russell © 1979

Let me hold you tight	(A)
If only for one night	(A)
Let me keep you near	(B)
To ease away your fears	(B)
It would be so nice	(A)
If only for one night	(A)

Publisher: Almo Music Corp., Inc.

"I Can See Clearly Now," written by Johnny Nash © 1971

I can see clearly now the rain is gone	(A)
I can see all obstacles in my way	(B)
Gone are the dark clouds that had me blind	(C)
It's gonna be a bright, bright sunshiny day	(B)

Publisher: Nashco Music, Inc.

"Beautiful Surprise," written by India Arie Simpson © 2002

It's like yesterday I didn't even know your name	(A)
Now today you're always on my mind	(B)
I never could have predicted that I'd feel this way	(A)
You're a beautiful surprise	(B)

Publisher: Warner Chappell Music, Inc.

"Yesterday," written by Lennon/McCartney © 1965

Yesterday	(A)
All my troubles seemed so far away	(A)
Now it looks as though they're here to stay	(A)
Oh, I believe in yesterday	(A)

Publisher: Sony/ATV Music Publishing LLC, Kobalt Music Publishing Ltd., DistroKid

Songs Referred to in Chapter 6

"I Can't Make You Love Me" © 1991
Songwriters: Michael Reid, Allen Shamblin
Publisher: Universal Music Publishing Group, Amplified Administrators

"What Goes Around" © 2005
Songwriters: Timothy Z. Mosley, Floyd Nathaniel Hills, Justin R. Timberlake
Publisher: Warner Chappell Music Inc., Universal Music Publishing Group, Songtrust Ave., Reservoir Music Management, Inc, Anthem Entertainment LP

"In My Life" © 1965
Songwriters: John Winston Lennon and Paul James McCartney
Publisher: Sony/ATV Music Publishing LLC

"I Don't Wanna Live Forever" © 2016
Songwriters: Jack Antonoff, Samuel Joseph Dew, and Taylor Alison Swift
Publishers: Sony/ATV Songs, Ducky Donathan Music

"Every Breath You Take" © 1982
Songwriter: Gordon Sumner (Sting)
Publisher: Gm Sumner

"Million Reasons" © 2016
Songwriters: Hillary Lindsey, Mark Ronson, and Stefani Germanotta
Publishers: Sony/ATV Songs LLC, BMG Gold Songs, House of Gaga Publishing LLC, Songs of Zelig, Rezonate Music, and Concord Music Publishing LLC.

"She's Always a Woman" © 1977
Songwriter: Billy Joel
Publisher: Universal Music Publishing Group

"Baby, It's Cold Outside" © 1944
Songwriter: Frank Loesser
Publishers: Warner Bros Music Corp., Frank Music Corp., Scaramanga Music

"Wide Awake" © 2012
Songwriters: Max Martin, Katheryn Hudson, Bonnie McKee, Lukasz Gottwald, and Henry Walter
Publishers: Warner Chappell Music, Inc, Kobalt Music Publishing Ltd, Concord Music Publishing LLC.

"7 Years" by Lukas Graham © 2015
Songwriters: Christopher Brown, Lukas Forchhammer, Stefan Forrest, Morten Ristorp Jensen, Morten Pilegaard, David Labrel
Publisher: WB Music Corp.

"Tears of a Clown" © 1967
Songwriters: William Robinson Jr., Henry Cosby, and Stevie Wonder
Publishers: EMI Music Publishing, Sony/ATV Music Publishing LLC

"My Girl" © 1964
Songwriters: Ronald White, William Robinson Jr.
Publishers: Hipgnosis Sfh I Limited

Songwriter Spotlight

DJ Toomp

DJ Toomp. Photo by Ben Rose/WireImage.

Grammy Award–winning DJ and record producer Aldrin Davis, aka DJ Toomp, is credited with discovering rap artist and actor T.I. DJ Toomp along with T.I. helped to bring trap music into the mainstream. He produced T.I.'s hit single "What You Know," which peaked at number three on the Billboard Hot 100. The song earned both Toomp and T.I. their first Grammy Award. DJ Toomp went on to work on four more projects with T.I. DJ Toomp co-produced the singles "Can't Tell Me Nothing" and "Good Life" for Kanye West's *Graduation* CD, as well as projects for Jeezy, Ludacris, and Jay Z.

Batiste: In what environment are you the most creative?

Toomp: I write a lot when I'm around my music equipment. It's almost like the instruments call my name when I walk into the room [laughing]. I use various music sequencers, keyboards, and software. But I can write anywhere. I wrote the melody to the song "Motivation," recorded by T.I., while riding in the car whistling. I whistled that melody for about two hours until I was able to get to my studio. I didn't have my digital recorder on me.

Batiste: What is your process for collaborating with an artist?

Toomp: One of the first things I do is study the artist, pull them up on YouTube, catch a few interviews; see what they've gone through in life, and listen to some of their music. With rap and R&B, I try to present the music with the hook already written, unless the artist is an experienced writer or when working with an experienced writing team. When Kanye and I did the *Graduation* album, I had three songs on there, "Good Life," "Can't Tell Me Nothing," and "Big Brother." The whole album was straight collaboration. The only track that I did by myself was "Big Brother." Collaboration makes it more exciting. What makes collaborating great is that you always learn something from another producer or another writer.

Batiste: What would you tell a young mentee who wants to get into the art and business of songwriting and production?

Toomp: Don't get into this business if you just see it as a new way to make money. Be sure you love songwriting and are willing to put in the time perfecting your craft and make the personal sacrifices it takes to succeed. You must be fully passionate, determined, and committed to the art and business of songwriting and production.

7
Rewriting

Just when you think you have completed your masterpiece, you hear a voice that says, "Hold on. Not so fast." If you do not hear that voice, you must seek it out. Allow your inner voice to call you out to re-evaluate what you have written. The art of fine-tuning the song is the most crucial part of songwriting in terms of creating the final product.

Why is rewriting one of the most crucial steps in the songwriting process? The answer may lead you to understand an unfortunate situation. We live in a society where good is not good enough. Songwriting is a very competitive business, and you would be remiss if you didn't ask yourself, "Why do the people have to have my song? What would compel a person to download my song for purchase as opposed to streaming it and giving it a kind nod?" You must ask and answer this question for yourself before you put your song out there in the universe for others to appraise.

Analyze your song for interest and continuity. The rewrite of the song requires you to ask yourself a series of questions about each area of your song. Some of your evaluation should include the following questions:

- Are there any words that feel weak or do not strengthen the meaning of any phrase?
- Is there a lull or emptiness in the music at any point?
- Is the story expressed authentically?
- Do the sections of the song follow the song function ideology for story development?
- Do the sections have enough distinct contrast from one to another?
- Does the story develop in a way that excites you?
- Do the lyrics answer the five big questions: Who, What, When, Where, and Why?
- Are the melodies accompanied by chords that best support them?
- Are all the vocal and instrumental parts arranged cohesively?
- Are you bored at any point during the listening?
- Can all weak areas be replaced with stronger ones?

Use these questions as a launching pad as you discover new styles, trends, and techniques in the development of your future writing styles.

Flexibility

How far are you willing to bend to get it right? In other words, how flexible are you? Do not fall in love with every element you write during the inspiration phase of the songwriting process. As inspiring as the idea was when you first gave birth to it, you must be willing to detach from it to nurture and mold it into a masterpiece.

Detaching is hard to do, especially when it seems like the initial inspiration of the idea felt so strong that the idea can't be better. No matter how great the original brainwave was in creating the music, characters, situation, and story, it is only a starting point. The best approach is to step away from your song after the initial creation and work period. Revisit your song a few minutes, hours, days, or weeks after the initial enthusiasm has been out of your mind for a time. This process in most cases will allow you to discover flaws and ways to strengthen the composition.

I've surprised myself many times by letting go and being open to possibilities. The art of rewriting is refining and reinforcing an inspired idea with the same enthusiasm and emotion from which you started. When it's all said and done, your work must relate to a human being's authentic and perfectly imperfect nature. Don't be afraid to change your mind for a new idea that gives the song more meaning and clarity. Remember that we live in a very diverse world consisting of various cultures, lifestyles, and tastes that are both alike and different. What works for one song in the songwriting process may not work for another depending on the song's genre, style, attitude, and audience. Some songs may require precise rhythm, perfect English, and a rhyme scheme, while others may not. Take for example the opening two lines of the song "That's What I Like" by Bruno Mars.

> *Hey, hey, hey, I got a condo in Manhattan*
> *Baby girl, what's hatnin'?*

Another way of writing the first two lines by another writer might have been as follows:

> *"I've got a condo in Manhattan*
> *Oh girl, tell me what's happening?"*

Both phrases have the same meaning. However, the way Bruno Mars chooses to express his idea best resonates with his audience and the music genre. Methods of rewriting are done on a song-by-song basis. Effective communication always rules over that which is rigid or complicated.

Momentum

Let's keep the song moving! It does not matter if the song's tempo is fast, medium, or slow. For the listener to become absorbed in your song, it must maintain a steady level of energy. The impetus and driving force musically, melodically, and lyrically must be felt throughout the development of the composition, from first note to last. In all areas of the rewriting process, you should take notice of what elements enhance the momentum and what seems to cause a drop in the energy.

Your song's momentum should start right at the beginning by ensuring that the introduction is not too long, preferably four to eight bars in length. With technology, social media, work, family, and many other factors competing for attention, it is difficult to keep the listener engaged if your song's introduction is too long. Keep it short and to the point, no matter how musically satisfying the performance may be. The story from the beginning of the first verse to the end of the last chorus should consist of words and phrases that capture details and imagery in a cohesive order. "Guess Who I Saw Today" by Nancy Wilson and "Neither One of Us" by Gladys Knight & the Pips are good examples of cohesive stories unfolding from beginning to end.

Rhythm

When I think of the word *momentum*, I get the feeling of motion, velocity, and a sense of going somewhere. One of the best ways to achieve the feeling of motion is by varying the rhythms to make sections of the song contrast from one to another.

For example, in the song "Crzy" by Kehlani, she exchanges the note value lengths in the music and melodies by varying rhythms from short to long, and vice versa. As a result, the song offers a combination of miniature catchy hook phrases.

This method can also be exercised within a section as demonstrated in "Needed Me" by Rihanna. Changing rhythm patterns or adding pitches in the melody and sing-along chants or nonsense words are also great contributors in keeping the song's momentum going. For example, Ed Sheeran's song "Shape of You" has a chord progression that moves with a continuously infectious, hypnotic, steady pulse within two bars (C#m–F#m/A–B). This boy-meets-girl story is told with detail, imagery, and word choices that are relatable, conversational, and true to life.

> *The club isn't the best place to find a lover*
> *So, the bar is where I go*
> *Me and my friends are at the table doing shots*
> *Drinking fast and then we talk slow.*

The melodies are fun and easy to sing in each section of the song. As a bonus, the audience is treated with a fun chant ("Oh-I-Oh-I-Oh-I-Oh-I") to sing along with at the end of the chorus right before the payoff line, "I'm in love with your body."

Tempo

Take a close look at the tempo of your song. The original tempo may have worked well while you were writing because you were focused on other aspects of the song, such as lyrics, melody, chords, and so on. However, in the end, you want the tempo of your song to reflect the mood and energy that you're expressing. Play around with the tempo to ensure that it is not too fast or too slow.

In addition, you will achieve more clarity by keeping the music and melodic structure similar in each section. For example, if your first verse is eight bars and contains four melodic lines, write your second verse with the identical number of lines and bars. The same method applies to lyrical rhyme schemes and phrases. At times there are deviations or vocal inflections that may occur to emphasize a certain word or statement, but in general, simplicity is the most effective way to deliver your song with clarity.

Embrace boundaries and structure as you create musical art. It makes sense that we have guidelines in composition such as we do in the English language. It allows us to communicate effectively. Just because we are charged with generating the most compelling, powerful, and creative way to convey our song doesn't mean we have to reinvent the wheel.

Music

During the rewriting process, you should keep in mind that the song isn't just for you to enjoy, but for others to love and appreciate as well. Therefore, it is crucial that you refine the song's structure. Check the length of all sections of the song, especially the introduction, to make sure it is not too drawn out. Examine the arrangement to ensure that all parts work well together as an entity and that you're using the most effective chords to support and complement the lead melody.

Does your music incorporate an element of surprise, or is it predictable? If you find yourself getting bored with the music, try varying the instrumentation by interchanging, blending various instruments to develop new textures, adding a musical motif played with a unique sound, adding musical or drum breaks, incorporating silence, adding rhythmic parts and/or percussion, creating an alternate section, or creating a new musical riff.

Lyrics

The most important part of the lyric rewrite is to make sure the message the listener receives and the one you intended when you wrote it are identical. Ask yourself if you're using the best words and phrases that give an accurate description, focus, and imagery for the thought that you are trying to express. For example, "She danced all night in his football jersey" instead of "She danced all night." The inclusion of the words "in his football jersey" paints a much clearer picture of the situation.

> **Lyrics Rewrite Checklist**
>
> - It is a great idea, title, and concept
> - It is clear what the narrator is talking about
> - The story develops with new information in each verse
> - All lines lead to the song's title (chorus)
> - The chorus lyric and melody work well together
> - The chorus has a payoff line or title lyric that is meaningful enough to stand on its own.
> - Chorus is easy to sing and remember (catchy)
> - Continuity is maintained through solid structure and order of conversational lines
> - There is action, detail, and imagery in the opening line of the verse
> - The verse sets the tone and moves the story forward with descriptive language
> - The song incorporates opposites and twists
> - The bridge introduces a new idea or deviation from the verse and chorus
> - The pre-chorus builds and sets up the chorus
> - Phrases do not take too long to get to the point
> - Lyrics address the questions: Who, What, When, Where and Why

Check to make sure your phrases and rhyme schemes aren't predictable or loaded with clichés. You want your listener to think, "Wow, that was a nice way to say that." For example, the John Mayer song title and chorus, "Your body is a wonderland," paint a more vivid picture than if the title were, "I love your body." Using the word "wonderland" instead of "body" stretches the imagination a lot further. Stay focused on the topic of the song by replacing words that are vague with words and lines that support the theme. Be sure to review items on the lyric checklist above for the best results.

Melody

Too often songwriters forget how important the melody is in making a solid connection to the listener, so it is important not to settle for the first melody you come up with just because it works okay with the lyric at the time of creation. You must ensure that your melody not only grabs the attention of the listener but that it is also a perfect marriage with the words, while being easy to sing along with.

If your melody seems repetitious to the point of boredom, experiment with alternating notes and changing patterns and rhythms as discussed in the rhythm section of this chapter. Repeat and modify melodic shapes that exist in your song by skipping notes within the scale that are moving in an ascending/descending stepwise motion. Sometimes you can emphasize important words by placing them on the highest or lowest note of a melodic phrase. For example, on the soul classic, "Midnight Train to Georgia," written by Jim Weatherly and recorded by Gladys Knight & the Pips, the lead melody exercises the right to use alternative notes to emphasize the word meaning as the song develops.

In most cases, the melody establishes contrast from one section to another. Therefore, be sure to create a distinct melodic and/or rhythm change from the verse to the chorus sections. Usually, the chorus melody is in a higher note range in contrast to the verse. The chorus melody should be written so that it is obvious by the melodic shape of the phrase where the title goes without hearing the lyric. For example, the melodic phrase for "Somewhere over the Rainbow" is very distinct and fitting for the lyric. It is impossible to imagine the title lyric being sung to any other melody in the song.

Less Is More

Your main objective is to communicate your song's message to the masses in the most effective manner, and you are in a better position to do this with fewer notes and words. Choose straightforwardness rather than overcomplicated phrases. In other words, cut to the chase.

The prominent elements of a song are the chords, melody, and words. Instrumental parts and background vocal arrangements are enhancers that function as accompaniment for the prominent elements. Therefore, your rewrite may include eliminating parts that conflict with the main elements.

A great expression of simplicity is demonstrated in the Stevie Nicks–penned song "Dreams," recorded by Fleetwood Mac. The song's entire foundation is based on two chords, which repeat. These two chords (F and G) accompanied by a sparse rhythm arrangement consisting of a steady bass guitar and matching kick drum create a driving and solid pulse, along with the snare drum backbeat on beats two and four. The melodic phrases perfectly match and strengthen the storylines, making the scenario true to life.

When Is the Song Finished?

Knowing when your song is complete can be tricky. Music is subjective. You should use your gut instinct based on your knowledge of what a hit song sounds like. You must be satisfied that you've fulfilled the hit song elements criteria and have answered the ultimate question: "Is my song a *must-have*?" If you are satisfied that the answer to this question is "Yes," then you know that your song is finished.

A final word of caution: Beware not to *over-rewrite* a song. One of the best pieces of advice I received from one of my mentors, Quincy Jones, was "Be careful not to polish the shine off." So, make sure that the changes you make truly strengthen the song's momentum, clarity, and connection with your audience. Otherwise, leave well enough alone.

Songs Referred to in Chapter 7

"That's What I Like" © 2016
Songwriters: Ray Charles II Mccullough, Philip Martin Lawrence II, James Edward Fauntleroy II, Christopher Brody Brown, Peter Gene Hernandez, Jeremy L. Reeves, Ray Romulus, Jonathan James Yip
Publishers: Warner Chappell Music, Inc., Universal Music Publishing Group, Sony/ATV Music Publishing LLC, BMG Rights Management

"Crzy" © 2016
Songwriters: Denisia Andrews, Brittany Coney, Kehlani Ashley Parrish
Publishers: Warner Chappell Music, Inc, Concord Music Publishing

"Needed Me" © 2016
Songwriters: Songwriters: Robyn Fenty, Khaled Rohaim, Adam King Feeney, Dijon McFarlane, Nicholas Valentino Audino, Lewis Beresford Hughes, Te Whiti Te Rangitepaia Mataa Warbrick, Rachel Derrus, Brittany Hazard, Charles A Hinshaw Jr
Publishers: Almo Music Corp., Warner-Tamerlane Publishing Corp., EMI Blackwood Music Inc., Songs Mp, Mustard On The Beat Publishing, These Are Songs Of Pulse, Electric Feel Music, People Over Planes, Monica Fenty Music Publishing, Nyan King Music, Shay Noelle Publishing, KMR Music Royalties II SCSP, Songs Of Universal Inc.

"Somewhere over the Rainbow" © 1939
Songwriters: E.Y. Harburg, Harold Arlen
Publisher: EMI Feist Catalog, Inc.

"Shape of You" © 2017
Songwriters: Kevin Briggs, Kandi Burruss, Tameka Cottle, Ed Sheeran, Jonny McDaid, and Steve Mac
Publishers: Polar Patrol Music Limited, Universal Music Publishing LTD, Sony/ATV Music Publishing (UK) LTD, Pepper Drive Music, and Tony Mercedes Music

"Midnight Train to Georgia" © 1973
Songwriter: James D. Weatherly
Publishers: Bibo Music Publishing

"Dreams" © 1977
Songwriter: Stevie Nicks
Publishers: EMI Longitude Music, Welsh Witch Music

Songwriter Spotlight

Bonnie Hayes

Bonnie Hayes. Photo by Shervin Lainez. Used with permission.

Songwriter, musician, and record producer Bonnie Hayes has written "Have a Heart" and "Love Letter" by Bonnie Raitt, "Some Guys" by Cher, "Bottomless" by Bette Midler, as well as songs for Natalie Cole, Robert Cray, David Crosby, Adam Ant, Huey Lewis & the News, Billy Idol, and Booker T and the MG's.

Batiste: How do you go about your songwriting process?
Hayes: I don't write the way a lot of writers write. I don't write from content. . . . I don't write to an idea. Usually what happens to me is I'll get a little line. For example, I was reading a magazine today at my hair appointment and I read—"Roller Coaster Romance." And I was like, "That sounds like kind of a good idea. I know what they're talking about." So, I write those down on my phone. I just write down these little phrases or fragments or ideas and then I hang on to them and maybe a few days or like every other week I'll kind of just go through it and

see if anything just gives me that "zizz." It's just all resonance.... If it gets me excited or interested, I go toward it.

Batiste: It seems like the words or ideas come first and not necessarily the chorus. Is that right?

Hayes: Absolutely. Yeah, ... the chorus doesn't always come first, that's not fair. A lot of times what's going on for me is I always start with what I call *seeds*. My friend Mark Seimos taught me that the seed is the guide, which is like anything, an image or words, but sometimes it is just a little thing on the piano. I'll be playing like [plays an I–IV–V chord progression on the piano] and some little melody or rhythm that's repeating around and around. It may be a rhythm that I just like playing that sounds neat. Those things are what I call seeds.

Usually, the song will start building like I hear it coming from far away. But it comes from one of those ideas. It just starts haunting and attacking me and then suddenly, I write it and it happens. I know that sounds like magic, but I do a lot of pre-work for it. I think about it a lot. I do some writing on it, meditating, and thinking about stuff and then it just happens, and it happens fast.

Batiste: It's like how a spark turns into a raging flame from a little idea.

Hayes: A little tiny idea. And some of them don't go anywhere. A lot of them I've had for 10 or 15 years and I'm just like "Hmmm ... that's still sort of an idea" and I don't know what or when I'm going to be ready to write that idea. I find that for me there is this process where usually that idea will pick up steam, like something in my life. For example, If I was having a roller-coaster romance at the time, I might be more inclined to write that song. Right now, there are no roller coaster romances ... but there are many other roller coasters. So, you know, if I'm having that experience, or just had that experience or about to have that experience, I'll be more inclined. The song will build more energy. I do a lot of walking and I spend a lot of time just letting my mind play with ideas like that.

Batiste: How did you know that you were going to be a songwriter?

Hayes: Well, it took a long time. You got to remember I came up when, first, there were no women doing rock & roll and there were very few women working in this world. I was raised in the seventies and I remember distinctly having Neil Young's *After the Goldrush* album and looking at the picture on the back cover. I remember at first, I was like "I want to be his girlfriend." That was like kind of the highest ambition I could think of was being Neil Young's girlfriend. And then I was like "Hmmm ... I kind of want to be in Neil Young's band." Then when I started playing seriously; it was like, "I want to be Neil Young. Forget being his girlfriend!" And so, it took me a long time to be able to articulate that dream. I started as a jazz piano player. I was playing with my brothers. We had a band playing jazz-fusion. I did not think about writing songs at all until I was in my early twenties. And you know what else happened? I saw the Sex Pistols and thought I could do what they were doing. Then it occurred to me that I'm not a singer. This is one of my challenges.

Batiste: Uh ... Excuse me? Are you *not* a singer?

Hayes: You know, I'm a singer now. But at that time, I wouldn't sing, and I thought that singers were dumb and stuff. I was a player! I went and saw the Sex Pistols, which was like a horrible concert. I saw it in Atlanta, and it was their first show in the United States. I remember looking at them and thinking "If they can do it, I should be able to write a song. I mean how hard can it be?" And by the way, I love the Sex Pistols, but at the time it was sort of encouraging because they couldn't play then; they couldn't sing. So, I was like, "Oh, I'm just like them!" [laughter] And so that's when it started occurring to me that maybe I could have some autonomy or authorship in my work, and I just didn't have to play other people's songs. So really for me, it came out from being a musician more than being a songwriter.

Batiste: Is your songwriting instrument of choice the piano?

Hayes: I wrote for about eight years almost solely on guitar, when I started playing guitar. But now I go back and forth. Usually, I'll start an idea on one instrument, or another based on the rhythm because I do a lot out of the groove. So, that for me is sort of like the chords, the groove, and then the words. Like little pieces of words, depending on sort of how I feel like doing, you know? If I'm doing a more rock & roll or folk thing, I'll feel like playing guitar. A lot of times I write from beats, which is an amazing way to start a song because it gives you a rhythm foundation to work from. I don't have one specific place to start from.

Batiste: Many of your songs are inspired by the instrument you start with. How about when songwriting turns into a business—like when you have a job to produce someone, and they don't have material. How do you deal with the business of songwriting?

Hayes: I do a limited or special kind of production. I usually only produce songwriters. I have one client that has been recording covers. Everyone else is a writer. There may be a situation where they have a bunch of songs that are too much the same or they have undeveloped choruses; they may have all their songs in the same key or the same tempo. That kind of stuff. So, in that case, I review everything that is in consideration and pick the best songs. Like I'm working with the songwriter Tracy Blackman right now on her record. We are trying to work up a couple of the songs, bring them into focus, and clarify them. She's a very talented songwriter, so I sit and do that with her. For example, if I listen to a song and feel like I space out at a certain point, I may say that I don't get what you're saying here so let's talk about how we can maybe make it clearer? Overall, I want the song to have a great refrain and story, a great arrangement, a good beat, and a message that's digestible for most people. You must make people want to buy it.

Batiste: What are your thoughts on collaborating?

Hayes: I never really liked collaborating. I was a real solo, lone wolf songwriter for many years. My many publishing deals kind of forced me into collaborative situations, which were generally kind of hard for me.

Batiste: Why is that?

Hayes: Because I didn't like anything that I didn't think up or didn't have to say. If you believe that you have something to say and a way to say it that's authentic, and then somebody else has something to say that isn't what you wanted to say—it's hard to get on their page.

Batiste: Well, I know that it is like a marriage. You have to court a little bit and figure out if you have the same tastes and philosophies.

Hayes: Yes—whether you can get along, whether you have the same ideas and the same values. There are some people that I love writing with. When I'm writing with clients, I am doing their thing. I am on their page; I am trying to make their songs do what they need them to do, not what I need them to do. So, I'm not doing that Svengali, "I'm the boss, you are going to do what I want."

When I'm doing an even collaboration, like when I write with Steve Seskin [Tim McGraw, Kenny Chesney, Waylon Jennings], sometimes and he and I have a very even collaboration where we both work super-fast. We both work in all frames. We both switch from lyrics to melody simultaneously. I go "Well, let's change the melody!" and he'll say "Okay! Let's change the lyric!" You know, we just flip back and forth, and we will run eight possibilities by each other. What I love about working with him is that he is there with me. He doesn't get behind.

Batiste: Let's say you take on a project producing a seventeen-year-old. You want the record to sound authentic, but still, want to put the Bonnie Hayes stamp on it. Do you find it challenging to be authentic and still have commercial success?

Hayes: So, that is part of why I am here in Northern California and not in Los Angeles. Part of why I don't do those kinds of records. That's because for me that is a broad question. I mean I moved to Los Angeles and was signed to several big publishing deals. They... wanted me to kind of seduce other artists and producers into writing with me and they wanted me to write commercial hit songs. And up until then, all my hit songs, even the Bonnie Raitt songs, were written from pure soul art. I wasn't thinking about her when I wrote the songs. I was thinking about myself. I was in it, and I believed it, and I believe audiences can feel that. I believe listeners know when a song is written from the truth. So, when I had to start manufacturing songs to make money it started hurting my real work. I floundered in Los Angeles as a writer because it was difficult for me. I couldn't figure how to make decisions about songs anymore when I wasn't motivated by pure raging luck or truth. That got confusing and when I moved back to the Bay Area; I tried to quit music. I told a friend that I'm going to go to school and become a psychologist. He said, "You're crazy, you hate school. You are music!" And so, I did finally come back to music. Now the work I do is with people that I get. I only write songs that I want to write. I have the luxury of being able to do that, you know.

Batiste: I love it. Your friend was right. You are music! It's hard to believe that you quit writing songs for a while. Do you think it was better for you to quit music and regroup?

Hayes: For me, it worked out great. It cost me money, but it bought me time with my daughter, which I would have never had, and it brought me back to my music. I think that is a good question to ask people. And I know that lots of people can make this kind of commercial music. It's not that there is something wrong with making commercial music. It's that for me when that was the motivation, it changed the way that I wrote.

Batiste: I think the audience is sophisticated. They are great listeners. They can detect real art, the real artist, as opposed to something that is manufactured.

Hayes: I think they can. I was reading about this young girl, Ester Dean, who is a top-line writer for Rihanna. They have like twenty tracks, and they go in. And the girl, she does . . . what I do. She has her seeds on her phone. She goes through her ideas, starts singing, and makes up a hook. All while they are still playing. It sounds like she is having fun when she is doing that. I think the writing needs to be motivated by fun, and passion, and life.

Batiste: That is true. I think there is something for everybody.

Hayes: Yep!

Batiste: When and how do know that you have a great song?

Hayes: For me, I know that I have the makings of a possible great song when there is enough of a lyric that there is an actual idea. Not just "Roller Coaster Romance," but there is a story that I have sort of created around that. You know, like "Have a Heart." When I first wrote that title all I had was [turns to the piano and plays and sings the "Have a Heart" chorus line]. All I had was the melody. I had no words and no ideas, but I had that little thing. But I knew every time I sang it for some reason it made me sad. It's weird because it is so happy and cheery sounding. But for some reason, it made me sad.

    I just wrote it the way it was coming out. What I will say is when I get a lyric that is enough of an idea and it is sort of a snapshot of a bigger idea, like the title or the refrain. Whatever it is when you say it, and you go "Yeah!" That's when you know you have a great song or a great idea. And a melody, that when you sang it, you want to sing it again. Not only do you want to hear it again, but you also want to sing it because people like to sing along with the songs. And if I am going to sing that song, like I have sung that song 18 million times, I want it to be fun to sing.

Batiste: How do you go about creating a memorable and hypnotic melody, one that makes the listener want to hear it repeatedly?

Hayes: There are things that I notice that happen in melodies that people gravitate toward. Like the interval leap, long-held notes, and stepwise motions. Such as Sheryl Crow's chorus melody of the song, "If It Makes You Happy," or like, "Somewhere over the Rainbow." You have these leaps that catch you that make you listen. There are certain tricks that if I am struggling to find a melody, I will sort of evoke those tricks. I will go, "Let's try the leap. Okay, let's try the stepwise motion. Let's try melisma. Let's try working with the phrasing. Let's try flipping it around." So, I have these sorts of tricks that I use.

Batiste: You produce a lot of vocalists. Once you get an idea of their range and where they are coming from, are you better able to help them?

Hayes: Yeah, then we rewrite the melodies. And that is sort of a specialty of mine. You want to get that contrast between sections, you know.

Batiste: Yes. You want them to show off where their climax is.

Hayes: Right. So, you want the verse melody to be lower so that it has somewhere to go. Sometimes I will rewrite or restructure a melody if I know its range. But usually, I try to get the money, the chorus up in the higher part of their range.

Batiste: Did you say something about money? [laughing]

Hayes: Yes, the money, the feeling, and the emotions.

Batiste: You have an advantage. You mentioned before that you are not a singer. You didn't consider yourself a singer. You had a band. But a lot of what you do is your writing and working with artists.

Hayes: It is so singery. I agree.

Batiste: So, it's about the singer. You try to bring out the best of them. You sort of end up being a vocal coach, right?

Hayes: Yes, I do.

Batiste: So that's a lot of hats. When we think about songwriting, we are also thinking about making the connection. How did you develop all these talents and develop as a singer?

Hayes: I'm a piano player, arranger, and I work with Pro Tools. Then I started singing and writing songs. I got another singer for the band. I was thinking about all these things. And we kept getting all these singers that weren't right for the band. And finally, I said, "Gosh, I'll do it." You know. . . . I started singing and taking vocal lessons at that time because I couldn't sing. I'm telling you. So, I had to work on it! [laughing]

We played every weekend. I feel like I have performed a million shows as a singer. So, you learn, you learn how to save your voice. You learn how to take care of yourself. You learn how to set your songs, so you are not going to hurt yourself singing them but they are still feeling emotions. I learned a lot about the setting, finding the right key. The guitar players hate me and they [hollers out] "F sharp!" They put a capo on. But you know it is just that crazy thing of getting it in the right key where the notes are going to sing, which I learned from my voice, which has a very narrow golden place. So, when I must get the note in there, I'm going to do what I have to do to get it in there. Making myself sound good is what it is all about.

So, then the Pro Tools comes from making my own demos. My demos were huge in selling my songs. I was an early adopter to all that digital recording. I had a Teac DMA. I had a Teac four-track cassette before anybody had one. I was like really an early recorder and had microphones and stuff super early on. I was interested because I wanted to work from home and didn't want to have to go into the studio to make a demo. So, I just got better and better. I got good at Pro Tools and the more producing I did, the better I got.

Batiste: Absolutely! You're a great engineer. I have been lucky enough to have been hired by you for recording sessions as a background vocalist, and I'm amazed when we start working and get a chance to see you wear multiple hats in the studio. Most of the time, you're the producer, the arranger, and the engineer.

Hayes: Yeah, I think producing and engineering is all a part of writing. Part of making sure when I talk to people who have never made a record, and they are like, well do we really have to? Production is the last stage of songwriting. It is where you bring your music. I mean if I make a demo of "Have a Heart" with me playing it on the piano and squawking it out, you . . . may not be able to hear that song for what it is. We put it in a form where people go, "Oh my God, that is so beautiful. What is that?!" And that has to do with production. So, production, to me, is just another phase of writing.

Batiste: So, somewhere in your consciousness, when you start to write a song, you are thinking about the result, the production, and how things are flowing?

Hayes: Yes. Production is one of the few places where I still feel super creative. . . . I have no idea what it is going to be like. But I know it is going to be cool because I trust myself now. But I will . . . get a cello player and have him come in. And will say, "I want you to play the piano part on the cello." And they go, "Okay." And they play the piano part on the cello. And either it works, or it doesn't. If it doesn't work, no harm is done. . . . I learned something. And if it does work, it is so cool.

Batiste: What advice do you give upcoming, aspiring successful singers/songwriters?

Hayes: I think you should pay attention to the songs that you love. And learn from them. That's important. And you should also not let anyone tell you that what you are doing is wrong. I can't tell you how many times people have told me to change the first line of "Have a Heart." They told me to change the most beautiful chord of "Shelly's Boyfriend" that made the song so golden for me. I learned early to say no to that stuff and I think it was a saving grace for me. As an artist, I feel we put too much effort/emphasis on people trying to be like other people and trying to make music that is already successful. I think if you go toward the songs you love, that have inspired you, you just can't go wrong.

Batiste: Beautiful!

PART II
THE BUSINESS

8
Building a Songwriting Career

At first glance, building a songwriting career seems like a fun and easy job. Writing songs, getting them heard by the right people, making money—a piece of cake, right? Well, this dream job can become a reality if songwriting is your passion and you're willing to make sacrifices and put forth the dedication, diligence, and tenacity it takes to make your songwriting career successful.

The reality is that building a songwriting career is a full-time job that is both challenging and rewarding. You must think of yourself as a business, where you are the CEO and director of operations. You must be willing to embrace responsibility, educate yourself in business practices, stay on top of trends, and know how to protect your rights. Like any other successful self-owned business executive, you must be wired with an entrepreneurial spirit.

You should also be open to reprioritizing or adding some skills, how you can:

- be organized
- be innovative
- know your target market
- develop a basic understanding of marketing and strategic planning
- develop an operations and implementation model
- find a way to finance a finished product or demonstration
- be willing to constantly meet new people
- develop effective communication skills
- develop strong collaboration skills
- find a mentor
- differentiate yourself
- not be afraid to learn and unlearn
- take action

Your career can't begin without you, so set a designated time and place to work each day and commit yourself. Remove distractions such as phones and social media during your designated work time. If you work from home, avoid bills, household tasks, or outside obligations and distractions. Make a task list and set deadlines. Being respectful of people's time and establishing a foundation of trust will maximize business opportunities.

If you work each day at applying everything you've learned about crafting a song and establishing current business practices, a career can begin to slowly build. Although the business of songwriting may seem like a huge undertaking, it is simply about getting started by putting one foot in front of the other, while keeping your eyes on prized opportunities and your ears open to all possibilities.

It is equally important to always remain realistically optimistic about what could occur. A big part of being realistic is being able to identify your basic living needs and expenses and finding ways to address them. You need your creative energy to flow freely and smoothly. It is impossible to focus if you are worried about where you are going to live and where your next meal is coming from.

Phase One: Business Housekeeping

Protect Your Investment

Register your song with the Library of Congress Copyright Office (www.copyright.gov) before distributing or making it public. A copyright protects original works of authorship such as written works (books, articles, screenplays, blogs); musical and dramatic works (songs, plays, and choreography); artistic works (photographs, paintings, and sculptures); and software (computer programs, systems, and applications). You may register a group of up to 10 works at one time if the authors are the same on each of the works in that group of songs. Copyright does not protect ideas, systems, facts, or methods of operation.

Contact the U.S. Patent & Trademark Office to protect *trademarks* (i.e., names, logos/symbols, and slogan/phrases) and *patents* (i.e., inventions and discoveries). This includes your band name. To protect your domain name, use the Internet Corporation for Assigned Names and Numbers (ICANN), a nonprofit organization that assumes the responsibility for domain name system management.

Song versus Sound Recording

The song and the recording of the song are two separate properties. One entity is the "song or composition" (words and music), and the other is the "sound recording" of the song (the tangible product). The owner of the song and the owner of the sound recording have a right to say who and how their property is used. Copyright Form PA (Performing Arts) is used to register the song, and Copyright Form SR (Sound Recording) is used to register the sound recording.

The combination of the songwriter (creator of work) and the publisher (administrator of the song's copyright) represent one property and are automatically considered equal (50/50) partners at the point of the song's creation. In other words, a whole song consists of one-half writer's share and one-half publisher's share. The songwriter oversees the song's total ownership, including publishing administration duties, unless they assign all or part of the publishing duties and share them with another party.

The sound recording of the song (often referred to as "the master") is owned and controlled by the person or entity that owns the finished recording of the song. The owner of the sound recording is usually the financial backer of the recorded product. This person or entity could be a record label or the songwriter if they both wrote the song and financed the recording.

The songs and the sound recordings are considered "intellectual property." Each property is protected by a *copyright*, which is granted by United States Copyright Law. A copyright gives the owner of the song or its recording the right to copy and reproduce them. The owner of the copyright is the only one who can grant permission to others to reproduce their song. Therefore, the publisher owns and controls the copyright of the song, and the owner of the sound recording owns and controls the master of the song.

Permission granted by the owner of these intellectual properties for duplication and/or distribution is called a "mechanical license." A mechanical license is typically issued between the publisher and the record label or media company selling the product. For each sale of a composition, the owner must be paid a "mechanical royalty."

Royalties

Mechanical Royalties

A mechanical royalty is a per-unit payment made by a record label to the publisher and writer of a song when a song is sold physically, or by download, streaming, or on-demand. A mechanical license gives the record label or media outlet the right to reproduce the song for sale. This consent from the publisher must be given to a record label before the label transmits or distributes a song. After the recording is first released and distributed to the public, the song can be covered (recorded and released again) by another artist without permission if the artist or label releasing the song signs a compulsory mechanical license with the publisher.

The mechanical royalty rate established by the Library of Congress Copyright Royalty Board for physical recordings and permanent digital downloads is 12 cents per copy sold of songs that are 5 minutes or less, and an additional 2.3 cents per minute or fraction thereof for songs over 5 minutes. This is called the *statutory rate*. For example, if your song is released on a physical or digital download format as a single or as one of the songs on a product that contains multiple songs and it sells 1 million copies, the label must pay the publisher $120,000.00 per the mechanical license. The publisher keeps its share and pays the songwriter(s) the remaining share.

Many artists who record covers of previously recorded songs acquire a mechanical license through the Harry Fox Agency. The Harry Fox Agency issues mechanical licenses for physical and digital music formats and collects fees on behalf of music publishers in the United States. SOCAN (Society of Composers, Authors, and Music

Publishers of Canada) provides mechanical licensing services to Canadian and international writers and publishers. Special permission must be granted from the publisher if a newly recorded version of a song contains new or additional lyrics. Mechanical royalties from digital downloads are virtual mechanical reproductions and are paid the same as physical sales—the statutory rate of 12 cents.

Mechanical royalties for streaming are mainly licensed and paid by streaming services. For ten years, streaming services paid songwriters and publishers fractions of a penny per stream. Streaming mechanical payments were averaging about $0.06 per 100 streams. In 2023, the Copyright Royalty Board ruled in a settlement between publishers and Digital Service Providers (DSP's) a new rate that incorporates increases over a period from 2023 to 2027. The streaming rates are as follows:

2023: 15.1% of DSP revenue
2024: 15.2% of DSP revenue
2025: 15.25% of DSP revenue
2026: 15.3% of DSP revenue
2027: 15.35% of DSP revenue

Performance Royalties

Performance rights organizations, also known as PROs (ASCAP, BMI, and SESAC) track, license, and collect fees from TV networks, commercials, radio stations, films, digital streams, and venues for performances of songs, and then pay its affiliated songwriter members. ASCAP and BMI are both nonprofit organizations. SESAC is a private and for-profit PRO. Its members are invited to join.

All businesses that play music publicly must purchase a license from a PRO, which serves as their permit to then do so. PROs use the money collected from the license fees to pay their writers and publishers. Various methods are used in tracking song performances. It is important that you register with a PRO to receive money collected for performances on terrestrial radio (AM/FM), film, venues, and broadcasts. PROs do not collect synchronization fees or mechanical royalties.

If you are the publisher or co-publisher of one or more songs that are released commercially—meaning, available for sale to the public in any format for broadcast or performed in any licensed venue—you are eligible to join either BMI or ASCAP. To join a PRO, identify your publisher type (i.e., Individual/Sole Proprietor/ or Single Member LLC; C Corporation; S Corporation; LLC-C Corporation; LLC-S Corporation; or LLC – Partnership). Create and submit five names for your publishing company in order of preference. Be careful not to create a name that sounds like an existing publisher or entertainment name to avoid rejection.

For radio, a combination of logs and digital technology is used to determine payment. For television, cable networks, and film, PROs rely heavily on *cue sheets* to ensure that stakeholders in a song are compensated fairly. A cue sheet is a very detailed log of a song's usage on a television or cable broadcast, film, or any type of audiovisual production. The cue sheet is generated by the production company and is given to the appropriate PRO.

Cue sheet information includes:

- Series/Film Title
- Episode Title/Number
- Estimated Airdate
- Program Length
- Program Type
- Company Information
- Network Station
- Cue Title (Song used/where it's used)
- Music Length
- Composer
- Publisher
- Percentage
- Performing rights society

Although all the PROs do an equal job of collecting and distributing public performance revenue to publishers and writers, they all have slightly different methods of calculation. Here are links to detailed explanations of how each one of the PROs pays its publishers and writers for their song performances.

ASCAP—http://www.ascap.com/members/payment.aspx
BMI—http://www.bmi.com/creators/royalty/how_we_pay_royalties/basic
SESAC—http://sesac.com/WritersPublishers/HowWePay/PaymentInfo.aspx

SoundExchange (Digital Performance Royalties)

SoundExchange collects and distributes internet royalties for and to the sound recording, featured artists, and non-featured artists—such as session musicians and background vocalists—of a recording. When songs are used on satellite, internet, and digital television radio services, a playlist of songs played is sent to SoundExchange, along with a fee. Upon receipt, SoundExchange examines the data and distributes the payments to the rights holders (owners of the masters), featured artists, and non-featured artists.

It is important to register with SoundExchange to receive digital public performance royalties from non-interactive streaming as a participant on a recording. Digital performance royalties are for sound recordings only and do not include publisher or songwriter's royalties. Royalties are collected by SoundExchange, which holds the funds until the appropriate parties register to claim the monies. Monies must be claimed within three years before it gets passed on to major labels and artists based on their market share.

SoundExchange non-interactive royalties are paid out as follows:

- Sound Recording (Label/Owner of Master): 50%
- Featured Artist (Main Performing Artists): 45%
- Non-Featured Artist (Backing Vocalists and Musicians): 5%

Synchronization Licenses and Fees

A synchronization license allows the licensee (usually TV, film, video game, or advertising production companies) to synchronize visual media and music together. The copyright owner(s) of the song is/are paid a fee for usage. In addition to the fee, all the other royalties from mechanical and performances apply, if applicable. The fee amount negotiated is based on how much of the song is used in the production, its prominence and significance to the production, and the music budget of the project.

In other words, if your song is titled "We Are Family" and the name of the film is *We Are Family*, or if your song is a major hit record, the negotiated amount for usage would be at an all-time premium. On the other hand, if your song is the tune playing in the background while the main characters in the film are engaged in a heated argument, the song is more of an incidental use and the sync fee may be drastically lower.

Remember, a song has two components: the *composition*, which is owned by the publisher and composer, and the *recorded audio*, which is commonly referred to as the *master* and is usually owned by the record label or artist. Therefore, there are two types of licenses required to protect these entities.

1. Synchronization License: For the composer to protect the composition that is synced to video/film.
2. Master License: For the owner of the master (label/artist) to protect the recording that is synced to the video/film. master license fees are negotiated based on the same usage conditions as the synchronization license.

The owner of the composition and the master can be the same or different entities.

Music in Film and Television

Music is an essential element of the filmmaking process. We couldn't imagine seeing a motion picture without it. Music that is used for film and television production is logged by the production company on a cue sheet. The cue sheet documents detail such information as the title of the composition, composer, publisher, production

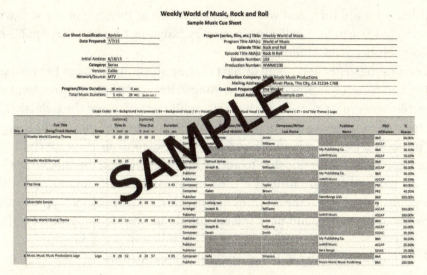

FIGURE 8.1 Cue Sheet sample titled "Weekly World of Music, Rock, and Roll" from ASCAP and BMI's Template. Courtesy of BMI Archives.

company, the title of program, date, episode, duration, network, and so on. Without a cue sheet, it would be difficult for the PROs to compensate the songwriters and publishers for their work.

Establishing a Publishing Company

The job of a publishing company is to make sure that songwriters are paid for their work when it is available for sale to the public or used publicly. As a songwriter, you are automatically the publisher of your song. Once again, a song consists of two parts, the writer's share and the publisher's share, and the songwriter owns 100 percent of both.

All business transactions and creative decisions are conducted through the publisher, who owns and controls the copyright. The basic reasoning for the publisher acting as the business entity of the song is that many licensees of music prefer not to deal with individual songwriters who may or may not understand the business of administering a song. Licensees would rather operate business-to-business. It is okay for the songwriter to retain publishing if he or she is willing to learn how to administrate songs, which includes having or developing the necessary resources to take advantage of opportunities for the song. By retaining your publishing rights as the songwriter, you share in both publishing and writing income generated from your song.

However, some songwriters choose to share publishing percentages in exchange for administrative and/or song placement services. If the songwriter chooses not to act as their own publisher, they may assign 100 percent of its publishing share to a publisher, who will then deal with the business side of the song or the songwriter may elect to share in the publishing income by assigning a percentage of publishing to a co-publisher or an administrator.

When a songwriter assigns all or part of the publishing to his or her own publishing company, or another party, the songwriter must sign an agreement with the publisher (even if the songwriter self-publishes) granting the publisher, co-publisher, or administrator the rights to control the copyright of the song. At this point, the publisher/administrator owns and controls the copyright. This agreement enables the publisher to administrate and act on the songwriter's behalf. All deals and negotiations for the song must come through the publisher. The publisher collects the monies from sales and licensing opportunities, keeps his or her share, and pays the remaining monies to the songwriter(s) or their heirs.

The main administrative duties of a publisher are as follows:

- Copyright the composition
- Register the song with the Library of Congress Copyright Office and with performance rights organizations (either ASCAP or BMI). SESAC is a private, invitation-only performance rights organization.
- Exploit the copyright: Promote song for placement on projects such as for artists, filmmakers, radio stations, games, ringtones, digital, and advertisements, as well as seek out new sources of income.
- Negotiate licenses: Secure mechanical licenses for physical sale and downloads; synchronization agreements for television and films, and make sure contracts are legally solid regarding terms of use.
- Collect monies due to publisher and songwriter.
- Manage the song: Make sure all the basics are covered in terms of collecting from all income sources, conducting audits if necessary, and representing the song; also, act as an agent for the song by identifying new opportunities. The publisher also aligns with foreign affiliates that collect foreign-use royalties. Foreign affiliates monitor and collect monies in foreign territories, keep their percentage, and send the rest of the monies to US publisher(s), who then keep what remains of the publisher's share and send the writer's percentages to the songwriters or their heirs.
- Accounting: Bookkeeping and distribution of shares of monies to the songwriters.

If you are a self-administered songwriter and not sure how to go about securing a traditional publishing administrator, you may want to consider joining the Mechanical Licensing Collective (MLC), a nonprofit organization appointed by the U.S. Copyright Office per the historic Music Modernization Act of 2018. The MLC administers blanket mechanical licenses to certain digital service providers and streaming services and pays songwriters and publishers. The service is free.

Getting Things Started

File a Fictitious Name Statement

A fictitious name statement (d.b.a., Doing Business As) grants an individual or company the right to do business under a name other than their legal name. Create an original name that is not like any existing business names. This is a process that you would have already gone through when creating your publishing name to submit for your PRO registration. You can check the online database of registered business names kept by your state's Secretary of State to see if someone already has the name you've chosen.

To officially own the name, file a fictitious name statement. Most counties offer this form online. If you choose not to file online, request a fictitious name statement form from your local county clerk's office, and file your fictitious name statement along with the DBA filing fee. The cost will vary. Most cities require you to publish an announcement of your intent to do business in a local newspaper.

Tax Identification Number

You must have a Tax Identification Number to start a business. The Tax Identification Number is like a social security number for your business so that you can be identified by the IRS for tax purposes. It is a nine-digit number supplied by the IRS, often under the common names Tax ID Number or EIN (Employer Identification Number). They are the same thing. Once you acquire a Tax ID Number, you must file tax returns. I recommend that you wait until you're doing business before taking this step. Otherwise, you're obligated to file tax returns with no activity, which is busy work. Who needs that?

If your principal business is in the United States or U.S. territories, you may apply for a Tax Identification Number online at IRS.gov. The individual applying must have a social security number. You can file online at irs.gov or pick up an SS-4 form at the local Federal Building in your area.

Three easy steps:

- Decide on your entity type (individual, partnership, corporation, LLC, non-profit, etc.)
- Fill out an SS-4 Form
- Submit the one-time processing fee

Bank Account

Your business will receive performance royalty checks from your PRO and mechanical royalty checks from a record label, distributor, and product licensing establishments. Therefore, your business will need to open a bank account to deposit these checks. The fictitious name statement and your tax identification number are required to open a bank account.

Educate Yourself

Most meaningful careers require a lifetime commitment of both time and finances. Thus, it pays to know what you're getting into before you leap. You must educate yourself about all aspects of the songwriting, the record and entertainment business, and trends. An excellent place to start is with a clear understanding of how this constantly evolving system operates. More specifically, you want to have a broad comprehension of ways to exploit your copyright and know how income participation and royalties work.

At the same time, make it a common practice to follow artists and business activities on social media such as Twitter, Facebook, Instagram, Tumblr, Google, Pinterest, and forums, chats, dialogs, and related blogs and video blogs. Immerse yourself in the social media movements on multiple levels, which will provide real-time interactions and feedback. Any source that offers information about opportunities for song placement will be significant to advance to the next step in building a songwriting career.

In summary: The main sources of income come from mechanical royalties (download, physical sales, streaming) paid by the mechanical licensing entity, performance royalties (music performed on radio, television, clubs, and restaurants), synchronization income (music performed in television, film, video games, and commercials), and numerous ancillary sources of income that includes ringtones, sheet music, commissions, digital performance royalties (artist revenue paid by Sound Exchange when sound recordings are played on internet or satellite radio), merchandise, and other unknown income sources created from the forever evolving music industry.

Phase Two: Personal Housekeeping

Setting Goals

Set goals for yourself, put them in writing and review them frequently. Dreams are not goals. Create a strategic plan and prioritize the order of tasks needed to accomplish each goal and have a specific date that you intend to complete it. You must act on your goals every single day. Distinguish what is important from what's irrelevant, or a distraction. Post your goals and task lists where you can see them. I prefer a calendar. Set up reminders for daily tasks on your phone or computer.

Concentrate on focused areas and attack each one with precise actions. These focused areas vary and may include writing and recording, musicianship, developing your fanbase, song placements, branding/marketing, booking, management, social media, and/or money to support your career.

To ensure success, goals must be reasonable, measurable, and achievable, and you must get them done on time. But pace yourself. Think about the most common goal in the world. If you want to lose weight, you must have a plan of action (exercise and reducing calorie intake) that runs over a course of time. You are not expected to achieve every goal overnight.

Whether your goal is to become a successful songwriter who writes for various artists or to launch a soaring career as a singer/songwriter, you are essentially creating your business empire. It makes sense to create manageable goals for yourself, including timelines and action plans. Goal setting involves envisioning where you'd like to be in three months, six months, 12 months, or three or four years from now.

Dream big but keep it realistic. Once your goals are identified, work backward in terms of plotting a plan to obtain them. Note that from time to time you may need to re-evaluate your goals to assure that they are in alignment with your efforts. I suggest that you develop both short-term and long-term goals; it helps to keep the big picture in mind while you focus on short-term success. Remember, life is a work in progress.

Collaborations

Collaborating with other artists and producers is one of the best ways to get a song placement on a project. More than likely, the song that you co-wrote with the artist or the producer will make the final cut on the project because your collaborator will have a piece of the action in terms of writers' and publisher's royalties. It is important to be secure in your talent, know your strengths, and have great listening skills to complement your collaborator. Someone who has a similar musical taste and complementary talents is a great candidate for successful collaboration.

Often collaborations are arranged by management and/or record labels to widen the audience of artists. It's an opportunity to introduce and share one another's fans and resources. It's also a good way of helping you to keep scheduled writing commitments. You are more likely to keep a planned writing time if you've committed to another person. Collaboration is also a great means of support to yourself and your fellow songwriter trying to navigate a business that could seem very unstable at times.

A Way of Life

If you do not have a track record of placing songs, you may initiate it by implementing the following steps into your daily first-year plan:

Prepare: Appropriately prepare yourself to accomplish your goal. If your goal is to place songs for other artists' projects, make sure there are a variety of songs in your catalog. Your catalog of songs should contain a variety of themes, tempos, and musical styles, ones that would attract a wide array of artists. Take all the time needed and the necessary steps to create an exceptional song that will entice and engage the listener. Work on product presentation (i.e., graphic design, logo, image, photos). Being prepared to present the most appropriate song to a potential client will not only give you a better chance for song placement but will open the door for future song submissions. Become an expert at preparation and presentation.

Research all music playlist platforms on terrestrial and internet radio opportunities to exploit your music. Research live performance opportunities such as house concerts, clubs, festivals, fairs, benefits, showcases/ conferences, and network with event planners and promoters.

Act: Remember that time is your most valued resource. Take care of at least three business tasks per day, just like eating three meals a day. Imagine the relationships and knowledge you would gain and benefit from by making more than 1,000 business decisions or actions per year! The most basic daily business tasks you should accomplish are: Follow up with potential clients/ collaborators, return calls and emails, and enhance social media activity (post, organize photos, prepare/share information).

Join: Join songwriting and music industry organizations such as the West Coast Songwriters Association http://www.westcoastsongwriters.org, the Recording Academy http://www.grammy.com, or the American Association of Independent Music https://a2im.org. To find an organization in your area, start by simply searching Google for "Songwriting Organizations." To help figure out which organization to join, attend events, meetings (if possible), and meet members of the organization to get a feel for which group will be the best match for your career area and point of service interests.

Joining a professional organization helps to provide more networking and employment opportunities, advance professional development skills, promote opportunities to mentor and be mentored, and increase chances for songwriting collaborations with other proficient songwriters. Most important, having a support system in place while navigating through the maze of the music industry and business trends is priceless. I will share a personal example that proves my point.

At the West Coast Songwriters Conference in 1986, I met Andre Pessis, hit songwriter for Bonnie Raitt, Huey Lewis and the News, Tim McGraw, and several others. We sat next to one another at lunch, introduced ourselves, and engaged in a casual conversation about the weather, the conference, and life in general. Although our past musical histories are in different musical genres—his success is in the field of rock and country, and mine in rhythm & blues and jazz—we both admired all genres of music and one another's work. Our humor was very similar and our taste in music was almost identical in terms of what we deemed to be of quality.

We hit it off fabulously and decided we would schedule a songwriting session. Our collaborations resulted in song placements for R&B artists the Stylistics and Lenny Williams, as well as a solid catalog of songs for future song placements. I consider Andre to be one of my best friends and collaborators. Our families are close, and we affectionately identify ourselves as "Brothers from Another Mother." If I had not joined this organization and attended that conference, our paths would have not likely crossed.

Also consider joining and meeting people in organizations that are non-music-related that could be a supporter of your music in collaboration with promotional campaigns that support their mission. For example, you may have a song that has a topic that supports causes such as health, bullying, community building, education, sports, or world events.

Follow Up: Follow up on contacts and submissions by returning emails, setting up meetings with prospective clients, and constantly refreshing your research on music styles, artists, and industry activities. Just as we become busy with projects and details of our lives, potential clients are no different. When you're "out of sight," you are "out of mind."

Walk the Walk: If you want to have a career as a songwriter, you must act as if you already have a career as a songwriter. Your destiny is in the palm of your hands. Take control of your career by creating a sound body of work. Construct a daily work schedule and follow it rigorously and religiously. Commit to writing a new song each day, creating an idea or concept, or revisiting, rewriting, and/or completing a pre-existing idea. Although you may have periods where you write songs and make demos, and periods where you do not write at all, you can NEVER stop attending to daily business tasks.

Thrive: One often overlooked step is remembering to refresh and nourish relationships you already have cemented. Keep learning, innovating, and remaining relevant. Keep up on your relationships.

Your Network Is Your Net Worth

Put yourself and your services on Front Street for others to see who you are and what you have to offer. Take advantage of all networking opportunities. Attend seminars, workshops, and events where you can engage with music industry professionals. Make your best efforts to meet the artist you aspire to work with. In addition, you should become acquainted with anyone remotely close to that artist's daily operations including the manager, producer, recording engineer, music publisher, stylist, driver, road and stage crew, secretary, assistant, and family members. Introduce yourself to new contacts; identify yourself as a songwriter.

Make it a habit of researching artists and projects for possible opportunities. Look to participate in songwriter conferences and showcases. Take time to learn the professional backgrounds of the workshop leaders and/or panelists so that you can approach them with a relatable conversation. If the event includes song critiques or placement opportunities, be prepared to submit the most appropriate song that may appeal to them. If a person is telling you about an artist or project that is looking for songs, pay close attention to what type of songs are needed, production submission requirements, and deadline dates. Listening to what is being requested and delivering a song that meets the specific request will strengthen your chances of your song being used in the final project, as opposed to submitting your favorite song. Be sure to only use the instructed method of contact. Missteps in this approach can derail the prospects of your project before it even gets started.

Do not overlook your peers and up and coming artists. Interaction with your music community allows you to create goodwill, spread awareness of your talents, and develop friendships. You can go further by donating your music services for worthy causes in your community. Remember to publicize your charitable efforts as well as take advantage of every opportunity to make people aware of your activities, songs, and products via your website, email newsletters, and social media. A large part of maintaining a healthy social media following is having plenty of new content. Use your smartphone to document and post your activities for your followers. People do not follow people who are not active, so create as many Kodak moments as possible.

Implementation (Your Team)

Tasks are completed faster when more people are working together. Therefore, the support and participation of a team are greatly needed to implement your career goals. The composition of your team should reflect the areas of expertise needed to achieve your goals. Team members should feel challenged and empowered with the freedom of ownership necessary to make innovative contributions in their work within the guidelines set by the common goals. To hold productive and efficient team meetings, organize and prioritize your next steps of implementation well in advance of the meeting, then set the agenda accordingly. Depending on your goals, you may want to pay close attention to the following:

- Music/Art and message: Product relevance to the audience
- Content development: Photographer, videographer, editors
- Presentation production: Graphic design
- Manager: To quarterback and help navigate the appropriate players on the team

- Publicist/Social Media Team/Manager of Tools: Facebook, Google, Twitter, Instagram, YouTube, Singersroom, Vimeo, blogs, etc., with the addition of print, posters/flyers, newsletters, email lists, live appearances, music industry panels, and workshops
- Booking agent: Live performances
- Business administration: Manager/coordinator/accountant
- Merchandising
- All: Constant refreshing of engagement methods

Your team is an extension of your voice and brand. As you develop your brand, your message must stay consistent. Therefore, your representation should always be aware of intimate aspects of your music and philosophies to properly implement them.

Phase Three: Getting Your Song Out There

The Song Demo

Once you have a well-written song, the next step is to make a demonstration (song demo) for presentation. Seeing and hearing are believing. There's no better way to say to others "I Am a Songwriter" than to have the song complete and in an audible or tangible form for them to reference. I relate the song demo to an audio business card. Without this essential tool, it's highly impossible to take the next step of your songwriting career. A good friend of mine has a son who is a very good songwriter. His son was invited to a dinner party at the home of a very well-known record producer. Toward the end of the evening, the producer invited the songwriter to play a couple of his original songs. The producer thought one of the songs was perfect for an artist he was producing. He asked the songwriter to send an mp3 of the song by morning so the artist and record executives could review it the next day. Unfortunately, a demo of the song had not been recorded and final decisions for the recording project were being made the following day. A perfect opportunity for a potential song placement was missed because the songwriter was not prepared.

As far as making the demo itself, one of the first things you want to do is review the elements of the song to ensure that your song is worthy of recording. In other words, you've developed the strongest idea for a song, you've hashed out the chorus, structure, melodies, lyrics, rhythm, and vocal arrangement, and chosen the best vocalist or instrumentalist to perform it. All instruments should be arranged so the parts are coordinated within the ensemble. Simultaneously, the instruments should support and complement the main vocal or instrumental melody while the overall sound of the recording should be pleasing to the ear. The same principles apply even if your demo consists of one acoustic instrument and a voice.

Choose your recording method. You may choose to record your music and vocals live all in one take (live recording), which gives you a live or rawer sound; or record each instrument and vocal independent on its track (multitrack recording), which produces a more polished/clean sound due to the ability to control the volume and sound of each track. Decide how and where you are going to record your demo. If you are making the demo at a home studio or on a laptop, buy recording software such as Pro Tools, Reason, Ableton, Garage Band, or any type of recording software that you can afford and feel comfortable operating. The best software is the one that works best for you and is within your budget. You will also need hardware such as a mixer and audio interface. In addition, you will need microphones, amplifiers, and cables if connections are not a part of your software. If you are new to home recording, get experienced people to help you and ask many questions to seek clarification. It will save you valuable time and minimize frustration. If possible, reach out to experienced engineers for professional advice. They will know best practices for microphone placement on an instrument, the best microphone to use for a particular texture of voice, and how to adjust the microphone placement for a person's height and the acoustics of the room.

Remember, you can record all the instruments and vocals at once, or one track at a time depending on the type of song you've written and sound you desire. Most ensemble or band types of recordings such as rock, jazz, heavy metal, and classical are recorded live with musicians playing all at one time. Other genres such as pop and hip-hop may lend themselves to recording programmed drums and individual parts played one at a time. If you choose the individual parts method in which you record one track at a time, remember that recording the demo is sort of like building a house. Start with the foundation (i.e., first the drums; then the bass) and work your way to the top. Simply follow your blueprint, which is the song outline you've already written. Be careful not to over-arrange the song with parts that are not significant to the basic idea or the vibe of the song. Music is subjective and although a person may like your song, it is possible that an over-arranged horn part or a busy string line, for example, could ruin your chance for song placement.

Mix your demo so that the frequencies, instruments, and vocal levels sound balanced. It is most important that the two basic elements of the song (the words and music) are heard with clarity. In other words, the lyrics and melodies are clear, the accompanying music is well blended, and the individual parts have their own space to be heard within the blend. To ensure the featured melody is heard distinctly, eliminate melodic parts that play at the same time and audio frequency range. This practice will avoid competition, conflict, and cancellation of the main melody and words. Do the same for the instruments accompanying the melody to ensure the main parts are distinct. You will need to give special attention to low, mid, and high ranges of instruments so that the song's frequencies are balanced. Although the quality of the demo does not have to be a final record master quality, it must be at a level that provides a satisfactory listening experience for the reviewer. Once the song is placed, it is the producer and mixer's responsibility to ensure the song is record-release quality before it is transferred to a data storage device (mastering) for duplication of copies. If you are a producer/songwriter attempting to get the production gig as well as the song placement, go ahead and produce and mix the song as if it were a final recording. If you plan on releasing your song with yourself as the artist, decide if your song will be an online distribution, physical release, or both.

Recording Budget

You must know how much you are able and willing to spend to produce your music before starting. Therefore, it is necessary to create a realistic budget. One of my favorite sayings is "The best surprise is no surprise," especially when it comes to money.

When creating a recording budget, you must first decide on the instrumentation of the songs and how you want your record to sound. For example, Is your music more suited for live or electronic instruments? Naturally, live musicians require you to hire personnel to play the various instruments. Does your music call for sparse arrangements such as drums, bass, guitar, and piano or big arrangements such as horns, strings, background vocals, etc.? Your typical budget line items in terms of expenses would be:

Producer
Studio
Engineer
Editing
Mixing
Mastering
Musicians
Vocalist
Guest talent (if applicable)
Equipment rental (if applicable)
Rehearsal facility rental (if applicable)
Meals, talent air and ground transportation, lodging (if applicable)
Hard drive
Post-production (art/design, marketing/promotion)
Legal
Manufacturing (if applicable)

Depending on your skills, you may be able to cover one or more of the line items yourself.

Become familiar with what online tools are available and decide which ones are most appropriate for you. I call this "being successful on purpose." Your strategy may differ from that of other artists based on your goals and target audience. Let's get started by identifying some of the marketing strategy tools available.

Song Placement

Many ask the question, "How do I go about getting someone to record my song?" I wish it were as easy as outlining an ABC plan; however, the answer isn't that straightforward. Finding a home for your song, typically referred to as *song placement*, is like leasing property in the real estate business. Getting someone to record your song could be a daunting task.

For some songs, it may be difficult to find a placement and could require some improvements or refining to suit a specific artist personality or fanbase before the mission is accomplished. In other cases, it may be as effortless as being in the right place at the right time. The ultimate situation is to write on a project with the artist who is releasing their product. Although collaborating with the artist or producer doesn't guarantee placement, it will stand a better chance of making the final cut because the artist or producer will share in the income participation of the song.

Building relationships with local artists is a great way to start. Find artists who are talented, dedicated, and show signs of potential success. You can't predict someone's success; however, if they show signs such as a growing live performance fanbase and social media following, as well as a good management team, a solid business structure, and great work ethic, they're most likely to be poised for success. If you're not a frequent performer, introduce yourself to the artist. Let the artist know that you admire their work and that you're a songwriter. Offer to share one or two of your best songs with them. If they like your material and do not write their material, pitch your song to them. If they write their material, offer to write a song with them. Building a relationship is not an overnight process. Show up frequently to support them and to develop a relationship. Also, build relationships with local music producers and good songwriters for song collaborations and submissions. Write for local radio, advertisers, and television. Invite local promoters to your shows either physically or through social media to get on shows as the supporting act for a popular local or a national artist when they come to town. Meet artists, managers, drivers, and anyone associated with a well-known artist, and stay in contact with them. Inquire about when their new recording project will begin and offer to submit a song or collaborate with the artist.

Rejection

Let's face it, we live in a bandwagon society. Once most people have given your song the stamp of approval, everyone wants to climb on board to be a part of the success. Everyone loves a winner. Be aware that once the spotlight is on you, you are vulnerable to as much criticism as you are praise. One way to show that your product is authentic and worthy of notoriety is to be open to feedback. The blogging part of social media provides the platform for an honest informal discussion about your material. Participants can also share links as part of the discussion. Trust your instinct regarding feedback based on both your knowledge and observation of techniques used by proven songwriters. These skills will give you the ability to differentiate between good or bad advice.

Keep in mind that song placement is a very competitive business and at times you may feel that your song should have been chosen for a particular project when it was not. Remember that rejection is all part of the game. There are several reasons why a song isn't accepted for a project. Take all rejections as an opportunity for a learning experience. Here are some of the reasons your song may not have been accepted:

Timing: Sometimes you have the perfect song but may have just missed the deadline for selection. It is easy to have missed opportunities due to a lack of making daily inquiries. Frequent monitoring of what is going on in the music world and organization generates better chances of staying on top of deadlines.

Good, but not exceptional (formula or familiar-sounding): This is when the songwriter has followed the rules of crafting a good song. All elements are present, but the song sounds too familiar, the idea or concept feels overused, or the element of surprise is missing.

Other songs with similar ideas lyrically or musically already on the project: This case occurs when the song you've submitted has a story or musical statement that has already been told on the project.

The song does not fit the theme or concept of the project: In this situation, you have an awesome song, but the direction or style is not appropriate for the project. This issue along with many of the others may be alleviated if you take the time to ask the right questions when making inquiries and respond appropriately. Many may ask the right questions (i.e., what is the concept, style, or instrumentation, etc. of the project), but make the mistake of trying to over-impress the client. The overzealous songwriter gives the artists everything plus the kitchen sink all in one song. Leave room for the artist to insert themselves. Be cautious and aware not to deliver a product that is something other than what has been requested. For example, my dear friend Michael Bearden, musical director for the late Michael Jackson, Lady Gaga, and a film composer enlightened me of a major rule to follow regarding delivering exactly what is requested of you. The director and/or film supervisor has a specific vision of what they're looking for and your song must complement the vision. In other words, if the scene requires a very light treatment, it would not be an appropriate time to show the supervisor all the heavy orchestration techniques you have under your belt. I think the way he put it was, "If the music supervisor asks for a peanut butter sandwich, do not deliver a steak because you think it tastes better." Just give them what they asked for: "a peanut butter sandwich," yum, yum.

Artist or producer does not have income participation from the song: Let's face it, song placement is a business. Although it makes perfect sense for an artist or producer to want to record the absolute best material for consumption, the reality is that most are willing to compromise art to ensure they will have a piece of the pie when the product sells. If the artist or producer has control over the selected releases, most likely the song in which they co-wrote will make it onto the final product. A win/win situation is when the artist and producer are strong writers.

Mood of listener: Sometimes the A&R person or decision-maker is just having a bad day. In this case, there is nothing to do but run!!

As much as we want to have our songs recorded by the artists of our dreams, the fact is that most of the time we have little or no control over the situation. We can only do our best to put ourselves in the best position for success. So, prepare and submit songs with the appropriate presentation, then follow up.

Building an Online Community

An integral part of building a songwriting career is developing an online community. This is the easiest way for people to become familiar with you, your music, and your songs. Meeting new people in the community makes it possible to receive immense help or for you to help others. Since the biggest challenge singer/songwriters face is creating awareness of their art, a great online community provides the most efficient platform for communicating with thousands of people for relatively minimal to no cost. The greatest expense is creating the actual product, content, and possibly a graphic design flyer for the selected method of presentation.

Make sure your music is downloadable, able to be streamed, and that your contact information is easily accessible for your audience. One of the most effective ways of directing targeted traffic to your website is to submit your website URL to search engines such as Google, Bing, and Yahoo. Again, the cost for this service is free.

Initially, you will need to identify the audience with which you want to engage. It is much easier for people to come together who share common music styles and related interests. Now that you've identified and made a connection with potential followers, create a comfortable environment for them to go to.

When people visit your website, immediately make your visitors feel welcomed. Keep your background simple. If you use a pictured background, make sure it's subdued and easy on the eyes. Moving objects, such as birds, cars, and animals, are huge distractions and should be avoided. If your music isn't at an amazing professional level yet, do not automatically play it as soon as your website opens. However, if you choose to do so, and even if your music is fabulous, provide a way to turn the music off (and make sure one doesn't have to hunt for the "off" icon). Too many advertisements are a deterrent. Non-working pages that read "Page Not Found" and "Error" are probably the worst offenses you can make as the site's owner. Make everything easily accessible. User-friendly tools make the best first impression. News, Tours, Shows, Video, Merchandise, Photo Gallery, and Contact (especially for new and independent artists) are pretty much the standard topic headings viewers want to see on your home page.

If your followers must navigate through the system to find this basic information, they may become frustrated and abandon your site. For example, I wanted to surprise an artist I'd met at an event by purchasing tickets to her upcoming performance. I thought I would go to her website, click on her calendar, find the performance date, and click to purchase tickets. Unfortunately, I was the one who received the surprise. The site was packed with lots of content to read, none of which I was interested in. The experience was quite irritating. The result was a loss of sale of two tickets. Remember, less is more. Make it easy to find what, when, where, and how. Include menus such as "Help" and "Frequently Asked Questions" to assist your follower, especially if you are introducing a new or unusual topic. If you chose to open your site with a pre-home page to advertise your latest song, CD, video, or merchandise, be sure the button to "Enter" the home page is conveniently available and easy to find. Before launching your website be sure all the kinks are eliminated. I suggest that you first test things out for yourself. Also have a friend go on your site and do a test run, then elicit their honest opinion regarding their experience.

Besides great content about yourself, be sure to post content that interests the music community and enthusiasts. The content should always be newsworthy, educational, inspirational, entertaining, and should include trending topics and tips on aspects of professional development. It helps to provide multiple opportunities for the community to engage in conversations. There's no better form of advertising than word of mouth and personal testimonials. Most importantly, your participation in the conversation and engagement with your network will make all the difference in the world as far as your benefits from this tool's usage. It is vital for people in your community to feel a connection and that you are truly engaging with them, as opposed to them thinking you've hired someone to manage your site. Set aside a certain time of the day to participate. I usually engage in social media once in the morning and again in the early evening. Do whatever is best for your schedule as long as you are consistent.

Consistency is valuable to your network. If normally you are in contact with your community regularly, you need to keep the pace going strong. If you were to suddenly drop off your efforts, followers would soon lose interest in your posts and your following will suffer.

Support, and celebrate other songwriters and artists by sharing their newsworthy posts. In return, you will receive support. Plus, your followers will become tired of only hearing your material and accolades. Celebrate others by sending them a quick note to let them know you are proud of their achievements. Also, be genuine with your support and praises. Do not say to the person that you are helping promote or supporting, "You owe me one." This cheapens your gift of encouragement and diminishes your good deed to an almost worthless level of giving.

Participate in workshops, conferences, and live speaking engagements, which you can promote to your network. This brings more attention and credibility to you and your work. It also helps you become a trusted community resource.

Lastly, always remember the friends you meet "off-line." The people you meet at casual or music industry networking events could also be of tremendous value to your online community. Face-to-face communication gives a person a more direct and personal connection, which makes them more comfortable sharing networks and personal contacts.

Maintain a Positive Attitude

I like to refer to songs as our children because we birth them, help them develop, and send them off into the world. We hope that they become the absolute most productive asset to themselves and society. We are sensitive to how they are treated and follow their every move when given the opportunity. As difficult as it may be at times, we must maintain an open and positive attitude when receiving feedback of praise or rejection.

If the feedback is positive, you should acknowledge the compliment gracefully. If the feedback is a constructive critique, you must sincerely listen for suggestions that may improve the composition. In both cases, you must communicate with appreciation. The most productive and humble position for a songwriter is to take the attitude that "My best song is my next one."

I frequently mention the importance of having a great attitude because ultimately, the music industry mainly thrives on relationships. The late Dr. Maya Angelou wrote, "I learned that people would forget what you said, people will forget what you did, but people will never forget how you made them feel." At the end of the day, most people only care about what they did, and who they did it with. If it felt good, they will have a desire to repeat the occasion.

Subscriptions and Education

The public usually thinks of Netflix or Spotify when thinking about subscription services. However, many singer/songwriters are offering subscription services to create more flexibility, creativity, exclusive engagement with fans, and a recurring revenue stream. A subscription service provides the artist with an opportunity to have a steady income in exchange for delivering something new and valuable to their fans for a monthly fee. An artist can trade songs, merchandise, exclusive invitations, private footage, early access to videos, memorabilia, etc. or anything fans deem as a value. Two of the most popular membership platforms for recording artists are Patreon (https://www.patreon.com) and Bandcamp (https://bandcamp.com).

One of the main rules of thumb is to read and absorb information from trusted publications and articles about industry activities, key players, music styles, and marketing trends. Here is a list of trusted publications for your review:

Music Industry Magazines
American Songwriter
www.americansongwriter.com
All musical genres; news and reviews

Billboard Magazine
http://www.billboardonline.com
Charts and news

Blues and Soul Magazine
www.bluesandsoul.com
Blues and soul—UK/Europe

Christ Community Music Magazine
www.ccmmagazine.com
Christian music, news, reviews, tours

Classical
http://www.classical-music.com
News and reviews on classical music

College Music Journal
www.cmj.com; www.cmjmusic.com
New music, artists, college and young adults

Clash
www.clashmusic.com
News, gigs, interviews, new artists, fashion, film

The Electronic Urban Report
www.eurweb.com
News and reviews

Froots Magazine
www.frootsmag.com
Folk and roots music

Gramophone
www.gramophone.co.uk
Classical—UK, news, reviews, festival

Living Blues Magazine
http://www.livingblues.com
Blues, news, charts

Music Trades Magazine
www.musictrades.com
New data subscription

Music Week
www.musicweek.com
Latest news, interviews, and music industry opinions

Music Connection Magazine
www.musicconnection.com
All musical genres. Music advice and support

Music Industry Quarterly
www.musicindustryquarterly.com
Urban news, videos, lifestyle, events

Music Row Magazine
www.musicrow.com
Country-Nashville

My Hit Online
www.myhitonline.com
Tip sheet

Pollstar
www.pollstar.com
Concerts, Venues, News

Song Quarters
www.songquarters.com
Pop and Urban musical genres; Tipsheet

Performer Magazine
www.performermag.com
Independent musicians in a DIY environment

Music Business News
www.musicbusinessworldwide.com
Global music business news

Digital Music News
www.digitalmusicnews.com
Global music business news

Music News: NPR
www.npr.org
Music news, artist, and album reviews

Books
All You Need to Know About the Music Business, 10th edition © 2019
by Donald Passman
Publisher: Simon & Schuster

How to Make It in the New Music Business © 2019
by Ari Herstand
Publisher: Liveright

Six Steps to Songwriting Success © 2008
by Jason Blume
Publisher: Billboard

Songwriters on Songwriting © 2016
by Paul Zollo
Publisher: Paul Zollo – Da Capo Press

How to Use Spotify Playlists to Launch Your Career in Music © 2017
by George Goodrich
Publisher: George Goodrich

Music, Money, and Success, 8th edition © 2018
by Jeff Brabec and Todd Brabec
Publisher: Schirmer Trade Books

Tunesmith: Inside the Art of Songwriting © 1999
Jimmy Webb
Publisher: Hachette Books

Great Songwriting Techniques © 2018
Jack Perricone
Publisher: Oxford University Press, Inc.

Free Online Songwriting Tools

- Autochords (https://autochords.com)—Chord generator that generates four chord progressions and all of the chords in every key
- The Method Behind the Music (https://method-behind-the-music.com)—Music theory terms and concepts
- LANDR's Collaboration (https://www.landr.com/music-collaboration/)—This allows you to share private links to your music for feedback and collaboration.
- Rhyme Zone (https://www.rhymezone.com)—Rhyming dictionary that includes synonyms, antonyms, and similar-sounding words
- Hook Theory Trends (https://www.hooktheory.com/trends)—Chord progression resource that shows which popular songs use the same chords.
- HumOn (https://hum-on-easiest-music-maker.soft112.com)—iOS and Android songwriting app that creates a song and score in various styles such as classical, R&B, etc., around a hummed melody.
- Songspace (https://songspace.com/about)—Enables you to share access to your songs with others. Also allows you to grant rights for others to edit.
- Song-Writer Lite (Lyrics) (https://appadvice.com/app/song-writer-lite-write-lyrics/447771549)—iOS organizer with digital folders ("Complete" and "In Progress"), titles, label sections.
- iO808 (https://io808.com)—TR-808 drum machine that's useful for plotting out rhythms.
- Bandlab (https://www.bandlab.com/?lang=en)—App-based digital audio workstation that allows you to record from your phone or demo on-the-go.

Songwriter Spotlight

Andre Pessis

Andre Pessis. Photo by Kimberly Beeson. Used with permission.

Andre Pessis is a multi-platinum songwriter, musician, and educator. He has written hits such as "Slow Ride" for Bonnie Raitt, "Walking on a Thin Line" by Huey Lewis and the News, "Wrong" for Waylon Jennings, as well as songs for Tim McGraw, Journey, Mr. Big, RatDog, Southern Pacific, Ben E. King, the Stylistics, and Laura Branigan.

Batiste: When did you start writing songs?
Pessis: I never wanted to be a songwriter, it just happened. I was in a rock & roll band in the sixties that did mostly original tunes like most bands back then. I started to write for the band and became the main writer. I put in my time and fell in love with the craft and art of it. When the band broke up in the seventies, I continued to write.
Batiste: How do you build a song?

Pessis: I usually build a song from a title idea. I write the music and lyrics for the chorus first and then the verses. I have a notebook full of title ideas. Sometimes I'll write a piece of music first, but I find it easiest to go with the title first and flesh out the storyline in my head before I write music. It doesn't matter how you do it. Everyone is different.

Batiste: How did your collaboration with Kevin Wells on the classic "Walking on a Thin Line," on the mega-selling album *Sports* recorded by Huey Lewis and the News, come about?

Pessis: Vietnam vets were not treated with respect in the sixties by a lot of so-called hippies even though my friends and I were completely sympathetic to their plight of having to fight for a war that nobody believed in. I had a friend named Doug who had his leg blown off by the Viet Cong. Doug drove our band to Monterey when we had a week booked at the Bull's Eye Tavern, a well-known hippie venue. I spent a lot of time with him talking about that war. I wrote maybe twenty pages of notes about the war and composed a piece of music for it and tried out some lines. I came up with the title first, as usual.

I went up to Kevin Wells' house to write and we were trapped there for a few days due to flooding. I played him my music for the song and told him about my ideas. He didn't go for my music and composed what became the final music, which I loved more than mine. While he and his wife were watching TV in the living room, I sat in the piano room alone for a few hours and wrote all the lyrics. I had thought about the subject so thoroughly and taken so many notes, that the lyric just poured out of me.

Batiste: Well, that writing session certainly paid off! The *Sports* album has sold over 10 million copies and is still selling. You and Eric Martin have been very successful as collaborators on projects for the band Mr. Big. What are your tips on what makes a successful collaborating team?

Pessis: A successful collaborating team is based on the chemistry between the partners. Eric and I have had over 44 songs recorded by Mr. Big. We have been writing together for more than 20 years and each of us brings a different set of skills to the table. I am mostly the lyric guy and Eric the melody man, but these lines blur all the time as Eric is a very good lyricist and I have many musical ideas. Eric is a world-class singer and writer and an inspiration to work with. If the chemistry is absent, then writing between partners never results in art, only craft. Inspiration comes from love and any strong emotion. When you find someone that you have chemistry with, hold on to them. That's the bomb, man.

Batiste: What are the key ingredients for a hit song?

Pessis: The key ingredients of a song are originality, honesty, and beauty. If you write the same lyric that others have written before, your song won't make it. If you have a good idea, story, and beautiful heart-grabbing melody, you are on your way.

Another key ingredient: you must have something in your song that is so attention-grabbing as to stop anyone listening in their tracks. Then you must command their complete attention for three minutes or so and leave them something to remember. Inspiration is also a key ingredient as it is the only engine that drives this train home.

Batiste: What advice do you give music creators interested in a songwriting career?

Pessis: My advice to young songwriters is to write a lot and ignore all those who love to tell you that it can't be done. Writing in some ways is like weight training: the more you do, the stronger you get. Be stubborn about it. If you keep at it long enough and love it, you will succeed. All through my career, I have heard that success in this business is almost impossible. This just means that it is possible. Of course, talent has a lot to do with it, but in all my years of teaching songwriting, I've rarely encountered someone without talent. You need to be obsessed with your art and learn to accept rejection as part of the learning process.

There are easier ways of making a living than songwriting, but ... I can't ever imagine not writing. It's too much fun!

9
The Business of Digital Music

Digital music is music that has been converted from analog data into digital data. The most common physical form of digital music is the compact disc and the mp3. Now that CDs are almost extinct, digital platforms, streaming services, playlists, and downloads of mp3 files are the most common ways for people to consume music.

Although the distribution of digital music has given artists more control over their careers, having to market and promote that music has considerably increased their workload in comparison to depending on a traditional label. However, control over finances, creativity, and new methods of fanbase outreach have proved to be far more beneficial for the independent artist.

Digital formats can be downloaded and listened to on computers and mobile devices and supported by other hardware products, including smart TVs. Digital music codecs allow steaming and various playback sound file formats via wi-fi.

Why Digital?

After going through the process of crafting a great song, arranging it, recording awesome performances using the best mics, preamps, and consoles at your disposal, and then mixing and mastering it, one might ask: why would you want to compress it into a digital format? The primary reason is that downloading, streaming, and mobile devices are the methods by which most individuals consume music. Also, the cost of producing a recording project has been drastically reduced. Therefore, the focus and expense become marketing: creating awareness for the song and artist via the internet and social media.

With digital music, an artist can release music globally without signing to a record label. But in today's fast-paced world, with constant demand for the next big thing, the biggest challenge is consistently producing and distributing content (i.e., music, graphics, fashion, video, photographs, locations, etc.) that is relevant and appeals to your audience.

Music Streaming

Streaming is a technology that allows a person to receive audio and/or visual content without requiring them to purchase or download files from the internet. Streaming also allows people to listen to music or watch videos in real time.

Interactive and Non-Interactive Streaming

With interactive streaming, the user chooses what songs are played. For example, services such as Apple Music and Spotify are interactive because the user can choose what they want to listen to. Interactive streaming services pay both mechanical and performance royalties.

Non-interactive streaming services function more like radio stations. The music is pre-programmed, and the user cannot choose the songs that are played. A few of the non-interactive streaming services are Sirius XM, cable television service Music Choice, iHeart Radio, and Pandora. However, Pandora is both interactive, with its launch of Pandora Premium and Pandora Plus, and non-interactive, based around its original model.

Getting Paid for Digital Sales and Performances

The traditional music royalty model generates income from three main sources: mechanical royalties, performance royalties, and synchronization fees. These traditional royalty income sources of revenue are now further extended to include digital formats such as downloads, streaming, ringtones, satellite radio, and performance payments from SoundExchange.

When songs are used on satellite, internet, and digital television radio services, a playlist of songs played is sent to SoundExchange along with a fee. Upon receipt, SoundExchange examines the data and distributes the payments to the rights holders (owners of the masters), featured artists, and non-featured artists (backup vocalists and session musicians).

Since consumers have become accustomed to listening to a lot of their music for free, it is increasingly more difficult to make a living as a songwriter. As a songwriter, you must acquire entrepreneurial skills if you want to be successful. Every time your song is sold, streamed, or played on the radio in any format, you should be generating income. It's up to you and only you to make sure that your business affiliations are lined up to get paid. The digital world is constantly evolving, so as more outlets are developed, you must take advantage of new opportunities.

Here are a few ways to get paid from digital sales and performances of your songs:

- Receive mechanical royalties by signing up with a distributor and making your music available for sale on iTunes, Spotify, Apple Music, Amazon, and as many purchasing outlets as possible.
- Register with SoundExchange to receive payments for internet airplay of performances.
- Have your music available on various streaming platforms.
- Register your work with PROs.

- Seek out music supervisors for placement in TV/film, games, and advertising agencies to secure sync fees/digital synchronization licenses.
- Develop ringtones of your songs and receive income from both the sale and public performance.
- Take advantage of social media monetization on YouTube (YouTube Partner Program), Facebook, Instagram, TikTok, Triller, etc.

How Do Streaming Services Generate Income?

Streaming companies generate income from three main sources:

Ad revenue: A website or platform sells advertising impressions based on the number of views the ad receives. These video ads may run pre-roll (before the main video shows) or mid-roll (the main video stops, and the ad will roll, then the main video will resume). The price is commonly based on Cost Per Thousand (CPM) views. For example, advertisers may pay $15 to $20 per thousand views that an ad receives.

Subscriptions: Users pay a monthly fixed amount, and the library of content is available to them.

Transactional Video On-Demand (TVOD): Allows users to access content without the constraints of a regular broadcasting schedule. Users pay on a pay-per-view basis and can download content.

Digital streaming royalty rates are established by local legislation. In the United States, the Copyright Royalty Board negotiates performance royalty rates with PROs.

Selling Your Music Online

The two main places to sell your music online are on your own website and through online retailers. Online retailers include Apple Music, Spotify, CD Baby, TIDAL, Amazon, Bandcamp, and many others, as well as stores that sell musical instruments, equipment, and accessories.

Your website is a great place to sell your music because you can also engage with your fans, giving them a chance to learn more about you and your performances. It also allows you to present your merchandise for purchase. But the big advantage of selling from your own website is that you will own the emails and data collected when making sales, which is crucial for engaging long-term with your fanbase.

The challenge for every independent songwriter is to balance the crafting of their songwriting skills while developing strong entrepreneurial skills to grow their business and fanbase. Many singer/songwriters are using e-commerce platforms for selling their products on the internet, such as Shopify, Bandcamp, WordPress,

Musictoday, and WooCommerce. Many of these platforms also provide promotion for your music by advertising on Facebook and Instagram, and they furnish built-in analytics to give you a sense of what is popular with listeners.

Having your music available with regular online retailers and playlists, along with your own website and store, is crucial. Online retailers help new audiences discover your music, increase your sales, and develop your fanbase. Another point to consider is that new fans of your music may feel more comfortable purchasing from an online store that they know and trust.

Digital Music Distribution

Distribution is defined in the name itself: It simply means sharing throughout the marketplace and making your music available for sale in a physical or digital form. With the presence of digital music, artists no longer depend on major labels and affiliations for their distribution platform.

You can use various distributors for different releases, but only one distributor per release. One-stop digital distribution companies such as TuneCore, DistroKid, Google Play, and CD Baby will get your project to the various services such as Rhapsody, eMusic, Apple Music, LastFM, Spotify, and so on to sell your music, collect royalties, and provide services such as promotion and marketing. No matter which company you decide to use, *always retain 100 percent ownership of your music master and copyrights*. It is acceptable for companies to take a commission for additional services, but nothing else. Many of these distribution services offer marketing, radio promotion, and data reporting, which are the same services a record label offers.

The ability to distribute your music gives you a tremendous amount of freedom, creativity, independence, and ownership of your music. The key is to make sure your music is in as many trusted digital music distribution outlets as possible.

Two of the most popular digital music distributors among independent artists are TuneCore and DistroKid. TuneCore has been around since 2005 and is well-branded. DistroKid was founded in 2013 and has an incredible service reputation, as well as competitive pricing.

Here are a few sample comparisons between TuneCore and DistroKid:

TuneCore

Costs
- Album: $29.99 first year/$49.99 each following year
- Single: $9.99 per year
- Ringtone: $19.99 per year
- You keep 100 percent of your music sales revenue

- You keep 100 percent of your rights
- Sell your music worldwide on Apple Music, Spotify, Amazon Music, Google Play (150-plus music partners)
- Daily sales trend reports with Apple Music, Spotify, and Amazon Music data.
- Monthly music sales reports.
- Create cover art if needed.

DistroKid

Costs

- Albums and songs (unlimited content): $19.99 per year
- You keep 100 percent of your royalties; get paid monthly
- Sell your music on Spotify, Apple Music, Pandora, Amazon, Google Play, TIDAL, iHeartRadio, YouTube, Deezer, and 15-plus stores and streaming services.
- Distribution to outlets faster than any other distributor.
- Allows you to create a party (group) of people that has an ownership stake in the sales of product and allocate/designate percentages to go directly to the desired party.

Online Marketing and Promotion

Talent, a great song, and stellar production are only preliminary steps to building a singer/songwriter's career. Your level of success depends on how well you can promote yourself and your music. Online marketing is the most cost-effective, convenient, and efficient way to promote and engage your fans instantly with your latest product and information you want to share.

One extreme example of the power of online marketing is when Beyonce released her fifth solo project, *Beyonce*, in 2013 without traditional promotion. Typically, artists released a single or two before an album's release to spark the interest of current and potential fans in anticipation of a full album of material to come. There was no radio single released prior to or in tandem with the *Beyonce* release, although she did release 17 videos simultaneously, which were available only if you purchased the digital album.

Despite having no previous marketing or promotion before its release, Beyonce's album sold over 800,000 copies in three days simply by announcing it on her Facebook page. Beyonce's use of surprise marketing also proved to be an effective marketing tool on her sixth album, entitled *Lemonade*, where she made a "save the date" announcement, declaring a world premiere event without divulging what the event was. This created a buzz among her fans who speculated if the event was a new movie, album, business venue, book, or personal crisis? The HBO special was a full visual concept album in which the songs were used to tell a story. She waited until the middle of the event to reveal the surprise announcement that this story was indeed the release of the album *Lemonade*.

Beyonce's innovative marketing style continued in 2019 with the promotion of her *Homecoming* documentary on Netflix and the simultaneous release of a new live album entitled *Homecoming* that featured live versions of the songs from her 2018 Coachella performance. She offered an additional song, a cover of the Maze featuring Frankie Beverly 1981 classic "Before I Let Go." She sparked a viral dance challenge on Instagram, requesting fans to submit their dance routines to the song. In return, Beyonce reviewed and responded to the submissions. Fans were ecstatic, and they responded by making *Homecoming* Beyonce's seventh hit solo album.

Granted, few artists have Beyonce's fanbase and few can pull off the mega-numbers she does, but she sets a positive example for creative ways to reach out to an audience.

Here's another example, from a recording artist who seemingly came out of nowhere and just a couple years later did TV commercials with Sir Elton John! Lil Nas X publicly rolled out the release of his first full-length mega-successful album, *Montero*, over six months, based around a carefully orchestrated marketing strategy that took nine months for Lil Nas X and his team to develop.

Lil Nas X rose to fame with the hit single "Old Town Road" in 2019, a song which as of the date of this writing holds the record for the longest-running top single in the United States. He dominated news headlines and social media trending topics and sparked controversy for a month when he announced that he was gay at the height of the song's popularity.

At that time, gay culture was not entirely accepted by country music radio. But Lil Nas X's team utilized the combination of backlash, support, and controversy surrounding his sexuality to capitalize and expand his brand through marketing across all social media platforms. Lil Nas X released four singles—"Montero (Call Me by Your Name)," "Sun Goes Down," "Industry Baby," and "That's What I Want"—before releasing the album. Each release leading up to the album proved controversial and immediately went viral.

One of the social media apps he used to promote the first single, "Montero (Call Me by Your Name)" was TikTok, the short form video sharing app that allows users to create and share performances that are mainly based on trending topics. He posted a pole-dancing challenge that linked to the video. In the video, he dances with the devil, gives him a lap dance, and incorporates religious and historic symbolism. This video had conservative politicians and Christians in a fury. He offered fans a $10,000 prize for using the hashtag #PoleDanceToHell and tweeted a threat to kiss anyone who made an offensive comment about him. This offering resulted in TikTok creators posting over 180,000 creations at 390 million views.

Lis Nas X responded to people critical of his lifestyle with marketing content that resulted in viral trends that attracted new fans with each response. In the case of "Montero (Call Me by Your Name)," his response to critics was to release three supplementary videos on his YouTube channel: "Satan's Extended Version," "But Lil Nas X Is Silent the Entire Time" and "Bathroom of Hell."

He sparked more controversy when he offered his fans 666 pairs of Nike Air Max Satan Shoes containing human blood within the soles of the shoes. After a two-day uproar including a threatened lawsuit by Nike, he responded with a fake apology video featuring a clip from the video of the single, which garnered more than 8 million views. This promoted the song even further. This single has more than 360 million views on YouTube to date.

Along with promotional skits and teasers, Lil Nas X posted several parody billboards. This unexpected traditional method of marketing was controversial. One billboard showed him dressed as a cheesy lawyer. It read, "Are you single, lonely and miserable? You may be entitled to compensation and Lil Nas X is here to help." The billboard then directs the viewer to the pre-sale site for the album.

Just before the album's release, Lil Nas X announced that he was pregnant and released photos of himself sporting a fake baby bump symbolizing the birth of his album. The photos spread throughout social media outlets like wildfire. He set up a baby registry where fans could donate to his favorite charities.

Also, on the day of the album's release, Lil Nas X partnered with YouTuber Zach Campbell to post a reaction video to the album. A reaction video is essentially a video review of a product. Zach Campbell has 600K subscribers on YouTube.

Lil Nas X's brilliant marketing strategy is based on knowing his audience and eliciting fan engagement, by taking advantage of controversy and by using both traditional and new social media methods. His marketing strategy has created a blueprint for queer brands and creators. His fundamental marketing strategy was innovative and successful. All artists would be wise to look at how he reaches fans.

Establish a Solid Social Media Following

The main reason for using social media is to inform, invite, attract, and retain fans, so it is important to incorporate the following elements in your messaging on your social media platforms:

- Documentation: Fans want to follow your journey and feel like they're taking part in your experience. Video and photographs help the fans' experience.

- Education: Fans like to learn different things about you that perhaps the public doesn't know. This education could be as varied as an unknown talent or an inside look at your songwriting process—even a picture of your studio or your favorite piano!
- Entertainment: Provide your fans with quality, entertaining content (i.e., exceptional music and production, behind-the-scenes footage, exclusive access to non-commercial live video performances).

Online Marketing and Advertising
Paid Advertising
Paid online advertising is used to increase the visibility of you and your product by driving fans to your website or other platforms where they can listen and purchase your music. Before spending money on advertising, be sure to know your target demographic (who you're trying to reach); know the value of what you're offering your consumer (i.e., product, performance ticket, merchandise, etc.); let fans know how to take action (i.e., purchase instructions, "like" fan page, vote in the contest, etc.). Instagram, Facebook, SubmitHub, and YouTube are some of the most successful and popular paid ads for songwriters.

Pay-Per-Click Advertising
With this advertising model, the advertiser pays the publisher or website owner each time the ad is clicked. This model is used to drive traffic to websites.

Affiliate Marketing
Affiliate marketing is referral marketing, where you share profits with fellow marketers in exchange for promoting each other's products. An online retailer pays a commission to an external website for traffic or sales generated from its referrals.

Email Marketing
Email marketing is the use of email lists to promote products and/or services. Although some may consider email marketing to be old-school, it is still one of the most effective advertising channels. Almost everyone checks their email several times a day.

Mobile Marketing
The most "reachable" method of connecting with fans is through their mobile device—smartphones, tablets, smartwatches, and other mobile devices. Almost everyone owns a mobile device and nearly 100 percent of mobile device users keep their mobile device in their possession most of the time; 80 percent of internet users'

access is through a smartphone. New music can easily be discovered at any time of the day or night.

Video Marketing

Visual content is one of the most used tools in digital marketing. YouTube is the second largest search engine after Google, followed by many others like TikTok, Yahoo Screen, Bing Video, and AOL Video. YouTube is also the number one site for discovery of new music; it reaches viewers instantly. If you're trying to promote music or introduce yourself as a new artist, sharing your video online is an effective way to disseminate your songs, projects, and electronic press kits to millions of viewers. Video marketing was instrumental in launching the careers of successful artists such as Justin Bieber, Tori Kelly, Avery, Shawn Mendes, Charlie Puth, among countless others.

One quick video marketing tip: film 70 percent of the audience on one of your songs at a live performance. Then let the audience in attendance know that you're posting the video of that song on your website. There's a good chance that members of that audience will visit your website and tell their friends to visit, as well. Once on your website, they will have an opportunity to hear other music, view photo galleries, interviews, performance calendars, receive giveaways and make discount purchases on merchandise, performances, and other exciting items.

Also, make use of Facebook's Music tab in its Watch menu, which enables you to add a music video library to your page.

Cross-Marketing and Collaboration

The concept of cross-marketing is to take advantage of every opportunity to get you and your music seen and heard everywhere possible. List links to your sites on all your social media platforms so that each one of your sites lists one another. Your Facebook page should also list your Instagram, Twitter, blog, and website addresses, and vice versa. Don't forget the basics!

Collaborating with other entities such as artists, organizations, promoters, event planners, and television, radio, and advertising agencies allows you to share links as part of promoting the product and/or event. Don't forget to link your offline world to your online world by listing your sites on printed materials. Once the viewer is on your website, their email address will be required to receive the promotional item or discount. Then add the email addresses to your email marketing campaign.

Time for Release

The first order of business before diving into marketing and promotion of any type is to create great music. Without amazing music and a recording of it, you will be forever climbing an uphill battle. I can't emphasize this fact enough and will take the liberty of mentioning it several times in this section.

Okay, moving forward. Now that your songs are well-written, arranged, and professionally produced, you are ready to share your music with the world! Naturally, your next inclination is to rush to release your product soon after its completion. However, unless you are already a superstar, you must wait until all steps and plans for their implementation are in place to gain the most listens for your song.

Here are a few reminders of things you might still need to do:

Independent Record Release Checklist and Timeline

Three Months Before Album Release
- Create awareness of the album while it is being recorded
- Copyright all music and master (Forms PA and SR)
- Register with ASCAP, BMI, or SESAC
- Register with SoundExchange
- Document the creation and behind-the-scenes journey for fans
- Collect contacts of your fans for your newsletter
- Decide on marketing and PR plan (identify and recruit team members)
- Create a timeline calendar that outlines details leading up to the release
- Update bio for website

Two Months Before Album Release
- Photo session with three or four images
- Complete single/album/EP artwork
- Research and select Spotify pre-save/marketing platform
- Select and register with distributor (TuneCore, DistroKid, CD Baby, etc.)
- Announce single release date
- Launch a pre-order and pre-save campaign to generate interest. Register your UPCs with MRC Data to get credit for your pre-orders for music charts.
- Produce a video for a single; produce a short video to announce a single release
- Announce album/EP release date
- Social media posting (Facebook and Instagram three to four times per week; Twitter three to four times per day; YouTube frequently)
- Website: URL links to all your social media platforms; contact info easily found
- Media content (photos and videos)
- Maintain high visibility on social media

One Month Before Album Release
- Release the single and video
- Produce a short video to announce the release of the album/EP
- Set a date for a live or virtual album/EP release event

- Continue to engage with fans
- Download Spotify artist app
- Spotify pre-save campaign
- Create an ad in Spotify Ad Studio
- Sign up for Apple Music for artists
- Update profile and post reviews on Amazon
- Sign on to SoundCloud, Bandcamp, Pandora, TikTok

Two Weeks Before Album Release
- Schedule premiere countdowns on social media and YouTube
- Post daily on social media
- Write album/song release newsletter
- Complete media flyers and "Available Now" banners
- Create a contest to win free music or merchandise leading up to the release date
- Recruit friends, family, and close supporters to commit to posting about your release on the day of its release
- Distribute marketing and music with informational one-sheet to radio, blogs, reviews, and interview outlets.

Day of Album Release
- Replace all current social media ads with "Available Now" flyer/banner updates
- Send out newsletter
- Remind friends, family, and supporters to post
- Create Instagram and Facebook Stories
- Have a party

After Album Release
- Continue to conduct as many interviews as possible
- Thank press and post on social media
- Add press articles or clips to your social media and website
- Release a new single/video or promote the most popular song from the album/EP
- Announce promotional performances
- Perform and collaborate with other artists to expose your music to a wider audience
- Engage with fans on social media and merchandise booths when performing live

Livestreaming

Platforms with streaming features such as Bandcamp, Apple Music, Instagram, and Facebook are used by artists and fans to engage with one another. You can get an instant reaction from your fans about your music, and fans feel special when they're able to be a part of your journey, whether it is from the recording studio, traveling, or participating in a trending discussion.

Playlists

Create your playlists, develop followers, and share and enjoy playlists curated by playlist sites, other groups, or individuals. Since this method is how millions of listeners receive their music experience, your success depends on having your music on as many playlists and pitching it to as many curators of playlists as possible, especially playlists which have a huge number of followers. Various online radio platforms such as Last.fm, Pandora, and many others are a good direction to head for music promotion.

Here are a few tips on ways to popularize your songs and attract playlists that have many followers:

- Promote your music on your website.
- Share your songs on playlists and other playlist curators among your network of friends.
- Target event organizers, internet radio stations, websites, and curators that service your genre of music, television, DJ's, producers, promoters, and established artists who could be possible mentors and supporters
- Paid advertising
- Release songs often and in similar styles to build consistency. To retain fans, stay in the same genre for a while to establish your fanbase
- Join networks like A2IM, and website playlist curators or pitching services such as Fiverr, Playlist Plugger, Streambeet, Soundplate, or Topsify.com
- Release new music on a Friday to be a part of the new Friday playlists
- Make songs that get added on compilations from well-known artists or projects.

There are multiple playlist-building sites such as Spotify, Apple Music, Pandora, Google Play, Slacker, Napster, Favtape, Tidal, and Grooveshark.

Playlist-building sites make their money from advertisers and/or subscribers. Advertisers are attracted to playlists that have many followers. This makes getting added onto a playlist with a considerable number of followers downright competitive. In most cases, you must have a substantial fanbase, buzz, and music already being played on multiple smaller but notable playlists. Some artists and record labels go as far as hiring a publicist or paying curators of a large playlist to get added to their playlist.

Another benefit of securing placement on a playlist with many followers is the likelihood of being discovered by random listeners. Many non-musicians or non-creators of music don't have the interest or time to curate a playlist of songs that appeal to them. Most hobbyists prefer to find one of the many existing playlist sites such as Spotify, Apple Music, and Pandora, pick their music genre and mood, and enjoy listening to new music mixed in with songs they're familiar with.

Although playlists such as Spotify, Napster, Apple Music, Tidal, Deezer, Pandora, Amazon, and YouTube are a lifeline for artists in terms of exposure, they are a nightmare in that their pay out rates vary at any given time.

YouTube remains the best resource for listeners to discover music and playlists due to its mass exposure from subscribers and random listeners. Artists complain that the pay for streaming on these sites is very low, but still participate because aside from mainstream terrestrial radio, playlists remain the most popular way for their music to be discovered and exploited.

The business of digital music and its evolving technology continues to create platforms for independent songwriters. With digital technology music creators are better able to develop entrepreneurial skills, engage their audience, capitalize on income opportunities, and gain creative and financial control over their career. Decide which distribution, marketing platforms, and streaming services works best for your product and incorporate them into your record release strategy.

There are always new and exciting things going on in the digital world and it takes a lot of work to stay on top of it. Staying on top of it requires that you learn and share information with others and reach out to colleagues for advice. We're all in this together.

Songwriter Spotlight

Peter Asher

Peter Asher. Photo courtesy of Peter Asher.

Iconic record producer, musician, artist, manager Pete Asher has been involved with many hits and hitmakers including "Lady Godiva," "I Go To Pieces," and "A World Without Love" by Peter and Gordon, "Sweet Baby James," "Fire and Rain," and "How Sweet It Is (To Be Loved By You)" by James Taylor, "You're No Good," "Blue Bayou," and albums *Heart Like a Wheel* and *Simple Dreams* by Linda Ronstadt, as well as artists that include J. D. Souther, David Sanborn, Bonnie Raitt, Neil Diamond, Cher,

Diana Ross, Olivia Newton-John, Ringo Starr, Kenny Loggins, Wilson Phillips, Carole King, and many more.

Batiste: I know that you had a fabulous career as a child actor. It seemed as if you were destined to be a famous actor. Can you tell me a story or an experience that led you to know that you wanted to be a music performer, producer, and songwriter?

Asher: I never really knew what I wanted to be—the various aspects of my career sprang not so much from any experience or story but from a willingness to jump on every opportunity that came my way and take it seriously.

When an agent told my mother that my sister and I might be able to get some acting work we jumped at the chance and enjoyed doing it. When I met Gordon Waller at school and we tried singing together, people seemed to like the way it sounded so we worked very hard at it. The first time I was in a real studio I loved every minute of it. Once I figured out what a record producer does, I made that an ambition and did everything I could to achieve it. The details of each effort were long and complicated, but the overall theme was (and remains) "When you see a chance, take it!" kind of thing!

Batiste: You have a brilliant gift for recording great songs, starting with being a member of the mega pop music vocal duo Peter and Gordon, followed by the huge roster of successful artists that you've produced and managed over the past few decades. What "must-haves" or key ingredients do you look for in a song when choosing material for yourself and your artists?

Asher: I do not quantify or analyze—I just must love the song and feel inspired by it to come up with arrangement/production ideas.

Batiste: What special characteristics did you see in James Taylor that convinced you to sign him as an artist while you oversaw A&R at the Beatles' Apple Records?

Asher: Everything! A unique finger-picking guitar playing style that drew from the classical guitar as much as from folk (throwing in a few kinds of R&B chord changes underneath), an extraordinarily rich and mellifluous baritone voice (kind of folky in tone but with a lot of Sam Cooke and Ray Charles in the phrasing!) and amazing original songs. Not to mention [he was] highly intelligent, charming, and handsome!

Batiste: How much does the artist's ability to write his/her material play a role in your decision to manage them?

Asher: Well, I don't manage anymore these days—but some artists are brilliant enough, like Linda Ronstadt, without writing their material so there are no rules.

Batiste: What are your thought process, considerations, and preparation when writing for a particular project or artist opportunity?

Asher: Too variable and hard to define. I approach each assignment/project differently, whether it be production or writing or directing a stage show (as I did for Hans Zimmer) or working as a music supervisor. The one thing they all have in common is that you do spend a lot of time on preparation, pre-production, and advance work of all kinds. Many notes are taken, and many plans are sketched out *before* a project begins—I like to be *ready*!

Batiste: For example, "Love Always Comes as a Surprise" from Madagascar 3, written by Dave Stewart and yourself. How did that project come about?

Asher: Hans was working on the M3 score in London and had put a little band together to try out some ideas; Sheila E, Dave Stewart, a couple of Hans' keyboard geniuses from LA, Yolanda Charles (brilliant UK bass player), and me (playing a bit, producing a bit). The movie team was there too and when a certain scene came up for discussion, they mentioned that they were considering it as a possible spot for a new song, which would become the love theme for those two characters. When the session was over, Dave and I decided to write the song they described that very evening before anyone else got the gig. So, we did. We played the movie people a rather drunken (there were martinis involved) iPhone demo the following morning and they loved it and asked me to produce a proper track back in LA. I did so and sang a demo vocal. They put that version in the movie as they put it together and, in the end, it was Jeffrey Katzenberg who decided (in a subsequent meeting) that I should sing it for real rather than bringing in an outside singer. Again, just a question of making the most of it when an opportunity presents itself.

Batiste: What vocal production techniques do you use to get the best performance from an artist?

Asher: It varies from artist to artist, so the art is in finding out what works best for that artist.

Batiste: What advice do you give music creators interested in a career as a songwriter, performer, and producer?

Asher: The inevitable question and one I am asked all the time. Just do it! Write, create, sing—as much as you can, anywhere you can, with anyone you can, and so on. Keep at it. Face the fact that the odds are against you. You have to not just be better than everyone else, you must work harder—*and* be luckier as well!

10
Building a Fanbase

In 1967, the Beatles, one of the biggest rock groups of all time, recorded "All You Need Is Love," an infectious song that lifted the hearts and souls of all who heard it. In today's climate, a slight adaptation of that famous song title provides a more realistic motto for singer/songwriters: "All You Need Is Fans" who love you and your music.

Considering the advances in social media, it is impossible to be a successful professional singer/songwriter without a loyal fanbase. There's nothing better than enthusiastic fans who are devoted to you and will support your career by attending your shows, recruiting other fans, purchasing your music and merchandise, and contributing to your causes.

The importance of writing great songs is a given, and it's likely built into your DNA, but you must remember that your fans are supporting your image, personality, fashion, and views, along with your unique creativity and approach to writing songs. In other words, your personality, songwriting, recording, and performance need to all match one another.

To succeed as a singer/songwriter, there are two things you absolutely must have in hand: (1) quality music, and (2) plenty of enthusiastic fans.

To attract and retain fans, you must know your audience. In other words, know the type of people who are attracted to your style of music and lifestyle. Your fans demand excellence regardless of your level of commercial success, so it's your responsibility to always present your audience with musical authenticity, quality, and integrity. If you can do that well and see your numbers going up, then simply continue doing whatever you are doing to attract them. It's working. But keep in mind the quote authored by Zig Ziglar, "There is no elevator to success; you have to take the stairs." Take your efforts to the next level by surpassing your fans' expectations with each musical creation.

Social media networks provide the most efficient and least expensive means to build a fanbase. For the most part, social media networks are free. Expose your songs in every form of media and live performance as possible. Start establishing your fanbase one relationship at a time until you've built a group of loyal supporters. As you continue to build up to a large group of supporters, nurture them, and continue to seek new fans. Your fans are more than important, they are everything.

Launch your website and fan sites on social media (i.e., YouTube channel, TikTok, Facebook, LinkedIn, Twitter, Instagram, etc.) to showcase your songs and live performances, while also providing daily news and updates. Frequent engagement with fans, cross-promoting, and link sharing with friends, and making sure you follow up right away on any questions or requests will increase both your exposure and the strength of your connection with fans.

Recording artist Tori Kelly was eliminated from *American Idol* but went on to be discovered by the label head Scooter Braun after he saw her videos on YouTube. Later, she signed with Capitol Records, was nominated for a Grammy Award for Best New Artist, and later went on to win a few Grammys. Long ago, Justin Bieber's mother posted dozens of his performances on YouTube. Eventually, he was approached by a manager, which led to his discovery by Usher, one of the world's top recording artists. It all must start somewhere!

There is no "right" or "wrong" way to build a fanbase—every songwriter and artist is unique. But there are a few elements you can focus on to get started and point yourself in the right direction.

Image

Does your image tell a story? One of the important elements of a good song is a great story. But it's not enough that your story be told only in your songs. It is vital to create an image, one that tells your story while building your brand. Your image and music combined represent your complete package as an artist. You've chosen to enter the world of show *business*.

I emphasize the word *business* because this is the word that many creative people forget about when deciding to pursue a career. As an artist, you and your music are considered commerce. To compete with other products, you must have a compelling image or brand perception that represents your music, tells your story, and prompts a consumer to purchase. Your audience wants to follow every aspect of your life, which includes your lifestyle, fashion, philosophy, and interests.

This does *not* mean that you should try to project a superficial image for some persona's sake. I'm saying that whatever image you decide on, make sure that it fits your lifestyle authentically and that you are consistent. An artist whose brand is genuine and popular is more likely to secure musical and financial opportunities.

Once your image is established and your audience is vested in you as an artist, they expect to hear and see what they've purchased consistently. This aspect of giving your audience what they want is the aspect of the business that truly separates the artist with a lengthy and solid career from the one-hit wonder.

For example, rap artist and songwriter Cardi B uses her raw and candid personality along with her music to create an image that leaves her audience thirsting for more. She is known musically for her unapologetic and unfiltered authenticity. Her fashion is bold, vivacious, risk-taking, and outrageously fabulous. Fans love her provocative and innovative music, and they also anticipate a fashion experience. It simply would not work if Cardi B showed up for a performance in ripped denim jeans and a cotton shirt. Her clothing and music form equal parts of her image. Remember, *art* makes up half of the word *artist*.

On the other hand, recording artist Daniel Powter had huge commercial success with his song "Bad Day" in 2005. His image was inconsistent, as he appeared nonchalant about his fashion, performance, and message. His stage and everyday street appearance seemed to be the same, and he often performed wearing similar or identical casual outfits. Listeners liked his song, but they had no idea who he was as an artist.

"Bad Day" was number one in the United States on the Billboard Hot 100, Pop 100, Adult Contemporary charts, and Adult Top 40. It was the most played song on European radio and charted in the Top Five in more than ten countries worldwide. The song was used in various television and radio commercials, multiple television shows, and was the recipient of a ton of awards. Despite the success of the song and Powter's extensive media exposure, his inconsistent image, and his lack of stage presence in print, social media, and concert appearances, often left his fans disappointed, which resulted in the inability to retain his audience. He's made many records since, but he's mostly dropped off the radar.

Developing a public image that suits who you are as an artist and as a person can be incredibly challenging. Here are some tips to help you get started:

- Identify what is unique about your music style and message. Define your values and philosophy. Then develop an image with fashion and stage presentation that authentically reflects that music and message.
- Write a short biography (bio) that tells your fans who you are. Be sure it is personal and compelling. Your followers will connect and stay with you if they can relate to your story by getting a sense of your influences and experiences.
- Be consistent with your music, messaging, performance, and image. It is very important to give your fans the quality of product and experience they expect.
- Be sure to use professional photography for your photo shoots! Your headshot and your stage shot both define your image. Pictures convey a crucial element of your brand and identity by representing you in the best light. Make sure that your photographs, whether taken for your own website or for sending out to media properties, are shot with proper lighting and are in high resolution (300 dpi is common). If you can't afford a professional photographer, try aligning with a college student majoring in photography or an up-and-coming photographer looking to build a portfolio.

One note about photography: Before you even begin a photo shoot, make sure to establish an understanding in writing regarding ownership of the copyrights to the photos coming out of the session. It is most beneficial for you as the artist to treat the photographer's work as a "work for hire" so that you retain all the rights, which will enable you to use the photos as you desire. The more well-known the photographer, the more he or she might insist that they copyright the photos, and you purchase the copyright from them, or that they license the photo to you for a particular use.

Audience and Message

Now that your music has been recorded, your image developed, and the message you want to send to the public well-established, the next step is to identify your audience. Music is a highly subjective art form, and it is impossible to please everyone's taste. Your time, therefore, is best spent focusing on a particular target audience. What age group, gender, and types of personalities does your music most appeal to?

Analyze your target market. What is that market's music culture? What other artists are in the market, particularly those who have a similar music style to yours? What makes you different from the competition? Then once you've identified artists who have a similar sound as you, research the marketing methods and techniques they use to connect with their audience. There's a good chance that the fans of a popular artist, working in the same style, will also like your music. Find out which platforms they use, then make sure your music is added to those platforms.

Once you have a good understanding of your music market, it's time to create a meaningful, monitorable, results-oriented strategy to promote your music to the world. This is simply a step-by-step plan as to how and where to advance to the next step of achieving your end goal. Let's presume that your end goal is to be a successful songwriter. You are confident in your songs, you have quality recordings in hand, and your image has come together where you feel genuine and creative. Now it's time to get the message out.

Creating a consistent message starts with establishing what type of content your audience should expect when they follow you on social media. If they expect cultural and lifestyle items from the worlds of entertainment, fashion, education, and social trends, they might get confused if suddenly you start posting items geared toward religious or political topics.

The overall goal is to create awareness of you and your music by identifying what it is that makes you unique. Repeat that message until it sticks. Brand and control your images across all media platforms for a significant period so that your messaging is consistent. Keep in mind that your fans on Snapchat might have completely different dynamics than your fans on Instagram, YouTube, or Facebook.

Yes, I have recommended that you link all your social media accounts, and yes, fans should be able to see everything that you do. That's part of your image. I'm simply saying that you might not want to put photos from late night at your 20th annual high school reunion front and center on your LinkedIn page. It only makes sense to tailor your message so that it appeals to the taste of your fans based on the platform involved.

Feel free to stagger your messaging and build as you go along. You don't want to bombard your new fans all at once. Start with shorter messaging until you establish a wider audience. Most viewers will not want to see an eight-minute video piece if they're not all that familiar with you as an artist. You stand a better chance of a person watching 15 to 20 seconds—a whole minute if you're lucky—of an entire piece. Once you're more established, fans will start spending more time with you.

Streaming Music and Promotion Platforms

Make sure that your music is easy to find. There are many platforms you can use to promote your music. Here are some of the most common ones:

- **Spotify** is a free and subscription service for streaming and downloads. These services allow great access, but there is no fixed per-play rate for artists. The average per-play payout is between $.006 and $.0084.
- **SoundCloud** is a good platform for people to discover your music. Besides content sharing, other opportunities include networking, groups, reposts, and enhanced private messages. Tip: Choose the genre tag carefully from the "Explore" section to increase visibility in genre-specific searches and browses.
- **Amazon Music** is the first music store to sell music without digital rights management for major and independent labels.
- **Apple Music** allows users to stream content to their devices on-demand (in stereo or Dolby Atmos immersive formats) or listen to existing curated playlists. It also includes an internet radio station.
- **TIDAL** offers high-resolution sound quality, high-definition music videos, and curated special feature content by music journalists. Subscribers pay a higher fee for this service.
- **Bandcamp** offers a platform for selling albums and tiered bundles. It enables artists to offer free downloads of music in exchange for a fan's email address.
- **YouTube** is still the number one streaming music service and the most common way to attract new followers. Keep in mind that the number of views accumulates based on how many minutes your video is watched. In other words, your video must be watched until the end to count as a view. Tips: Include names of featured artists, credits of talent in video, and a description.
- **Facebook** may be most useful for its advertising function, video, livestreaming, text posts, images, and behind-the-scenes footage. Due to its operating system, not all your followers will necessarily see your latest posts. Tips: Post the scenes footage, announcements, and previews of upcoming projects; create a fan page; initiate dialog with your followers.
- **Twitter** is good for having short, instant conversations with your fans. However, due to the volume of users, only a small portion of your total fan base will receive your messaging in that instant. Engage fans with short statements and questions, along with a short video or photo. Tips: Leave space for your fans to retweet or make comments by not using all 140 characters; join in on conversations; put links at the beginning of the tweet; use action words.

- **Instagram** is quick and easy. Users prefer visuals over discussions. More and more imagery. Note: You can't link to your latest video without running an ad unless you add the link to your bio. Tips: Build your following by focusing on imagery and relevant hashtags; overcasting will spam your audience; use hashtags that are most relevant to your audience.
- **TikTok** is one of the most-used video platforms, with users regularly uploading their own videos, as opposed to other platforms where most of the users only watch videos. TikTok is unique in that everyone is an audience, and everyone is a creator.
- **Blogs** are great for discussions and engaging with fans. Create your own blog and promote your music. Also, research other blogs that comment regularly on your music genre, and if you find a few that you like and respect, send the blogger your music and a personal note. It can't hurt.

In general, you can't go wrong with any of these platforms. The next step is to then link all your platforms together for increased social reach. Your Facebook video snippet and Twitter should absolutely link to your full-length YouTube video, Instagram photos, SoundCloud songs, and your own blog post.

Promotional Tools

It is important to note that every other artist out there is using the same tools, so it is essential that the quality of your product (i.e., music, film, voiceover, and photographs) and your promotional information is superior—something that your fans, and potential fans, would want to receive.

Electronic Press Kit

An electronic press kit (EPK) is a great tool for booking gigs and introducing a new recording project. The EPK is a true multimedia resume that may include your press releases and one-sheets, a brief bio, information about your new music, videos of live performances, interviews, snippets of tracks, insights on how the music came about, and future dates or plans.

The EPK provides a vehicle for setting forth a realistic insight into your songs and into you as an artist. It's a message that you control, and it's what you would send in advance to journalists, podcasters, or bloggers, especially if you are in the middle of a tour and scheduling multiple media events. With the elimination of printing, postage, and housing of materials, the EPK is a far more effective and cost-efficient tool for both the artist and the audience.

Press Releases

The press release is an important tool for singer/songwriters seeking free or paid publicity for their upcoming music release or live performance. Media outlets, including print, digital, and local radio, are necessary in helping spread the news about any product or activity you are trying to promote.

Here are a few items to keep in mind when writing a press release that will draw the attention of journalists, DJs, bloggers, and fans.

Newsworthy events will receive top priority. Present your press release to media outlets that are most relevant to your news. This request research to find the proper media sources that will care about your music or event. If you don't do the research, you're wasting your time. The better you become at finding the perfect fit between the media outlet and the type of news you offer, the more successful results you will have in terms of appropriate coverage of your event.

A familiar format is expected when competing for attention among business media companies. Begin the heading with "FOR IMMEDIATE RELEASE" or "FOR RELEASE (DATE)." This heading should be followed by your contact information. A journalist or editor's interest in printing your story may require a conversation with you before running the announcement. Be sure to leave a phone number that will be answered promptly.

A creative headline will pique someone's interest far faster than a dull one. The headline must prompt the reader to read further. Creativity along with bold headlines are great devices for grabbing the reader's attention. For example, "Building Houses for the Homeless, Song by Song," is far more engaging than, "Stanley Startup Plays Homeless Fundraiser."

A good press release should also include the following information:

- The details of your story, which is the heart of the press release. This should be able to be summarized in a few sentences. You don't want to make it hard for a journalist or music editor to understand your unique story.
- The Who, What, When, and Why should read like an article or news story.
- The press release should be written in the voice of the third person (using He, She, and They, as opposed to "I," "You," or "We").
- Use quotations to add more interest. For example, "My goal is to create more business opportunities for creators of music," Batiste says.
- Include an "About Us" section: This information identifies the sender and adds to the comfort level of media outlets in terms of endorsing the sender's event.
- "For Further Information": Provide appropriate contacts at the end for those seeking more information.
- The press release should be one page, or two pages at maximum.

One-Sheets

A one-sheet is a document that would typically accompany the product (i.e., the album, the song) at the time it is delivered to a retailer. Although brick-and-mortar music retailers are quickly disappearing, a few do still exist, and the content of the traditional One Sheet is equally applicable when artists distribute and sell songs in the digital age.

A one-sheet is like a CD press release in that it includes information that helps the retailer decide if it will carry the product as a part of their online or offline inventory. They are called *one sheets* because they are one page in length. Retailers receive a lot of new material, and they tend to prefer a bullet-point version of the press release.

The usual sections included in a one-sheet are as follows:

The header: This is the quick reference section of the sales sheet, which includes:

- Label name
- Artist name
- Release (Title of CD) name
- Formats of the release (CD, vinyl, download, etc.)
- Catalog numbers
- Dealer price
- Logo and contact information at the bottom of the page

The body: All the important information—a brief bio, an expanded description of the singer/songwriter's style and influences, the music contained in this project—is included in the body of the one-sheet and should appear in news article form, like the press release.

Boilerplate information: You should include bookings, links to your website and social networking sites, your contact information, and so on. The one-sheet should also be included on your website.

Email Newsletters

The most effective way to target a specific group of people is still via email, so putting out a regular email newsletter can prove to be a tremendously effective way to keep your fans engaged in between your major events.

In a world where practically EVERYONE is using the internet as a marketing tool, your email headline and subhead must grab the attention of your audience. Most of the time, the headline will not be enough. A headline that reads "Jeff K. Smith" does not say very much and would probably be considered a lower priority for most when checking emails. But if the headline is accompanied by a subhead that reads: "Jeff K. Smith: Tour Canceled Due to Tragic Accident," one may be more inclined to open the email with urgency.

Writing good headlines takes practice. Here are some additional tips to make your newsletter more effective:

- Open with a greeting and make your newsletter read like an article or a conversation, as opposed to bullet points.
- Be clear on what you want to accomplish by sending out your newsletter. Whether you are advertising an upcoming performance or announcing a song placement, sharing excitement about a review or an upcoming interview, or just want your friends and fans to check out your new song or video, both you and the reader should be clear about the letter's intent.
- Do not send newsletters as attachments. They will most likely never be opened or will be seen as spam.
- Rank your subjects in the order of importance. The most important subject will be the leading article, then gradually work your way down to the least important story.
- Share new information about your latest project. This lets the reader know that you are actively working on your art and have a vibrant presence in the arts community. Do not forget to include direct links to your product and events so friends and family can easily make a purchase or get more information.
- Present a proper balance between visuals (i.e., graphics, logos, photographs, etc.) and text. Text alone might bore the reader. Too many visuals might make some think it is lacking in substance.
- Be sure to service your reader: How does your article affect them? Include information that is helpful or relevant to the progress of their career or lifestyle.
- Sections of your newsletter should be enlightening and entertaining.
- Always include links to your social networks for additional communication, along with CD Baby, iTunes, Amazon.com, TuneCore, DistroKid, or YouTube so that the reader has an option to purchase and hear your latest work.

Artist Website

If your website represents your premier presence, it should be a fully functioning cyber hub, ready to service the world before the release of any product. Design your website so that fans will be motivated to spend increasing amounts of time there. Make it feel like a community where like minds gather. This is your private space, where you invite your fans and friends to visit.

Wouldn't you want to show your friends your best stuff? Create high-quality and diverse content so that your fans are intrigued when viewing and not annoyed by poor-quality photos, videos, or redundant information. Fans and followers like to share content if they have had a quality experience, so make sure that all your content is of the highest quality. And make it fun for them! Create interactive elements of engagement, things like involving them in choosing the order of songs, selecting what song should be accompanied by a video or a contest, or making suggestions on artists to work with. You want them to feel like part of your community. You want them to stay for a while.

The length of time that a visitor stays on your website depends initially on the setup of your home page. Your home page should visually resonate with your target audience and be designed in a way that makes information easily accessible. It should be clear who you are, what you do, and why the visitor needs to be there.

Make sections as convenient to locate as possible so that your readers can retrieve the information that they are trying to find without multiple clicks. Contact information, music, reviews, discography, calendar, and links to friends and favorites—it is best to place essential information where the reader is expecting it to be.

Depending on the image you are trying to put forth, you might want more or fewer photos and graphics. You might want many SoundCloud song samples right up front, or you might want a larger news section. Maybe live performing is your specialty. The point is that you want to make it easy for your fans to know who you are, and you want them to be able to find out more. Even picking the right typeface says something about who you are and how your fans perceive you. Generating a QR Code and/or Linktree is probably the most efficient method of sharing your music and information about you.

Digital Promotional Tools

QR Code
A Quick Response (QR) code is a two-dimensional bar code consisting of several black squares and dots that provide direct links to music creators' online media information when users scan the code on a digital camera, tablet, or smartphone. The QR Code is becoming one of the most used promotional tools for songwriters and recording industry professionals.

Linktree
The application called Linktree is a great way to house all your social media platform links, website, portfolios, videos, and projects in one place. Linktree is a landing page that hosts multiple links and enables the user to access various social media channels like YouTube, Instagram, Facebook, Clubhouse rooms, TikTok, and analytics. You can share a Linktree on any of your platforms. Linktree has a free tier and a "pro" paid tier. Although the free tier has many features, users have limited control over the look of the landing page. A paid pro upgrade comes with additional features that includes advanced tracking of analytics, customized branding background options, animated stylings, email and phone number collection, e-commerce, and more. Whether you decide on the free tier or the pro paid tier all depends on what is important to you as a singer/songwriter. Linktree also comes in QR code form.

Driving Traffic to Your Site

The main purpose of creating a website is so that you have an online home where people can see what you're all about. Once there, you want to keep them engaged and coming back for music, merchandise, and more information. Some fans may seek you out on their own while others may discover you by accident. You cannot be passive about generating fans. They are your lifeline! You simply cannot exist without them.

If you want your career to thrive, you must be successful on purpose. Here are a few proven methods that will help you drive fans to your own website:

- Buying advertisements on social media networks
- Cross-promoting with personal and other social networks, with articles, events, and blogs linked back to your website
- Inviting guest bloggers to share their views on trending topics
- Interviewing industry leaders and publishing articles within your blog
- Posting content to LinkedIn
- Giving each page its title line and artwork. Title lines are important text for search engines and can be crucial in being discovered by new fans
- Using effective URLs, title lines, keywords, and descriptions
- Giving each image its own URL, individually searchable on search engines and linkable through social media posts
- Recording video of the audience at live shows, then using newsletters and social media to entice fans to visit the website and see the show again!
- Updating and maintaining the site regularly. Fans want new things. It takes effort to post something new each day, but it might just be the best thing you can do.
- Keeping up with your offline fans. Fans want to interact with the artist at live shows, meet-and-greets, and see flyers and cards as a promotion.

Live Performances

The ability to reach a live or virtual audience can be both gratifying (if you are prepared to give a professional performance) or crushing (if your performance skills aren't as developed as your social media skills). If you are in a rush to show off your talents before they are adequately developed, you may close a door that will take a while before it opens again. Take the time to study and develop your performance and showmanship. Develop the craft of performance with a small audience first, then build from there.

Each time you perform, opportunities are created for future shows, collaborations, and adding to your fanbase. Set a goal to expand your audience and performance venue size. With gradually increased performing experience, awareness, and popularity, the size of your venues could easily expand from a coffee house to a concert hall.

The initial focus must be on growing the audience and not necessarily on making money. Constantly develop and adapt your live performance by attending and studying professional concerts, watching live video performances, and taking notes on how an artist commands the show and sets the tone/vibe, mood, and tempo of the performance (i.e., song order, dynamics, audience participation, etc.). You want to give the audience the best experience of their lives, so you must constantly work on your performance and keep your style up to date.

Here are a few random details to keep in mind when you take on the role of live performer:

- Always give the best possible performance and choose the right venue acoustically for your audience to experience your performance.
- Word-of-mouth is the best possible form of advertising. Make that word-of-mouth positive all around.
- Be sure your stage image is consistent with the personality in your music, message, and PR campaign.
- Consider performing, hosting, and participating in community events to promote your music and shows.
- Always have email list signup available.
- Have merchandise available with both high and low prices so that you can have something that most people can afford.
- Make sure all your merchandise has your logo on it.
- Have free items available for those who sign up to the email list.
- Plug your merchandise at some point during your show.
- Create content (photos and videos) to share on social media and on your website. Fans support active artists.
- Take the time to engage with your fans by thanking them at the meet-and-greets or after-show signings.
- Post images or snippets from performances on social media either in real time or immediately following the show.
- Take photos with your longtime supporters and new fans as much as possible.
- Make sure your website information is visible at your shows.
- Mention future show dates
- Exploit your brand by including your logo on merchandising items. Fans are always proud to show off cool stuff. That can bring in new fans.
- Consistently produce content, content, and more content to share on social media.
- Make your QR code available for scanning.

Besides increasing your fanbase by putting on paid live performances, you may want to host shows or a specific monthly or quarterly event for songwriters (i.e., open mic, workshops, etc.) in your area. You can pay it forward by participating in community events such as benefits and artist showcases, or by creating a group on Facebook or a blog to share information that supports and advances the livelihood of all singer/songwriters. These activities could boost your positive image while producing opportunities to acquire new fans. Use your social media networks to document and increase your visibility.

Strategic Scheduling

Do not over-schedule public dates. When just starting out, you should play as much as possible to bring awareness of your gift and to hone your craft. Once you develop a decent-sized, dedicated following of 75 to 100 people, you might consider limiting public performances to once a month, and vary the venues to expand to different regions for exposure to new audiences. When your dedicated audience expands to 150 to 200, you might limit performances to once a quarter, then semi-annually, for more established indie acts, and once a year for the established act.

Effectively Promoting Shows

You've booked the date and the performance is well-rehearsed, now it's time to promote the show. Everyone knows that the most efficient and cost-effective way to advertise shows is through social media, so let's discuss some of the preparation materials needed before the promotion begins.

Here's a checklist of some of the promotional materials to collect for advertising and promotion of an upcoming live performance:

Materials
- Promotional photo
- Posters and flyers
- Video teasers (i.e., skits, music, announcements)
- Bio
- CDs or downloads, to sell or give away
- Merchandise
- Contacts: Journalists, bloggers, show promoters
- Volunteers/Team: a collection of email addresses
- Merchandise table

Digital Promotion
- Online ticketing
- Social media (flyers and banners)
- Facebook and Instagram Live

Make registration a part of your event. Then send monthly and weekly reminders as it gets closer to the event. If using Instagram, curate Instagram hashtags and use Instagram Stories to spotlight speakers and topics. Promote on Twitter in the same way. Create a buzz around the event.

Why Go Live on Facebook?
- Audience Engagement. Your audience can ask questions and you can answer them in real-time.
- Facebook video can be saved on your page once it ends so that fans can watch later.
- People prefer video over photos.
- Facebook Live videos receive more views and higher engagement than photos and regular videos.

More Tips for Digital Promotion
- Cross-promote with other friends and organizations on their social media platforms.
- Repost recorded video to your page as an ad and to re-target your audience.
- Embed your video links in your email newsletters
- Write blog entries (yourself and others)
- Post Save the Date announcements
- Announce agenda or programming
- Keep promoting up to and including the day of the event

Also, there are a few offline promotional tasks that may seem obvious but are sometimes easily forgotten in these times where the internet seems to rule the world of communication.

- Let your audience know about your next performance at your gigs.
- Post flyers and posters in surrounding areas of the venue where you're about to perform.
- Contact local radio stations for interviews and mentions of your performance by a disc jockey.
- Extend personal invitations (offline and online)
- Encourage band members to promote on their personal social media networks.

Fan Engagement and the Virtual Audience

Virtual events have steadily been on the rise, but not until the upsurge of the pandemic of 2020 did virtual shows and production become a way of life for the entire entertainment industry. The deadly virus forced songwriters and artists to broadcast using their mics and webcams from anywhere they chose via Watch Parties on Facebook Live, YouTube Live, Instagram TV, Stageit.com, Twitch, and the like. Most team business meetings, songwriting collaborations, interviews, workshops, even television news and talk shows were forced to use platforms such as Zoom, GoToMeeting, and Streamyard for communication purposes. Preferably, you should choose a platform that allows a chat to occur during the performance. Reviewing the chat section is good for receiving accolades and performance evaluations.

Monetizing virtual events is probably the most problematic area of virtual events. There are a few ways to earn money such as tips, making the concert a donation drive as opposed to asking fans to pay a regular ticket price, subsidizing with sponsors, ads, and exclusive shows for your paid Patreon subscribers. Unfortunately, many shows compete with one another in terms of scheduling, forcing audiences to choose one among two or three of their favorite artists that may be performing at the same time.

Virtual performance success as a singer/songwriter requires you to step up your social media engagement with your fans. Provide ways for fans to interact with you before and after the virtual shows by offering teasers and some views of behind the scenes and your personal life, and live chats. As far as performance, the challenge for the singer/songwriter is to come close as possible to delivering the same level of excitement, emotion, enthusiasm, adrenaline, and fan engagement via the computer as one would experience if they were attending a live concert.

Production is a key part of the experience: inspiring and interesting content, great mics, lighting, and a good director to keep things moving in terms of the show's tempo (i.e., setlist, timeline, variation, energy, and editing). These aspects are especially important if you're combining pre-recorded elements along with a live performance. After all, it is the experience that your audience is paying for.

Although nothing can replace the experience of a live performance, both artists and fans must admit that there are major benefits from virtual events. Some of the benefits include:

- Cost-effective—No venue or associated expenses (venue staffing, security, travel, ground transportation, hotels, catering, rentals, etc.); no-cost social media advertising
- Global attendance
- Flexibility in scheduling
- Easy attendee feedback—chat is built into the platform
- Convenience for attendees regarding restroom, food, drinking with no lines or distractions from the crowd
- On-demand capabilities make shows available to attendees anytime
- Eco-friendly—leave a positive impact on the environment.

Besides the expense of having a traditional stage manager if multiple acts are performing, other livestreaming expenses may include camera operator(s) and a video editor if the performance isn't a livestream.

Some tips you may consider when promoting virtual events on social media are as follows:

Facebook—Creating an "Event" will automatically remind the person who RSVP'd; it allows you to have direct contact with an attendee, and increases your exposure to friends of your attendees.
Instagram—Create countdowns and announcements for upcoming events.
Livestreams—Use livestreams on your social media platforms before the show or event.

I think it's safe to say that the inclusion of the virtual experience is likely to become commonly integrated with live performances and events.

Lastly, whether your concert is physical or virtual, you can consider the option of hiring or partnering with a professional event promoter to promote your performance.

Additional Streams of Income

You want to make a living as a songwriter, which means you need to extend your image, brand, and music into many new areas of commerce. All these outlets would benefit from the same press and promotional materials.

Here are a few of those brand-extending, money-making outlets you might not have thought about:

E-Commerce

E-commerce is the activity of electronically purchasing or selling products over the internet. As technology has allowed audiences to gain awareness and access to the artist and their music from all over the world, it has also allowed the consumer to purchase merchandise from artists, which not only helps to supplement their music income but also strengthens the branding of the artists. Two of the most popular e-commerce platforms for music artists are Shopify and StoreFrontier. They are most popular because they cover a gamut of sizes of businesses from small to medium to large. They are especially popular because they are the most user-friendly platforms for people who do not consider e-commerce to be their primary business.

Shopify

Shopify is an e-commerce platform for online stores and point-of-sale systems. You create the look, layout, and content of your website. You create and operate your Shopify store from anywhere. Shopify handles marketing, payments, secure checkout, and shipping. You are responsible for supplying all items for sale in your store. Shopify charges a subscription fee as well as additional fees.

StoreFrontier

StoreFrontier is a free web store that will sell your product at no upfront cost to the seller. You create and customize your free website with unlimited products. You set your prices, market and promote your products, and you don't pay for the materials or products. StoreFrontier will print, process, pack, and ship orders to your customers. Your products are produced on-demand; therefore, you do not have any extra inventory and you never sell out. The shipping cost is paid by the customer. StoreFrontier charges a percentage for each item sold. You must register and identify each item for the percentage breakdown.

Subscriptions

When most people think of monthly subscriptions, businesses such as Spotify, Netflix, and magazine publications come to mind. Subscriptions have proven to be a successful and profitable model for the singer/songwriter's additional income stream. With subscriptions and free streaming networks being the preferred method in which consumers receive music, it makes sense for artists to get on the subscription train as well. Plus, there's no better way to engage and develop your fan-artist relationship than to deliver something new to them on an ongoing basis. Devoted fans are willing to pay for personal, exclusive, and repeated interaction. Plus, a subscription would ensure that fans will not miss promotions or announcements from the artist. This is one way to have a predictable income stream in a climate where finances can be very unpredictable for an independent artist. For example, if you have one thousand subscribers that paid ten dollars a month, you would receive ten thousand dollars in subscription monthly income. If you spend two to three thousand dollars monthly on producing products for your subscribers, you can earn an income of seven thousand dollars monthly. Imagine if you had two or even five thousand subscribers!

Your job is to deliver something that has a more monetary, nostalgic, or unique value to your subscribers than the monthly subscription amount.

Potential Subscriber Benefits
- One to two new songs (i.e., songs from the upcoming project, live audio, or video recordings of covers) and/or music for members only per month
- Merchandise (i.e., shirts, hats, buttons, pens, bracelets, photos, memorabilia, limited edition items) that are not available to the public

- Exclusive previews of new music, videos, and interviews before it is available to the public
- Opportunity to make suggestions for artist collaborations, artwork, video choice, and song order
- Advance purchase on tickets before they are available to the public
- Reserved seating at shows
- House concerts or private performances at no or low cost
- Contests and reward opportunities for fans who help recruit subscribers.

Websites such as Patreon and Gumroad set up subscription services specifically for artists. Research websites to find the best ones to suit your subscription service needs.

Things to think about before implementing your subscription service:

- Set terms of subscription
- Payment methods: Portal to charge subscribers; payment schedule; method for processing credit cards
- Establish a process of how benefits are distributed
- Offer a cancellation policy—this would build trust and motivate initial sign-ups

Summary: Building Your Fanbase

As an artist, you are constantly looking to boost fan engagement, promote your brand, and increase and retain fans. In a world where there are so many things competing for people's attention, you must be consistent in creating an experience for your fans.

Below are ways to build a fanbase and keep them engaged:

- Be original and authentic—remember that delivering a unique and quality product is always the first requirement for success
- Take care of business. Copyright music, establish a publishing company, open a bank account, obtain a business license, register with a PRO, establish online distribution, and develop a logo and marketing materials.
- Get organized. The only action that is more important than meeting people is following up with them. There are some very valuable tools available to help you keep track of your busy schedule and potential clients. Some of the most popular tools include Google Drive, Trello, and Customer Relationship Manager (CRM). Develop a timeline and tasks list, which identifies the who, what, when, where, and why to implement your goals.
- Develop your team. Take a realistic evaluation of your strengths and weakness in terms of your skills, and then develop a team of individuals that can expedite tasks in areas where you are weak. Team members may include legal representation, social media, booking agents, etc.

- Understand your audience: Demographics (age, gender, income)
- Know your audience's personality (likes, dislikes, hobbies)
- Build a brand and story (i.e., logo that reflects your music and uniqueness, bio)
- Be consistent with your marketing and messaging and interaction with fans
- Post regularly
- Always express your personality in your music
- Continuously deliver a quality product
- Constantly build network/expand your market
- Engage often with your fanbase
- Creative fan incentives (i.e., free song downloads and merchandise, contests, and giveaways)
- Provide interactive content if possible (i.e., game, moving images)
- Create themed playlists from various artists as well as share other artists playlists
- Share resources (cross-marketing)
- Get your music featured on blogs
- Perform live and virtual: Publicize on all social media and non-social media platforms
- Post after performance photos and footage for fan engagement
- Create and share content (videos, photos, information)
- Stay current, active, and proactive
- Time management: Make smart decisions regarding how you spend your time. There are only 24 hours in each day.

It bears repeating: your network is your net worth. So, it is essential to establish and build relationships with people and entities by using social media skills to help move your career forward.

Remember the reason you want to be in the business in the first place. For most music creators, it is the love and passion for writing and performing songs and the ability to express yourself through creativity and share your music with others. You must work hard at anything worth having, so you might as well work hard at having a successful music career. Put as much energy into getting to know your fans as you do while creating your music. Enjoy the journey!

Songwriter Spotlight

James McKinney

James McKinney. Photo by Schyler, used with permission.

Acclaimed Grammy-nominated pianist/vocalist, musical director, songwriter, arranger, producer James McKinney is well known for bringing independent artists to significant prominence within the recording industry. McKinney has produced and recorded with, R&B legends such as Melba Moore, Freddie Jackson, Carolyn Malachi, the Isley Brothers, and Lenny Williams. He has also performed for three U.S. presidents, and with the likes of Stevie Wonder, Dionne Warwick, Maysa, Kenny Latimore, Raheem DeVaughn, Kenny Burrell, James Moody, and Grammy nominees Wayna and Kokayi.

Batiste: You write with a lot of the artists you produce. What is your approach when songwriting with an artist for a recording project?

McKinney: One of my favorite ways to collaborate is writing in the recording studio with the artist. I like programming the beat, playing keyboards, creating vocals with the artist, and tracking all at the same time. I record a scratch vocal of the lead melody then build the arrangement around it. I like a song that feels authentic, so I don't think about many tricks or formulas during the initial stage of the writing process.

Batiste: What is your philosophy on songwriting?

McKinney: I write on inspiration. If the song is inspiring to us as songwriters collaborating, me as the producer/songwriter, you as an artist/songwriter, and we are both inspired, the song is going to touch others. After the initial inspiration for the song, I go back and fine-tune the creation. I don't have a lot of rules for songwriting. My philosophy on songwriting is quite simple. A successful song has a great story that leads to a strong hook. But overall, it is most important that the song is easy to sing and remember.

11
Internet Radio

Internet radio is made possible by technology that transmits content via the internet, as opposed to traditional radio (also known as "terrestrial radio"), which is broadcast via wave transmission from a land-based location.

Terrestrial radio transmission requires equipment such as a connected microphone, console or controller of some sort, and a loudspeaker, followed by a transmitter, communications circuit or channel, and a receiver. This format has worked well, and still does, for distributing news headlines, music, weather, sports, and traffic reports to the home or automobile. However, the development of internet radio gives both distributors and listeners more variety, flexibility, and options for communication.

Cable-based radio stations began popping up in the late 1980s, but the first internet-based radio station was created by Carl Malamud, founder of Invisible Worlds, Inc. In 1993, Malamud launched internet talk radio, and in the beginning, he mainly hosted interviews with people in the field of computer technology. On June 23, 1993, he "streamed" (a verb that was about to enter the culture in a big way) the first concert delivered over internet radio.

Nearly 18 months later, on November 7, 1994, a student radio station, WXYC at Chapel Hill University, North Carolina, launched a system known as Ibiblio, which used software called CU-SeeMe to create and deliver the first stream that included sound and video (now known as "multicasting") on the internet. Another radio station, WREK, developed software called CyberRadio1 and launched on November 7, 1994, as well. This expansion was followed by the premiere of KJHK FM at the University of Kansas campus station, one of the first internet stations to send out a live and continuous stream. This development was the beginning of a new era of delivering music to the mass public in a more customized, self-selected manner.

In 1995, internet streaming media delivery software company Progressive Networks, today known as RealNetworks, developed a proprietary audio format called RealAudio, which provided the blueprint for streaming program material in real time. Eventually, Microsoft and other companies began releasing streaming audio players and offering free downloads. The ability to download streaming audio players for free led to a major increase in internet radio stations.

The world's first internet-only radio network was NetRadio.com, founded by Scott Bourne in 1995. Not only was NetRadio.com the first internet radio network licensed by ASCAP, but it also went on to offer an IPO in 1999 and paved the way for growth among internet radio providers in digital media.

The first United States internet radio station to be licensed by both ASCAP and BMI for 24-hour-a-day live broadcasting was Sonicaves.com, created by Edward

Lyman in 1996. Virgin Radio followed the same year with its 24-hour live internet streaming audio service, the first European internet radio station to do so.

Likewise, Radio306.com launched in Canada in 1997. It wasn't long before streaming prototypes such as Windows Media, Real Media, Shoutcast, and Icecast began to contribute to the advancement and popularization of streaming audio content, making it accessible to the masses.

Live365, founded in 1999, was among the first service providers to offer its users the ability to create their own internet radio stations, or listen to radio stations created by others. Live365, like many other internet radio stations, has a corresponding affiliation with terrestrial radio networks, as well.

By 2005, the launch of internet radio providers such as Pandora Radio, Spotify, Slacker, YouTube, TIDAL, iHeartRadio, Sirius XM, CBS Radio, TuneIn Radio, Apple Music, and Google Music, among many others, secured internet radio's position as a primary means of audio and music delivery.

One of the major advantages that internet radio provides is the flexibility and ability for listeners with special interests to create playlists and discover music that just isn't heard on traditional radio stations. The development of internet radio stations has proven a welcome alternative for independent singer/songwriters seeking an outlet for their music.

Benefits for the Independent Artist

Internet radio can provide a lifeline for independent artists, singer/songwriters, and musicians seeking to expose their music to a wider audience. Because submissions for play time on internet radio stations are mostly free, it is a great place for independent artists to start. It's a no-brainer: limitless access to "airplay," the opportunity for your music to be discovered, and the ability to boost awareness and brand identity.

Plus, internet radio stations have a vast range of "transmitting" power. Terrestrial radio stations are limited by the power of the station's transmission tower, usually expressed in watts. Many can only be heard within a 120-mile (or less) radius. By contrast, internet radio stations can be listened to in anywhere you can get online. This is extremely beneficial for singer/songwriters, as the audience can enjoy music or a podcast while doing other activities.

Perhaps the greatest benefit of internet radio for featured artists, non-featured artists, and owners of the master recording is the ability to get paid for their performances via SoundExchange.

How Internet Radio Makes Money

On the surface, there appears to be no, or few, expenses associated with operating an internet radio station, especially the smaller, individually operated, free internet radio stations. But there is an underlying cost to run and maintain the station, including expenses for maintenance, equipment, internet access, hosting fees, employees, royalty payments to artists and copyright owners (for larger service providers), and so on.

Internet radio providers adopt several different kinds of business models to earn money, the main ones being advertising, sponsorships, and subscriptions.

Advertising

The amount of money an advertiser will spend depends on the number of listeners the radio station has, their age range and demographics, and their type of lifestyle. Advertisers need to be assured that they are reaching as many of their targeted audience as possible.

Sponsorship

A sponsorship is like advertising, but more subtle. A sponsor may pay for a particular event, aiming for a particular demographic, endorsement of service, or type of programming that directly reflects their brand. They will also pay for signage, whether the radio station is promoting on a website or in-person at an event/concert.

Subscriptions

Licensed and secured online services such as Pandora, Apple Music, Spotify, Google Play, and so on sell tiered subscriptions that offer varying levels of access to music and content. A premium service at $9.99 a month might include the ability to stream high-resolution or Dolby Atmos immersive audio tracks. For $4.99 a month, a listener might be able to play music ad-free or create their own playlists.

The most important thing to know about subscription-based services is that they are required to pay a royalty to artists, labels, and copyright holders.

Other methods for internet radio stations to generate revenue include:

> **Donations:** An appeal to the generosity of people who support the radio's programming and efforts. The best method of payment is to have a button on your website that gives the option to donate one-time or in automatic monthly payments.

Merchandise: Selling custom merchandise (i.e., hats, t-shirts, coffee mugs, etc.) to earn money, as well as promote the station.

Memberships: Offering discounts on events, merchandise, and other benefits to your members.

Unfortunately, the money from advertisers, sponsors, and subscriptions has not translated into a fair and equitable amount of income for songwriters or artists. For example, Spotify pays anywhere from $0.003 to $0.005 per stream on average to the owner of the music rights. This rate must be split between the artists, songwriters, producers, and record labels. According to most musicians, there is no defense for the low pay distributed by the most popular online services. Music rights advocates such as the Recording Academy (Grammy organization), SoundExchange, Musicians for Musicians, and many others are working on legislation for fair pay for artists.

Getting Your Music Played

Now that we understand more about how internet radio works, let's move on to getting your music played. First, however, we must keep in mind that there are different types of radio airplay:

- **Terrestrial:** Commercial or public (FM and AM radio stations with a tower and signal)
- **Satellite:** Sirius XM
- **Cable/Programmed TV:** Music Choice
- **Internet/streaming**

Believe it or not, terrestrial radio is still the number one driver of music consumption in the United States; it's where artists can reach the most people at one time. Terrestrial radio remains important in the digital era, sometimes as a companion to internet services, sometimes as the leader. Stations such as iHeart can get their songs played on corresponding digital platforms, which drives digital track sales. Sometimes the opposite is true, where large streaming numbers can help to get a single on terrestrial radio.

Bear in mind that despite all the attention in the media, less than half of the radio listening audience have Apple Music or Spotify.

A sure way of knowing whether your music is getting radio airplay is to subscribe to Mediabase, a radio station airplay monitoring service that publishes music charts and in-depth analytics on terrestrial and satellite radio's most played songs in the U.S. and Canadian markets. This service defines the success and popularity of recorded music, consumer listening trends, and consumption. Mediabase subscriptions are pricey and are usually purchased by radio promoters.

The Radio Promoter

Radio promoters have established relationships with radio station program directors and are able to pitch new songs to them on a regular basis, both as "adds" and for regular rotation. The radio promoter is the best connection for music airplay on radio for major and independent artists, as radio stations rarely accept submissions and meetings from artists directly.

Radio stations are broken down into formats that appeal to specific audiences and music genres like Pop, Rock, Alternative, Triple A (Adult Album Alternative), AC (Adult Contemporary), Classical, Religious, Rhythmic, Country, Nostalgia, Urban, Urban AC, and College. Each genre has corresponding promoters. Due to experience and the relationship between the radio promoter and a station's format and program director, radio promoters generally have a good idea of what they will be able to get played.

Radio promoter duties:

- Pitch new songs to radio programmers and/or music directors
- Develop relationships with program directors and on-air personalities
- Review data from digital streams, charts, and social media activity
- Use data/analytics as a tool to pitch songs to radio music directors
- Establish appropriate relationships outside the radio industry, for example with concert promoters, managers, and booking agents
- Work with the artist, manager, publicist, and agent
- Coordinate promotions and radio/television interviews for artists with publicists.

The best way to find a legitimate radio promoter is to first be worthy of promotion and airplay. In other words, have a great song, quality recording, a strong brand and image as an artist, and have a reasonably established fanbase. Then seek referrals and do your homework. For the most part, avoid ads on social media that promise a bunch of services without specific details. Reputable radio promoters usually do not advertise on the internet.

DIY Radio Promotion

The cost of a radio promoter can range anywhere from $500 to $5,000 a month, which could be expensive depending on your promotion and marketing budget. The cost of radio promoters who work with large terrestrial stations for major record labels are even higher. If you are starting with a minimum marketing and promotion budget, you may try some of the following options first:

- Use your personal networks: friends, supporters, bloggers, podcasters, DJs, and influencers who will post your music links and story on their social media and send to their email lists.
- Collaborate with other artists on recordings to widen both audience and resources.
- Extend collaborations to film projects (students and local filmmakers), sports teams, and organizations.

Having a radio promoter can make it easier to obtain internet radio airplay, but it is not impossible to get added to internet radio at some level without one. There are many internet radio stations available for your use. Some may feature a regular rotation and specific shows that you can submit to. Before starting the submission process, you must prepare your content.

Song: Use high-quality MP3s and WAVs (preferably wav, 16 bits, 44.1 kHz). Be prepared to create specific formats for stations that require them.

Song length: To maximize the chances of getting your song played on a radio station's playlist, the length of your track should be between 2 minutes and 30 seconds and 4 minutes (2:30–4:00). If your song is longer than 4 minutes, produce a radio edit for your single.

Track metadata: Provide digital information about the music (title, performer, producer, composer, publisher, ISRC code, etc.).

Bio: Prepare a short version of your bio

Press and media materials: Prepare an electronic press kit (EPK) in case the station wants additional information for an interview segment. Include artwork and newsworthy information about the song.

Spreadsheet: You'll need to keep track of who, where, and when you sent your music to as well as follow-up and activity information.

Before submitting to radio stations, you should make some of the following considerations:

- Research internet stations that best fit the style of your music. Look for stations that may interview you or may preview or feature your music. Develop a targeted station list.
- Make a list or create a submission column (if using a spreadsheet) outlining submission requirements for each station.
- Research stations that have specialty shows as a part of their programming.
- Be personable when speaking with program directors.
- Include cover artwork and information about the song(s).
- Include ID3 tags for all tracks.
- Include social media links and URLs to download music for purchase.
- Include performance and current event information.

> **Streaming Service Meets Radio Station**
>
> Many of the streaming services also incorporate radio stations. They are all similar, though some features may vary. For example, Spotify Radio allows you to create a playlist based on any artist, album, or song you select.
>
> Apple Music Radio features three stations: Apple Music 1 spotlights some of the biggest names in popular music and includes shows that feature specific music genres; Apple Music Hits offers a full catalog of songs from the '80s, '90s, and 2000s; and Apple Music Country spotlights, you guessed it, country music. Apple Music Radio can be listened to on multiple devices, including iPhone, iPad, iPod, CarPlay, Apple Watch, Apple TV, Mac computers, HomePod, and on the Web.
>
> iTunes Radio is non-interactive and offers 200-plus genre-based stations, as well as Featured Stations. Your music becomes available for iTunes Radio once it is in the iTunes store. iTunes Radio is only available in the United States and on the following devices: iPhone, iPad, iPod touch, Mac, PC, and Apple TV.
>
> There are literally thousands of internet radio stations out there. Some of the most popular include Worldwide FM, Pandora Radio, FIP, NTS, Vintage FM, Soho Radio, Balamii, Dublab, KEXP, Power 105.1/WWPR, and Cinemax. If you're not sure where to begin, you might start with aggregator sites such as https://www.streamfinder.com, https://gotradio.com, and https://filtermusic.net, which can make it easier to find stations that fit your style of music.

When you succeed in making the playlist on a streaming site, be sure to send a thank-you to the program director, producer, and show host. This will help you to secure placing songs on their playlists in the future. Cross-promote by sending links to your friends and fans on social media. Publicize your success to show fans and supporters that they are not alone in supporting your music. Then go out and get the attention of other radio stations that may have been slow to respond.

Starting Your Own Internet Radio Station

If you're the type of person who likes to deliver your message personally, conduct interviews, share interesting information and relevant topics, and develop creative programming, then you may be interested in starting your own internet radio station.

The benefits of starting your own internet radio station include:

- Direct fan development and engagement
- Low operation costs
- The ability to broadcast without geographic restrictions

- No license is required in the United States from the Federal Communications Commission, nor equivalent agencies in other countries
- It is censor-free (remember, however, to always portray material that is in line with your image)
- Requires little technical knowledge to operate
- Includes fewer advertisements than terrestrial radio

Starting an internet radio station is easier than you might think. You basically need four things to get started.

First, you need a quiet room to set up and operate your station.

Second, you need some equipment, such as a computer with a reliable internet connection, a decent condenser microphone, headphones, audio software, and an audio mixer with a minimum of four channels to control input of a microphone for yourself, one for your guest, another for your music source, and another for your mobile phone to take calls. A mixer will allow you to control the volume of all inputs.

The third requirement is a streaming media server, and there are many to choose from. Some of the most popular include https://live365.com, https://www.shoutcast.com, https://icecast.org, and SAM Broadcaster.

Finally, the most obvious and most important requirement: you need an audience.

Licenses

If you play music, run commercials, and host talk-based shows with only royalty-free music, you don't have to worry about licenses. However, if you play commercial music, you must pay for stream licensing. Licensing organizations will monitor and track the performance as heard by your listeners. The terms and conditions of the licensing entities vary from country to country.

If your online radio station broadcasts commercial music in the UK, you will need to acquire both a Phonographic Performance Limited (PPL) and a Performing Rights Society (PRS) license. The fee depends on the size of the radio station's listener fanbase and on how much your station earns. If you earn less than 12,500 euro, you'll need a limited online music license (LOML). If you earn above 12,500 euro and below 200,000 euro, you will need a LOML+. Both the LOML and LOML+ require monthly fees. You will need a music streaming license if your income exceeds 200,000 euros. The annual music streaming license fee covers your online broadcast for the entire year.

To cover playing commercial music on your internet radio station for casting in the United States, you must apply for a statutory license with the performance rights organizations: American Society of Composers, Authors, and Publishers (ASCAP), Broadcast Music, Inc. (BMI), Society from European Stage Authors and Composers (SESAC), and SoundExchange.

Look for a licensing package that fits your radio station. Some copyright holders require a flat fee for a defined period of usage, and some require a fee based on the number of times used. If you're looking to play music from unsigned or independent artists, many of them could be found on platforms such as Bandcamp, SoundCloud, Jamendo, Hype Machine, and Tribe of Noise.

Internet Radio Directories

An internet radio directory is a list of stations categorized by music genre. This enables singer/songwriters to submit their music and for the listener to find the music they want to listen to. Use online radio directories to submit your radio station information.

Here is a short list of some of the best internet radio directories:

- Radio Forest (http://www.radioforest.net/)
- Dirble.com (https://dirble.com)
- Streaming the Net (http://www.streamingthe.net)
- Shout Cast (http://www.shoutcast.com)
- European Radio Stations (http://www.listenlive.eu/)
- Radio Tower (http://www.radiotower.com)
- Vtuner Internet Radio (http://vtuner.com)
- Nexus Radio (http://www.nexusradio.com)
- Filter Music (http://filtermusic.net)

As with more established internet radio stations, you might use advertising, sponsorships, and subscriptions to earn income, as well. If you're thinking about setting up subscriptions for listeners, be mindful of the following considerations:

- Terms of the subscription
- Set up a "My Account" portal for payment
- The process in which service is delivered
- "Cancellation Policy": Indicates you intend to provide a valued service and establishes trust.

Promoting Your Radio Station

One of the biggest challenges in launching an internet radio station is simply creating awareness. Here are some tips for attracting and retaining listeners for your internet radio station.

- Build an official website, a home base so that fans can link to the station, review playlist, share information, shop, and engage.

- List your station in internet radio directories.
- Create awesome programming.
- Create individual pages and incorporate search engine optimization.
- Develop an email list. People still check their email every day.
- Blog: Write about relevant topics that interest your listeners and include a link to your station.
- Promote your station on forums and discussion boards.
- Promote on social media.
- Produce quality shows and upload them to your social media platforms.
- Cross-promote with other stations (i.e., joint competitions, sponsorships, newsletters).
- Distribute posters and flyers.
- Run a contest or sweepstakes.
- Communicate with listeners; invite them to share your link and information about your station.
- Collaborate with other artists by playing parts of their playlists on your station. This helps to grow both artists' fanbases.

Whether submitting your music to internet radio stations, starting your own internet station, or both, internet radio is the most effective way for independent artists to connect, engage, and build strong relationships with fans. Developing a presence and audience on internet radio and social media, combined with delivering solid performances while playing live, is a winning formula, and it is crucial in increasing and retaining your fanbase and level of success.

Although navigating your way through all the aspects of obtaining success on internet radio may seem like a roller-coaster ride, it can be fun and exhilarating once you get moving. So, buckle up and enjoy the ride!

Songwriter Spotlight

Preston Glass

Preston Glass (left) and Larry Batiste (right). Photo by Bob White, used with permission.

Songwriter and producer Preston Glass is best known for writing and producing hits such as "Who's Zoomin' Who" and "Jimmy Lee" for Aretha Franklin, "Miss You Like Crazy" for Natalie Cole, "System of Survival" for Earth, Wind & Fire, and the album *Songbird* by Kenny G.

Batiste: How do you like to start and build a song?
Glass: Usually, I like to start with a title. That usually helps to guide me as to where the melody will go on the hook and then the verse and so forth. The lyric is usually the last thing I'll work on. Interestingly, I can be in a room with 20 to 25 people, and construct a melody. However, to construct a lyric, I prefer to be all by myself.
Batiste: What is your thought process, considerations, and preparation when writing for a particular project or artist opportunity as opposed to writing with no project in mind? For example, "Who's Zoomin' Who" for Aretha Franklin.

Glass: With the song "Who's Zoomin' Who," producer Narada Michael Walden and I got that title from a phrase Aretha said while in a phone conversation with him. It was easy enough to get Aretha to sing that one. It always helps to have an artist in mind when writing, because then you have a purpose, clarity, and something to focus on. Even when I may not be in the middle of a specific project, I'll pretend I'm writing for a particular artist—just to have that focus.

Batiste: How did your collaboration with Michael Masser and Gerry Goffin on the classic "Miss You Like Crazy," recorded by Natalie Cole, come about?

Glass: "Miss You Like Crazy" was an idea I had sitting around when Narada Michael Walden and I were working on the second Whitney Houston album. Michael Masser contacted my co-publisher and asked if we could write something together. I showed him the idea—which he loved; and then, subsequently, he added some verse melodies and modulations. He then contacted Gerry Goffin to finish up the lyric.

Batiste: What is the key to your success as a songwriter and producer?

Glass: I think one of the main keys to success is recording a song that has a combination of accessibility and uniqueness. I tell young writers to always write and compose from their heart, no matter what music trends are going on currently. The verse and hook melodies should be so catchy that anyone anywhere can sing them. Also recording the best performance possible from the artist is crucial in making a connection with the listener.

When working with an artist in the studio, the comfort level between the artist and myself is very important. I try to make sure they are comfortable with me and comfortable in the studio. It's vital to consider the artist's needs and wants. So, if they want to start the vocal session every day at midnight because that's when they feel they can sing the best, well then, that's what we'll do.

12
D.I.Y. Masters—Finding Success Without a Major Record Label

A decade ago, the thought of an artist achieving success without the backing from a major record label or distributor was nearly impossible to fathom. After all, major record labels were the powerful force fueling most successful artists' careers, providing them with marketing, distribution, tour support, and worldwide visibility, which lead to rapid and massive fanbase growth, merchandising, product endorsements, and other financial opportunities.

A major record label is defined as a global company that, along with the companies associated with its group, has more than 5 percent of sales of music and videos in the world market(s). There are only three major labels in the music industry, Universal Music Group, Warner Music Group, and Sony Music. These major record labels are huge corporate parent companies that own a variety of several subsidiaries or smaller record labels operating under its umbrella. For example:

Sony Music Entertainment ownership includes Columbia Records, RCA Records, Epic Records, Legacy Recordings, Sony Music Latin, Sony Classical, The Orchard/RED Music, and many others.

Warner Music Group's ownership includes Maverick Records, Flagship Labels, Atlantic Records Group, Electra Music Group, Alternative Distribution Alliance, Rhino Entertainment, and Reprise Records, and many others.

Universal Music Group's ownership includes Interscope Records, Geffen Records, A&M Records, Motown Records, Polydor Records, Decca Records, Capitol Music Group, Republic Records, Island Records, Mercury Records, and Def Jam Recordings.

There are also many independent record labels signed to subsidiary labels. For example, Interscope Records is a subsidiary of the Universal Music Group, but smaller labels like Aftermath Entertainment and Top Dawg Entertainment are affiliated with Interscope Records.

The biggest advantage of being signed to a major label or a subsidiary of a major label is their ability to do the lion's share of the work in terms of financial backing, company departments, and the use of their many resources on behalf of the artist. The main departments of a record company and a brief mention of their operational functions include the following:

Business affairs—Manages the record label finances such as accounting and payroll

Artists and repertoire (A&R)—Searches for and secures new talent and works hands-on with the artists regarding song and producer selection, recording budget, and image. The A&R person is the liaison between the artist and the record label's other departments.

Legal—Administers the contractual matters such as contracts made between artists and record labels, contracts with other companies, legal issues such as lawsuits that may arise, and all other legal responsibilities.

Marketing—Oversees strategic marketing planning and coordination for promotion, including cross-promotion, sales campaigns, and publicity.

Promotion—The main job of the promotion department is securing both terrestrial and internet radio airplay as well as video outlets.

New media—This department is responsible for creating and promoting the artist's internet presence, such as streaming, playlist curation, and videos.

Sales—This department handles all aspects of sales of the product, making sure all distribution outlets are serviced with the product.

Public relations (PR)—This department arranges publicity opportunities such as television and radio appearances, online/print interviews, and online/print record reviews.

Art department—Oversees the production of the album cover design, layout, posters for advertising promotion, retail merchandise sales, and social media.

As you can see, major labels have many departments and sufficient finances to properly promote and market a product. In addition, they can provide the artist opportunities to connect with high-profile music industry professionals and media outlets. With all of the services and support a major label offers the artist, it seems that success would almost be guaranteed. However, despite these many advantages of being signed to a major label, there are just as many reasons an artist may not desire to sign with a major label. Some of the main reasons why artists are hesitant about signing with a major label are as follows:

- It's easy to get lost among a large roster of artists. If your record is experiencing slow launching sales, it is more likely that artists with a better selling product will rise to the label's priority status. The same will become true if the person who loved your music and signed you to the label loses their job. Now you may be in a position where no one is at the forefront advocating and pushing your music.
- There are not very many opportunities to develop personal business relationships with the team of people working with your music.
- You may lose rights of ownership to your masters and possibly publishing as well.

- You may lose creative control over music, merchandise, and artwork. Many major labels who make large investments in their artist want to obtain creative control over the artist's music.
- It's difficult to sign with a major label due to various reasons such as low fanbase numbers, age of the artist, or the music being non-mainstream or deemed by the record label as unmarketable.
- The artist royalty revenue is low. The artist royalty rate ranges from 10 to 20 percent of net profits. However, all of the monies for recording and marketing expenses such as the recording budget, marketing, promotion, and PR are being recouped from the artist royalties before the artist receives a penny. Unless the artist sells a large amount of product, they usually do not receive much revenue in the end. The independent artist who sells 10,000 copies at $15.00 per copy of their product, will gross $150,000 and will make a considerable amount more in revenue than an artist who sells 100,000 copies at $15.00 per copy, grossing $1.5 million on a major label. In this scenario, the independent artist in most cases will walk away with a $90,000 surplus if they can keep their expenses below $60,000, as opposed to the major label artist who stands a great chance of walking away with little to no royalties at all. The main reason for the huge discrepancy between the independent and major label artists is the recouping process of the major label.

The recoupable expenses are monies that are reimbursed to the record label by the artist and deducted from the artist's royalties before the artist is paid. For example, the recording budget, marketing and promotion costs, music video production, touring, legal, publicity costs, and royalty advances paid to the artist are all recoupable expenses. In many cases, a major label may spend well over a million dollars to market and promote an artist. This is how a recording artist can end up with little or no revenue from major label royalties. One of the most common factors that impact the bottom line of both the independent and major artists is the matter of the marked-up retail price versus the wholesale price. Also, both the independent and major label artists must factor in free and discounted promotional products, coupons, rebates, and so on. The royalty rate for the artist signed to the major label is based on the much lower wholesale price.

For these reasons, most artists have replaced the notion of seeking record and publishing deals and the idea of "being discovered" with the reality of building their empire from the ground level up using alternative avenues. Although the independent artist may not have the financial backing to support a large recording or marketing budget like a major label, technology has made it possible to make high-quality recordings at a much lower cost and to promote and advertise with internet marketing.

Grammy Award winner Chance the Rapper is probably the best-known example of an independent recording artist who had commercial success without selling physical copies of his music. His breakthrough album, *Coloring Book*, was the first streaming-only album in *Billboard* magazine charts history. Before his breakthrough album, he released a series of free mixtapes on DatPiff. DatPiff is an online distribution platform that allows users to download mixtapes for free. His motivation to release mixtapes for free derived from the desire to offer his best work without the restrictions of a major label. Chance the Rapper's marketing strategy was to simply build a loyal fanbase. He felt that a loyal fanbase was more valuable than selling his music. What fan wouldn't appreciate receiving quality music from one of their favorite artists for free? Making his music available for free gave Chance the Rapper an opportunity to be exposed to more listeners. He knew that collaborations with high-profile artists would strengthen his popularity. He was able to increase his fanbase by collaborating with popular recording artists, such as Kanye West, Lil Wayne, 2 Chainz, Jeremih, and Young Thug. Chance the Rapper released *Coloring Book* exclusively on Apple's streaming service for two weeks for free before making it available in other places. He mainly earns his income from selling merchandise, touring, and endorsement deals.

Chance the Rapper's team includes his manager Pat Corcoran, who had practically no management experience when he met Chance the Rapper through mutual friends; booking agent Cara Lewis (former agent at Creative Artists Agency), whose clients include Eminem, Khalid, and Travis Scott; and publicist, Dan Weiner (Weiner Media) whose clients include Childish Gambino.

Although it has become increasing easier for do-it-yourself artists to achieve success, the music industry remains very competitive for them in terms of sharing the streaming market and social media platforms with major artists. Being well-informed, creative, and strategic is needed to best the best advocate for one's career. Now, let's hear from a few D.I.Y. artists.

I had an opportunity to interview four other very talented and successful artists who are doing quite well without the help of a major record label. Eliminating a record label from the equation has been a rewarding experience for each of these artists and has allowed them the freedom to take more risks, create innovative marketing strategies, and ultimately create more stability and opportunities. Although their paths may vary, the common traits of courage, determination, discipline, critical thinking, charisma, patience, and tenacity are the vehicles they all used to arrive at their destinations.

Fantastic Negrito
www.fantasticnegrito.com

Recording artist Fantastic Negrito, born Xavier Amin Dphrepaulezz, is a multiple Grammy Award Winner from Oakland, California, whose music spans blues, R&B, folk, rock, gospel, and roots music. In 1996, he released an album under the name Xavier on Lexington House Records, distributed by Interscope Records. He was released from the label after a near-fatal car accident left him in a coma for several

FIGURE 12.1 Fantastic Negrito. Photo by Carol Dutra. Used with permission.

weeks. In 2007, he stopped making music. In 2014, he reinvented himself as Fantastic Negrito and returned to the music business, forming Blackball Universe, a multimedia collective created to serve as support for struggling black artists. Blackball Universe consists of writers, artists, directors, and editors as well as musicians. His first full album on his Blackball Universe label, *The Last Days of Oakland*, released in 2016, won a Grammy award for Best Contemporary Blues Album at the 60th Annual

Grammy Awards. In 2019, his second album, *Please Don't Be Dead* won in the same category for the 61st Annual Grammy Awards. His third critically acclaimed album, *Have You Lost Your Mind Yet?* won a Grammy Award in 2021. Fantastic Negrito is an international star who spends most of his time touring the world with his four-piece band and operating his recording studio and record label, Storefront Records, in the Oakland neighborhood where he grew up. Storefront Records opened in 2021 and is operated by a collective of artists and musicians.

Art

Batiste: Upon your return to the music business in 2014 after dropping out in 2007, you reinvented yourself musically and image-wise. What inspired you to form your own company, Blackball Universe, to handle the management and release of your music?

Negrito: I was inspired to form Blackball Universe because I never really felt like I fit in anywhere. I always felt like I was on the outside of the recording industry, and so I wanted to connect with other like-minded artists and creative types. One day I just finally admitted that I really couldn't do it by myself, that I needed to surrender some of the power and work with the other artists. I hope to build Blackball Universe into a powerhouse art-music-film collective one day. That is my alternate dream.

The team behind Blackball Universe's success is its co-founder, creative partner, and childhood friend, Malcolm Spellman; Fantastic Negrito's co-managers, Field and Phil Green; and audio engineer, Migui Maloles. His latest team with Storefront Records includes musician Tomas Salcedo, administrator/planner, Abu Abraham, and photographer, Carol Dutra.

Batiste: How did your professional name, Fantastic Negrito, come about?

Negrito: I came up with the name Fantastic Negrito to give the respect and honor to all of the human lives that lay the very foundation that we all build upon now. So many talented, brave, courageous souls with no names sacrificed their freedom, blood, sweat, tears, and lives so that we could stand here and pick from the beautiful garden of black roots music. When I imagined Fantastic Negrito, I was thinking of the greats Robert Johnson, Skip James, Howlin' Wolf, and Charlie Patton. These are amazing contributors and architects of popular culture.

Batiste: Tell me about your creative and recording process.

Negrito: I like to write and compose on the piano and guitar. I wrote my album, *Please Don't Be Dead* on an $89 bass guitar. In terms of perfecting my craft of songwriting, I am still learning. I am still reaching. I am still suffering. I am still striving. It is a very humbling process that is ongoing.

I am inspired by things that are happening all around me. This is usually very organic, and it just happens every day—life, death, stress, happiness, and sorrow, this is what inspires me to create. I am inspired by injustice. I am inspired by the underdog. I am inspired by perseverance, by human stories of surviving the worst. Taking the bullshit and turning it into good shit.

There is no set process in terms of my approach to writing songs. Usually, it's just an idea with a guitar or a voice on a piano. Very basic. This is step one. Step two is attempting to tell the truth, to tell the story, and that is usually the hardest part.

As a record producer, the most important thing for me in the recording process is comfort. It's important to stay connected to the vibration that got us all here. Tell the truth in that recording session. So that makes recording very cathartic. It can start with hand claps, humming—anything.

Batiste: You are a very charismatic performer! No matter the size of the venue, you manage to create a very intimate and engaging environment. Who is your audience and what do you think is the key to keeping them engaged?

Negrito: My audience is very interesting. I call them #negritonation. I feel like they are a lot like me—the ones that never really fit into the world's repressed fantasy of how people should be. I think they're people that felt left out. The freaks, the outcast, the rebels, the injured, the anti-hipsters. They are young or old, of every nation, every religion, every creed, every persuasion. They are my family. It's very humbling. The thing that matters the most is to make the connection with the audience. The human connection is the key to a great live performance. For me, a live performance, a concert, is a lot like group therapy. I call it to church without religion. I think I learned this from watching all the greats.

Batiste: What do you want most for your audience to experience from your live performances?

Negrito: Inspiration, human connection, group therapy, unity, liberty, inspiration. I hope that we can all get together in a live performance and exorcise our demons. That's why I call it the church without religion.

Meklit Hadero
www.meklitmusic.com

Meklit is an Ethiopian American vocalist, songwriter, composer, and cultural activist, making music that sways between cultures and continents. Known for her electric stage presence, innovative take on Ethio-Jazz, and her emotive live shows, Meklit has rocked stages from Addis Ababa (where she is a household name) to San Francisco (her beloved home-base), to NYC, London, Montreal, Nairobi, Rome, Zurich, Helsinki, Rio, Cairo, and more.

Meklit is a National Geographic Explorer, a TED Senior Fellow, and a 2019 Artist-in-Residence at both Harvard University and Yerba Buena Center for the Arts in San Francisco, CA. She has received musical commissions from Lincoln Center and the MAP Fund and is a featured singer in the UN Women theme song. Her TED

FIGURE 12.2 Meklit Hadero. Photo By Paul Chinn/*The San Francisco Chronicle* via Getty Images.

Talk—The Unexpected Beauty of Everyday Sounds—has been watched by more than 1.2 million people, and her music videos air daily on Ethiopian National Television.

Since 2010, Meklit has released three solo albums with a new one on the way, and three collaborative albums. Her most recent record, "When the People Move, the Music Moves Too (Six Degrees)" reached number four on the iTunes World Charts, number one on the NACC World Charts, and number 12 on the World Charts in Europe. It was named among the best albums of the year by the Sunday Times UK and Bandcamp and featured collaborations with world-renowned musicians Preservation Hall Jazz Band and Andrew Bird.

Art

Batiste: When did you know that you wanted to be a professional artist? Did you have an influence/mentor? Was there an experience?

Hadero: I always knew I wanted to be a singer. My mother says I sang before I spoke. . . . she says I was coo-ing in tune long before my tongue could form words. My father says that at three years old, I would ask people in the elevator or on the bus if they wanted to hear a lullaby. Many years later, with a degree in political science from Yale under my belt, I moved to San Francisco and finally let myself take the dream seriously. Here, I met visual artists and musicians who were creating art in a way that was meaningful and connected to the world around them. That community became my role model, my band, my audience. Things grew from there.

Batiste: What instruments do you play?

Hadero: I play guitar and krar, a traditional Ethiopian six-string harp.

Batiste: How did you learn the craft of songwriting?

Hadero: Once I moved to San Francisco I started taking voice lessons, which was a revelation to me. Soon after, I found the Young Musicians Scholarship at Blue Bear School of American Music. It was given annually to young musicians aged 12 to 25 to take classes there. I was in the last year of eligibility for the scholarship, and I got it. The photo for that year looks like I was the leader of a child band because all the others scholarship recipients were like 14, 12, 17. It was funny, but I didn't care. Whatever it takes. At Blue Bear, I took a songwriting class with Bonnie Hayes, which opened my eyes. My first album of songs just came naturally from there. After that, I had to get to the craft part. In 2013, I met multi-Grammy-winner Dan Wilson (Adele, John Legend, Nas, Pink) at the TED Conference where I was performing and speaking as a TED Senior Fellow. We became friends, worked on an album together, and are currently doing another EP together. Spending time with him is always serious songwriting school. For me, songwriting is a mix of discipline and mystery. It took me about ten years of writing to be able to understand that.

Batiste: Does your experience as a TED Global Fellow impact or influence your songwriting? If so, in what ways do they intertwine?

Hadero: TED has just taken me all over the world, which is a constant inspiration for songwriting. I've been to TED Conferences in Brazil, Scotland, Tanzania, and many in the US. Travel always opens your eyes.

Batiste: What is your songwriting process—(what idea generally comes first—title, lyric, music, everything all at once)?

Hadero: Melodies usually just come to me, and I sing them into my phone and keep a bank of them. Then, when it's time to make an album, I am in my studio every morning. I start first thing, no internet, no email, no news. Just straight from the dream world to the song world. Often, I'll start with that bank of melodies and just listen. What grabs my attention? What is speaking to me? I'll ask myself, is this a bass line, a horn line, a lead melody? I'll record a rhythm that fits, sing the melody on top, start improvising words. I try to ask what the melody is trying to tell me, what's its story. When I get stuck, water is usually a really big help . . . A walk near the ocean, but also simpler things like washing dishes, a shower, or splashing my face somehow always brings lyric ideas out. I love the excavation of it. The sense that you're finding something, not necessarily creating it. I love the humility of being a vessel.

Batiste: What is your collaborating process?

Hadero: It depends. When I was songwriting a lot with Quinn Deveaux we would always trade a piece of paper back and forth, try to finish each other's lyric lines, and sentences, really meld our minds so that you couldn't divide who did what.

Batiste: What is your recording process?

Hadero: I record live with a rhythm section. I love my band a lot and the feeling we have together has been developing for years. Recently I took them home to Ethiopia with me and that just deepened the whole thing. You can hear the hang and the friendship in how we sound. I want to give listeners the experience of our chemistry, as well as our musicianship. That happens from playing together and making that the basis of an album.

Batiste: Your music is a rich and tasty gumbo of African, folk, jazz, soul, and Ethiopian culture. How did you find your audience (discover who to target your music toward), and how much consideration do you give your audience in the creative process if at all?

Hadero: My early audiences were San Francisco–based and I found them by just playing all the time, especially at the Mission Arts and Performance Project (MAPP), a free street-level arts event that I was also co-curating. I got my first booking agent through Facebook. She found a post from a mutual friend and said, hey I love what you're doing—let me take you to some festivals. Things took off from there. Now, interestingly, my biggest audience is in Ethiopia. I'm such a huge star there that I can't walk down the street. My videos are on TV daily. That audience has very different needs than my American and European audiences. For them, I need to sing in Amharic. So, I'm always really aware of where things will hit. But sometimes they overlap! So for example, when I recorded my version of the Ethiopian traditional song "Kemekem (I Like Your Afro)," it was a huge hit in Ethiopia. At the same time, that love of the Afro and African diaspora black culture became big in the Black Lives Matter activist circles in California. So there are places where we can come together.

Batiste: How important is the art of live performance?

Hadero: Live performance is extremely important. For me, I want an artist to be better live than on the album. I want to feel their soul and spirit directly as an audience member. That's also what I try to give audiences. I try to be so free and so much myself on stage, that I invite others into that sense of expansion too. It's a blast.

Business

Batiste: How/when did you know you could have a successful career as an artist without the help of a major record label or distributor?

Hadero: To be honest, I never really thought about the major labels as my main goal. I thought a lot more about the life and lifestyle I wanted to live. First, I wanted to work for myself, set my schedule, be in charge of my own time. I wanted my creativity to be the engine of my life, to write great songs, to be in my joy and purpose. I wanted to be able to create socially meaningful projects that harnessed the power of music to help us grow as a society. The first label I signed to was called Porto Franco Records, and it was run by a father/son duo Peter and Sergei Varshavsky. I had known Peter for years. When he came to me and said, "Let's make an album," I said no. I told him I wasn't ready. Ha! A few months later, I was like—WHAT HAVE I DONE?? I called him back and told him I wanted to move forward. So, we did. Porto Franco gave me all the freedom and support, and my first record, "On A Day Like This," really did well in terms of press, sales, and launching my career. But I had zero expectations, so everything was like a wonderful surprise.

Batiste: What are your music education and business background?

Hadero: My music education has all been non-institutional. I didn't go to music school. I didn't start writing songs till I was 25 and I started playing guitar when I was 26. I've taken lots and lots of voice lessons. But I also feel that you learn by doing. In 2006 I started co-directing San Francisco's Red Poppy Art House and dedicating myself to making space for other artists. That turned out to be huge for me because I met a community of musicians who were open to being my band and my collaborators. They also became my teachers. I learned from them in all kinds of ways. In 2011, I co-founded the Nile Project, an initiative bringing together musicians from the 11 countries of the Nile (DRC Congo, Rwanda, Burundi, Kenya, Uganda, Tanzania, Ethiopia, Eritrea, South Sudan, Sudan, and Egypt). That was a music school in itself. That's where I learned to play krar (Ethiopian harp—By the way, I was born in Ethiopia). I also got deeeeeeeeep into polyrhythms, Ethio-Jazz, and just generally developed the depth of my East African sound. We would tour for months at a time, in East Africa and North America, thinking about, studying, and demonstrating the intersection of culture and ecology. That was a huge educational experience. It changed me and matured me as an artist. Those musicians don't mess around. I was surrounded by virtuosos.

Early on in my career, I also took a class at San Francisco's Women's Initiative for Self-Employment, which taught me how to run my own business. That was a whole set of skills I didn't realize I needed. As I said, you learn as you go.

Batiste: What skills other than music are required to be a successful independent artist?

Hadero: You need so many skills other than music. Sometimes it can be daunting. You need to know: accounting, financial planning, graphic design, video production, stage management, tour management, photo editing, social media management, strategic thinking, communications, networking and sustaining business relationships, band-leading, how to develop and hire a team, some understanding of what venues are looking for. You also must learn to talk about what you do and communicate why it's important to others outside of yourself. You can't just say—listen to me. You have to entice people to give you a chance. The skill sets you must develop are so numerous. I mean, it can be overwhelming. I always go back to—one thing at a time. Also—It doesn't mean you have to do all these things every day, but you have to know if the people you hire have the skills to fulfill these functions, and you must make sure they're doing a good job! On top of that, a lot of my success comes from the fact that I straddle the worlds of "arts and culture" and the music industry. So, for example, learning to write grants has been a huge support for my work. I also give lectures and workshops and work with students at universities around the country, mostly around cultural activism and social practice art. This has been what has allowed me to become a National Geographic Explorer and TED Senior Fellow, as well as doing residencies at places like Harvard University, NYU, and Yerba Buena Center for the Arts in San Francisco. It's allowed me to speak at the UN as well as be a featured voice in the UN Women theme song. It's also allowed me to get commissioned to write music from places like Lincoln Center and the MAP Fund.

Batiste: What percentage of time do you spend working on the business aspect of music; and what do you spend your time doing in both art and business?

Hadero: The pendulum swings on that. When I'm writing an album, it's a good 50 percent of my time on songwriting. Then after that, I usually have to shed the material I just wrote and that same amount of time goes to that. If I'm about to release an album, [I] have to clear [my] schedule because little things come up every day, especially around press opportunities. Then, I also have my grant writing seasons, where I'm on the computer most of the day. Every day is different, that's another thing I love about this life.

Batiste: In terms of selecting members of your team, what qualifications were you looking for to execute tasks?

Hadero: It depends on the role. Mostly, I'm looking for folks who are real go-getters, who can self-manage their time, and who are not afraid to just try and figure it out when they encounter a new problem. Honestly, that's probably the skill that's helped me the most in music. If I don't know how to do something, I'm willing to try and learn, ask for advice and help, and get better at new things. Also—there is so much uncertainty in the music industry right now, I need experimental people who have out-of-the-box ideas, but are grounded enough to answer emails when I write and be present around deadlines.

Batiste: What methods do you use to build and retain your fanbase?

Hadero: All the regular ones: social media, videos, touring as much as I can.

Batiste: What revenue stream(s) have been the most successful for you as an independent artist?

Hadero: It's all about diversification: grants, residencies, commissions, plus touring, private events, merchandise sales, giving talks to organizations and companies. Everything adds up when you put it all together, but you have to bring a lot of different bits of intelligence into your practice. Multiplicity is key.

Batiste: The way music is disseminated and consumed has changed so much over the years; what is your view on the future of the music industry?

Hadero: No one knows what's going to happen. Be experimental.

Batiste: What songwriting advice would you give to an up-and-coming artist?

Hadero: Leonard Cohen said—"If I knew where the good songs came from, I'd go there more often." In other words, embrace the mystery. Don't run from it. Also, good songs are all about volume. For every five songs I write, I keep one. Don't be discouraged by a few tunes that don't fit, and for goodness sake, don't play everything that you write. Ask trusted friends what the good ones are, keep those. As for the others, maybe you'll get a good bass line out of one, or one good lyric out of another. Just keep going. It adds up. Be patient. Be on the 50-year plan. Music is for life. Also—learn to play an instrument. Accompanying yourself and being able to communicate with other artists is so important.

Batiste: If you had to give three crucial pieces of advice about the music business, what would they be?

Hadero: Work with kind people who have your best interests in mind. Remember that that's a two-way street too.... Try to find out what is motivating others. if you help them to fulfill that, you can always create win-win situations.

Be an organizer. Don't wait for someone to come discover you. Make your momentum. Create your shows. Record in your living room. Do whatever you need to bring your music out into the world.

Know that at least in your heart, the music has to be its reward. The song itself, the lyric itself, the melody itself. The music industry has intense ups and downs, and if you get swept away by those, you'll lose your energy and bow out. Also—stardom is fickle. If the music is its reward, you will always have your motivation and you can be your light. Your light is what will attract others to you anyways. Sustain it.

Batiste: Do you have any other message (other than my questions) for songwriters regarding succeeding as an independent songwriter and/or recording artist?

Hadero: This is hard work. I work late most days, don't take too much time off, am constantly expanding my skills, growing, and stretching. It takes immense stamina. Hang out in marathon mind. Sprinters will struggle.

Cornell "CC" Carter
www.cornellcartermusic.com

Cornell "CC" Carter was born and raised in the San Francisco/Oakland Bay Area and has been recording and performing as a professional for over 30 years. Cornell Carter, professionally known simply as "CC," has been become an international success in Europe, gracing stages and entertaining thousands of fans with music released on his independent record label. He has shared the stage with the legendary James Brown, Ray Charles, and many others. He has also had the honor of recording with Grammy winner Narada Michael Walden, Carlos Santana, and the Isley Brothers, among others. He has released three highly acclaimed albums on his independent label, CDC Records. His album *One Love* is one of the hottest selling albums in the UK. The album and several singles from the album have reached number one on multiple charts. Besides CC's many performances in the UK to enthusiastic audiences and rave reviews, he is an Indie Soul Awards Nominee in several categories, including Album of the Year, Song of the Year, and Male Artist of the Year. He received the 2018 Soul Tracks Readers' Choice Award as New Independent Artist

FIGURE 12.3 Cornell "CC" Carter. Photo by Bill Gidda of Eye Media UK.

of the Year. In 2019, he released the album *Absoulutely*, which produced two UK number one singles, "I See Love" and "Say Yes." CC recently released his fifth album, entitled *Next Life*, to critically acclaimed reviews, including topping the UK charts.

Art

Batiste: As an independent artist, what music experiences were critical to your development in terms of music education, influences, and/or mentorship?

Carter: My first music experience was at the age of seven. I grew up watching my brother Donald rehearsing with his singing group and sponging it all in. I also remember at an early age seeing James Brown perform. Man, what kid wouldn't want to do the splits, get back up, and look cool doing it? However, the reality that I had a shot at pursuing a professional career as an artist was in my early 20s when I auditioned for a cover band and got the gig! My biggest drive before that had been to complete what my brother Donald started. He was a phenomenal singer and was headed for big things when, unfortunately, he was killed in an automobile accident at a young age.

I played congas as well as sung lead vocals in the cover band. One night an older gentleman pulled me to the side and said, "Son, you have a gift, and you need to get rid of those congas and come out front and take charge." At that point, I started researching by looking at footage of every great performing artist I could find to become a complete lead singer and band, frontman. I have been mentored by all the music I was exposed to while growing up. Ultimately, my two biggest musical influences are Stevie Wonder and Marvin Gaye.

Batiste: What is your songwriting process?

Carter: I usually start my songwriting process by creating the song title and/or the chorus, otherwise called the "hook," first. Sometimes I can hear a musical idea in my head and if I can't play it, I hum it to someone who can. I play a little drums and piano, which helps me express the chordal and rhythm feel when creating. My main instrument is my voice. Melodies, lyrics, and harmonies come naturally to me due to growing up in the Motown era. I gained quite a bit of knowledge from listening and watching the great R&B bands of the '70s along with some of the great musicians and songwriters in the San Francisco/Oakland Bay Area. Some of the many lyrics as well as some poetry that I have written down and forgotten about are sometimes revisited and are used in songs. I write songs based on things not only that I experience but what I see happening around the world. A songwriter should be honest about things that affect us as people of all races, cultures, and genders. I feel blessed that my music connects with audiences who love independent soul and jazz music in the United States as well as the UK, Japan, Spain, and other places in the world!

When collaborating with other writers and producers, I mainly write the lyrics, vocal melodies/harmonies, and vocal arrangements. The musical idea must speak to me personally for it to come to fruition or else it's just being forced, and I've learned through experience not to do that. The basic track must have plenty of space to create the lyric and melodic content. It's hard to write melodies and lyrics to a track that is fully produced with strings, horns, etc. because the prewritten instrumental melody lines can influence and limit your creativity. In terms of recording, record the basic music and vocal parts first, then take the time to build brick by brick, instrument by instrument, note by note, until the masterpiece is complete.

Business

Batiste: How/when did you know you could have a successful career as an artist without the help of a major record label or distributor?

Carter: My mom instilled confidence in me to always believe in myself to achieve whatever I wanted to in life. Therefore, I have always been a confident and independent-minded person. The inspiration to be an independent artist came from seeing so many of my fellow musicians who had early success with major labels and touring with big-name acts, then watching all of their success fade away, was a big lesson for me. I guess you could say that was the light bulb moment! Another light bulb moment was meeting and working with Grammy

Award-winning producer and songwriter Narada Michael Walden (NMW) in 2013. His productions include Mariah Carey, Aretha Franklin, Whitney Houston, and George Michael. Working with NMW and his company, Tarpan Records and Studios, taught me a lot about production and how to establish a team of people you can trust and rely on to implement tasks. His passion for business is just as fierce as his passion for music!

Batiste: Besides music, what other skills are necessary for an independent artist's success?

Carter: The necessary skills for an independent artist are:

- Effective communication and networking skills are the key components to success. The way you communicate with colleagues in the music industry demonstrates a certain level of professionalism.
- Marketing and promotion are essential skills that must be strategically expedited.
- Organization skills are imperative when working out the logistics of production, booking, air and ground travel, lodging, band itineraries, and performances.
- Do not be afraid to take risks. The process of putting yourself in a position to receive opportunities requires trial and error. To achieve a positive outcome, you must never be afraid to fail.
- You need the support of a trusted team of people whose enthusiasm, energy, knowledge, and work ethic are compatible with yours. Again, communication is important in team members achieving goals. You must engage in open, honest, and productive discussions that result in doing what is best even if everyone doesn't initially agree.

Batiste: What methods have been most effective in building and retaining your fanbase?

Carter: Some of the things I do to help build and retain my fanbase is speaking to as many people as I can, especially DJs and promoters around the world who play my music. They are the conduits for us as artists. I do as many radio drops and interviews as possible to promote shows. It's hard to get the outreach that you need to be successful in today's competitive market, so I go out of my way to cooperate with any idea a promoter may have to advance a show. I often have contests or give away free promotional CDs and T-shirts from time to time. However, the most effective way to build and retain your fanbase is to perform live as often as you can and to use your social media platforms to let your fans know that you are active and relevant.

Batiste: What revenue stream(s) have been the most successful for you as an independent artist?

Carter: Although Amazon, iTunes, and YouTube streams have brought in modest revenue, selling my music and merchandise at concert venues is the most profitable.

Batiste: What songwriting advice would you give to an up-and-coming singer/songwriter?

Carter: My advice to up-and-coming singer/songwriters is to be original and true to your authentic self. Too many times writers try to create a song that will sell as opposed to a song that is well-written and artistically crafted to last forever. Whatever your style is, stay with it and be as unique as you can because someone will always try to compare you to others who may have a similar style or a style that is trending at the moment. Never make the mistake of competing over creating art!

Take care of your business in terms of starting a publishing company, copyrighting, and registering your work with one of the performance rights organizations such as BMI or ASCAP. Register with SoundExchange. Create a budget for your recording and marketing, and stick to it. Keep good records of everything you spend and earn for tax purposes. Your endurance will be tested. You must be willing to hang in there through all of the disappointments of being told "No." Constantly research successful music industry marketing trends and apply those that are appropriate and relevant for your music and fanbase. Save all the money you can to promote your work because the mistake that many independent artists make is spending too much money on the recording cost (manufacturing included) and not having enough finances to promote the product. Do not release your product until the music and recording are solid, and you have a strategy and implementation plan in place.

Lastly, form your marketing and promotion team and find an independent distributor that believes in your vision and who has had some success with other independent artists.

Kev Choice
www.kevchoice.wordpress.com

Kev Choice is a rapper, educator, classically trained pianist, music and community advocate, and recording artist whose unique infusion of hip-hop, jazz, R&B, soul, and classical music puts him in a category of his own. He has released eight critically acclaimed albums and is everywhere in the San Francisco/Oakland Bay Area music scene. Kev Choice is recognized in the Bay Area for playing in venues as diverse as Yoshi's and SFJazz Center to Davis Symphony Hall, where he's performed with his Kev Choice Ensemble and jazz trio Black London; and from his touring and serving as musical director for hip-hop icon Lauryn Hill; or behind the keys accompanying or collaborating with global-local artists like Too Short, Rayana Jay, Mistah FAB, Jenn Johns, and Brookfield Duece; or touring the US and Europe with the Coup; or his commissioned compositions for the Oakland Symphony Orchestra and San Francisco Symphony orchestra; various recording projects; or musical directing live

FIGURE 12.4 Kev Choice. Photo by Ariel Nava, used with permission.

shows at events. Kev Choice is the epitome of a successful independent self-made artist!

Art

Batiste: At what age did you know you wanted to be a performer?

Choice: I think I was about nine or ten years old when I realized I wanted to be a performer. I was heavily influenced by music my mom played around the house and what I heard on the radio. That "aha" moment was watching the movie *Purple Rain*. I was so fascinated with Prince and his band and the energy and emotions brought to audiences when they performed in that movie, I started mimicking every move. Then when *Under the Cherry Moon* came out, in which Prince played the role of a piano-playing gigolo in the French Riviera, I instantly wanted to learn piano and speak French! That all made me want to be a performer and musician. I think I wanted to be a professional artist when I started going to studios and got booked and paid for my first shows and sessions in junior high school. I realized I could do this for the rest of my life and wanted to get rich and famous. My mom also worked for a local record label, so I saw some behind-the-scenes action of how a label was run, shows were booked, the artist recorded, etc. Also, seeing an artist I went to junior high and high school with start getting record deals and start having big records like "I Got 5 On It" and "93 Tip Infinity," I saw then that it was possible.

I started off writing poems, just to express my little crushes on little girls in elementary school. I had an uncle who was a rapper and he sat me down one day and started explaining to me how to write bars and verses and what a 16-bar verse meant. Then I started crafting raps and hooks like the songs I heard on the radio.

Batiste: Each of your project titles consists of compositions that are cohesively focused on a theme. When working on an album project, do you solely focus on that project, or do you work on multiple projects simultaneously?

Choice: I tend to work on one project at a time. I like to think of my projects as complete bodies of work that tell a story conceptually and musically. I may go back to old ideas musically and reshape and restructure them to fit into the current framework of what I'm working on, but I like to be in a certain vibe and mood when I'm working on a project to make it all connect.

Batiste: What is your songwriting process?

Choice: I have various methods of writing a song. Sometimes I sit down at the piano and start searching for chords and a progression and build a melody off that. Often concepts or ideas pop in my head and I just take out my phone and record a voice memo so I can work on it later. I also always keep a notepad on me and am often just scribbling down ideas or concepts that I may come back to later, or sometimes never. I'm often most inspired by what the music is expressing to me or how it is making me feel.

Batiste: What is your recording process?

Choice: I usually tend to produce a musical idea before I start adding vocals. Sometimes I go in after a vocal and chorus are recorded to a beat and add live instrumentation, more vocal sections, but if I did that I would usually go back and do the main vocals again to fit the feel. There are times when I just have a chorus and one verse and I may not come back and write the second and third verses until much later.

Batiste: Due to your very versatile artistry, your audience is very diverse in age, music genre, and gender. How much consideration do you give your audience in the creative process if at all?

Choice: The main thing I think about as far as the audience is how it will make people feel and if I'm being real and true to who I am. I don't think much about age or demographics. I do try to consider how it will connect with people, if it will have a positive impact, is it something I want the youth to hear and feel good about, will it shed light on something that needs to be spoken out about, am I being genuine to who I am, and am I pushing myself musically to a high level.

Batiste: What do you want most for your audience to experience from your live performances?

Choice: A journey, from beginning to end. A journey where you never know where it may go, but you can connect with it, learn from it, experience something new, and most importantly feel it and be inspired by it. I want them to experience something that is rooted in hip-hop, but incorporates and encompasses so many different genres, and in an authentic way. I want them to expect the unexpected and be open and free as I try to be when I create.

Business

Batiste: You are an emcee, educator, classically trained pianist, jazz and hip-hop musician, composer, producer, and performer. Most artists would choose only one of the disciplines to pursue at a time. By combining all of your talents into your artistry, you've created your very own unique category as an artist, which took a lot of courage, to pursue a career in uncharted territories. How/when did you know you could have a successful career as an artist without the help of a major record label or distributor?

Choice: Initially, I also had the hopes and dreams of getting signed and being on a major label. I think when I saw it wasn't happening, and I learned more about the business from other artists I worked with, from touring and performing on my own, I realized I would be best suited to push myself independently, but it was mainly out of necessity. I didn't want to wait for someone to recognize me or sign me when I knew I had talent, good music, and a vision. I decided I was going to go just as hard pushing myself, my music, my band, my message, as a label does pushing their artist.

Batiste: What is your music business background?

Choice: I gained most of my music business background from experience. My degree is in music (piano performance), which focuses heavily on the performance aspect of the instrument and hardly any on the business aspects. After graduating with my master's degree, I came home and had to start from scratch and learn how to get out and find gigs and build a career. I learned a lot just from being out on the scene, having mentors, and from making mistakes.

Batiste: What skills other than music (i.e., communication, organizational, etc.) are required to be a successful independent artist?

Choice: The biggest skills you have to have are more like personal qualities. You have to above all, have tremendous belief and faith in yourself and what you are trying to accomplish; without that, you won't get far. Of course, you need to be able to be a leader to help dictate and facilitate those who you will need to assist you, whether that be musicians or behind-the-scenes people. You must be a visionary, having the ability to dream something, execute it, then get out and push it to the people to garner support to be able to continue to create what you envision.

Batiste: What percentage of time do you spend on music versus business; and what do you spend most of your time doing in both areas?

Choice: I try to keep it balanced like 50/50. I have to spend a considerable amount of time working on the music and the craft, but it's also important to handle the business aspects. If I feel one taking over, I have to find a way to make up for it or compensate. In an ideal world, it'd be 80/20 in favor of the music. That's the goal for me personally, to push the art to high levels and create content that will garner more streams of revenue. For music, I spend the most time in the studio working on production, writing songs, or rehearsing with my band or various bands for shows and events. I also spend a considerable amount of time just trying to practice on the piano. Business-wise, I spend a lot of time at meetings, discussing partnerships, events, and strategies to push the music and build the brand. I also spend a lot of time online, sending emails, responding to gig requests, pushing, promoting, and providing content on social media and sites, which is very crucial. I also spend a lot of time networking, being at events, being visible in the community, being part of organizations in the music community and local community as well.

Batiste: What does your team consist of?

Choice: Right now, my team is my head, my mind, and my soul. LOL. But seriously, I don't have a manager, booking agent, or label, but I do have a great network of musicians, friends, and other creatives who assist me. I have an incredible band, and collectives or artists and friends who support me, and we work closely together performing, recording, doing community work, and supporting each other in every which way possible. I also have a solid videographer who helps document events, a photographer, and a business consultant, basically, a homie who I run ideas by. I'm in the process of meeting with a financial advisor and am always looking for a manager so I can focus on the music!

Batiste: What revenue stream(s) have been the most successful for you as an independent artist?

Choice: For me, it has been doing shows. As a bandleader, musician, and artist, I make the biggest bulk of my income from performing. Selling music doesn't garner as much income as it used to, so being able to create events, get booked at venues, festivals, private events, corporate events, and throughout the community helps me sustain and maintain.

Batiste: If you had to give 3 crucial pieces of advice about the music business, what would that advice be?

Choice:
1. You have to be willing to work as hard as possible, and just as hard or harder than everyone. It's not a competition, but you are always fighting to maintain relevance, keep an audience, and push your brand.
2. Learn from others, but also know everyone's path is different and unique. Some people blow up quickly then fall off just as fast and never reach that status again. Some people work hard all their lives and get a big break years later. Always, think about longevity and providing quality that will help maintain a career that will last as long as you desire to stay in it.
3. Never stop learning! Never stop mastering your art and learning more about how to get your art to the world and make a living from it. It's a never-ending process!

Batiste: Thanks Kev. I appreciate you!

Choice: My pleasure!

Although the artists in this chapter may have taken different paths, each one of them has embraced their independence with confidence and has managed to create and develop a satisfying and legitimate career path that has enabled them to express their individuality and maintain financial and artistic control. I applaud them and all artists who take the D.I.Y. approach to building a music career for all failures and successes are a direct result of their efforts, capabilities, and tenacity.

Index

For the benefit of digital users, indexed terms that span two pages (e.g., 52–53) may, on occasion, appear on only one of those pages.

Note: Figures and boxes are indicated by an italic *f* and *b* following the page number.

accents, 5, 14, 41–42, 43, 63–65
accidentals in music theory, 49
action, in opening lines, 97
adjective and noun exercise, 22–24
administrative skills, 10
advertising digital music, 157–58
affiliate marketing, 157
Amazon Music, 170
Apple Music, 170
Apple Music Radio, 193*b*
arrangements of songs, 4–5
artistic freedom, 20
Asher, Peter, 163*f*, 163–65
attitude in songwriting career, 142
augmented triads, 57*f*, 57

"Baby, It's Cold Outside" (Loesser), 96
"Bad Day" (Powter), 167–68
Bandcamp, 170
bank account, 130
Barias, Ivan, 30*f*, 30–33
bass clef, 50*f*, 50–51
bass line, 20–21, 34–35, 45, 58, 75, 86, 207, 210–11
Beatles, 90
Beyonce, 154–55
Black Eyed Peas, 27
Blogs, 171
bonding, as concept, 26–27
Bourne, Scott, 187
brain freeze, 22
Braxton, Toni, 92
bridge section, 36–37, 95
B section. *See* pre-chorus/B section

cable-based radio, 187, 190
call-and-response technique, 67, 77, 80–81, 96–97
Cardi B, 167
career-building skills, 5–6
Carter, Cornell "CC," 211–15, 212*f*
catchy title, 21
"Celebration" (Kool & the Gang), 81

Chance the Rapper, 201–2
character traits, 5–7
Childish Gambino, 27
chords
    diatonic chords, 55, 60*f*, 60, 61
    dominant seventh chord, 59*f*, 59
    in music theory, 55–57
    progressions, 61–62, 62*b*, 62*f*
    structure of, 4–5, 58
chorus/refrain
    lyrics in, 94–95, 96*b*, 97
    overview, 36
    pre-chorus/B section, 21, 34–35, 36, 94, 109
    title of song in, 22, 24
chorus-verse combination, 96–97
chromatic scale, 49*f*, 49
circle of fifths, 54, 55*f*
clefs
    bass clef, 50*f*, 50–51
    in music theory, 50–51
    treble clef, 50*f*, 50–51
coda section, 37
collaboration
    Barias on, 32
    Carter on, 213
    digital music, 158
    DJ Toomp on, 104
    Glass on, 198
    Hadero on, 207
    Hayes on, 114–15
    McKinney on, 185
    Pessis on, 148
    Remi on, 17
    songwriting career, 131, 138, 192
    Walden on, 85, 86–87
Coloring Book (Chance the Rapper), 201–2
communication skills, 9
composers, 20, 93, 98, 125, 126–27, 139–40, 192, 205, 218
concept development, 25–29

contrast
  in harmony, 67
  in melody, 66
  in rhythm, 65–66
  in song sections, 35
  in song sounds, 65–67
controversy, as concept, 27–29
copyright, 122–23, 127–29, 183
countermelody, 67–68, 80–81
country music genre, 70–71
creativity
  Barias on, 31–32
  DJ Toomp on, 103
  Fantastic Negrito on, 204–5
  of lyrics, 93
  Remi on, 18
"Crzy" (Kehlani), 107
cue sheets, 124–25

demo songs, 135–37
detail, in opening lines, 97
diatonic chords, 55, 60f, 60, 61
dictionary use, 90
digital music
  advertising, 157–58
  collaborations, 158
  cross-marketing, 158
  defined, 150
  distribution of, 153–54
  income from, 152
  livestreaming, 160–61
  marketing and promotion, 154–56, 157–58
  payment from, 151–53
  playlists, 161–62
  reasons for, 150
  release of, 158–60
  selling online, 152–53
  social media and, 156–57
  streaming music, 150–51, 170–71
digital performance royalties, 125–26
diminished triads, 57f, 57
disc jockey (DJ), 40–41, 48, 70, 103–4, 214
distribution of digital music, 150, 153–54
DistroKid, 154
Dixie Chicks, 28
DJ Toomp, 103–4
dominant seventh chord, 59f, 59
Dozier, Lamont, 44f, 44–46
"Dreams" (Fleetwood Mac), 110
drivers in songwriting, 34–35

e-commerce, 181–82
education for songwriting career, 130, 143b
Electronic Dance Music (EDM), 40–41

electronic press kit (EPK), 171, 192
email marketing, 157
email newsletters, 173–74, 179
ending section, 36, 37, 79, 88
essential elements in songs, 42
euphemisms, 22
"Every Breath You Take" (Sting), 93

Facebook, 170, 181
false rhyme, 99
fanbase
  audience message, 169–70
  building of, 183–84
  e-commerce and, 181–82
  Hadero on, 210
  image and, 167–68
  importance of, 166–67
  income streams, 181–83
  live performances, 176–81
  promotional tools, 171–75, 178–79
  scheduling strategies, 178
  social media and, 166–67, 169–70
  subscriptions, 182–83
Fantastic Negrito (Xavier Amin Dphrepaulezz), 202–5, 203f
fear of nonacceptance, xiii
feminine rhyme, 99
fictitious name statement, 129
film music, 126–27
first position of note, 58, 59f
first-year plan, 132–33
Fleetwood Mac, 110
flexibility with rewriting songs, 106
friendship, as concept, 26–27

Glass, Preston, 197f, 197–98
goal setting, 10, 130–31
good times, as concept, 27
gospel music genre, 73
Graham, Lukas, 97
grand staff, 51f, 51
"Grenade" (Mars), 75
groove, 36, 45, 63–65, 65f, 69–70, 74, 84, 86, 114
guitar riff, 20–21, 36, 68

Hadero, Meklit, 205–11, 206f
harmony
  contrast in, 67
  lyrics and, 41
  understanding of, 4–5, 41–42
Harry Fox Agency, 123–24
Hayes, Bonnie, 112f, 112–18
hip-hop music genre, 70
hit songs
  elements of, 20–21

Index

Hayes on, 116
Pessis on, 148
Remi on, 17
Walden on, 84, 86

Ibiblio, 187
"I Can't Make You Love Me" (Raitt), 92
"I Got a Feeling" (Black Eyed Peas), 27
"I Kissed a Girl" (Perry), 27–28, 29
image, 167–68
imagery, 24, 97
imagination, 14–15, 17, 90
improper grammar, 92
income streams, 181–83
independent recording artists
    benefits of being, 188
    Carter, Cornell "CC," 211–15, 212f
    Fantastic Negrito, 202–5, 203f
    Hadero, Meklit, 205–11, 206f
    Kev Choice, 215–20, 216f
independent record labels, 199–202
"In My Life" (Beatles), 90
inner rhyme, 99
innuendo, 22
inspiration
    Barias on, 31
    cell phone use in, 21
    Dozier on, 45
    Fantastic Negrito on, 204
    finding of, 13–14
    Hadero on, 206
    Hayes on, 113
    in hit songs, 20–21
    Kev Choice on, 216
    Lawrence on, 74
    for lyrics, 13
    for music, 14, 35
    for titles, 13–14, 21–25
    Walden on, 83–84
Instagram, 171
instruments
    Hadero on, 207
    Hayes on, 114
    importance of playing for songwriting, 4
    playing by ear, 4–5
    as tools to create emphasis, 41–42
    Walden on, 84
intellectual property, 123
interactive streaming, 151
internet radio
    advertising on, 189
    airing music on, 190–93
    benefits of starting, 193–96
    directories of, 195
    DIY promotion on, 191–93

    donations through, 189
    earning money through, 189–90
    independent artists and, 188
    licensing of, 194–95
    memberships through, 190
    merchandising through, 190
    overview of, 187–88
    promotion on, 191–93, 195–96
    radio promoters, 191
    sponsorships through, 189
    streaming services and, 193b
    subscriptions through, 189–90
intervals in music theory, 48–54
introduction section, 36, 94
inversions, 58, 59f
iTunes Radio, 193b

Joel, Billy, 95–96
journaling, 29

Kehlani, 107
Kelly, Tori, 167
Kev Choice, 215–20, 216f
key signature, 54, 55f
keywords in songwriting, 29, 90
Kool & the Gang, 81

Lady Gaga, 94
Lawrence, Donald, 73f, 73–74
leadership skills, 8
Library of Congress Copyright Royalty Board, 123
Lil Nas X, 155–56
limited online music license (LOML), 194
lines and spaces on music staff, 50, 51f
Linktree, 175b
listening to music, 3–4
literary skills, 9
Live365, 188
live performances
    fanbase and, 176–81
    fan engagements, 179–81
    importance of, 176–81
    scheduling strategies, 178
livestreaming, 160–61
Loesser, Frank, 96
long-term goals, 10
love, as concept, 25–26
Lyman, Edward, 187–88
lyrics
    in bridge, 95
    call-and-response technique, 67, 77, 80–81, 96–97
    in chorus/refrain, 94–95, 96b, 97
    concept development, 25–29

224 Index

lyrics (*cont.*)
   creativity of, 93
   for existing music, 99
   harmony and, 41
   Hayes on, 113
   importance of, 47
   improper grammar, 92
   inspiration for, 13
   Kev Choice on, 216–17
   Lawrence on, 74
   as memorable element, 34
   opening lines, 97
   opposite meanings, 98
   outline for, 95, 96*b*
   pronoun usage, 92–93
   Remi on, 18
   rewriting, 108–9
   rhyming, 98–99, 100*b*
   song sections and, 93–95
   story concept, 91–92
   structure of, 95–99
   tools for writing, 90–91, 91*b*
   twists on words, 98
   word selection process, 89
Lyte, Eliphalet Oram, 76–77

major key, 54, 60*f*, 60, 85
major record labels, 199–201
major scale, 52*f*, 52–53, 53*f*
major triads, 56*f*, 56. *See also* dominant seventh chord
Malamud, Carl, 187
marketing. *See also* promotional tools
   affiliate marketing, 157
   Barias on, 32
   cross-marketing, 158
   digital music, 154–56, 157–58
   email marketing, 157
   mobile marketing, 157–58
   promotional tools, 171–75
   skills needed, 9
   streaming music, 150–51, 170–71
   target market, 121, 169
   video marketing, 158
Mars, Bruno, 75, 106
masculine rhyme, 99
master license, 126
McKinney, James, 185*f*, 185–86
Mechanical Licensing Collective (MLC), 128–29
mechanical royalties, 123–24, 130
Mediabase, 190
melody
   Barias on, 32
   chord progressions and, 61
   concept development, 25, 27, 28
   contrast in, 66
   countermelody, 67–68, 80–81
   Hayes on, 116–17
   as memorable element, 34, 75–78
   note use in, 78
   pauses in, 78
   phrases and, 67–68, 80
   repetition in, 76–77
   rewriting, 109–10
   surprise elements in, 79–80
   uniqueness of, 75–78
   variation in, 77–78
   vocal range, 79
   Walden on, 84
memorization, 5, 88
metaphors, 22
middle eight section, 36, 37
Midler, Bette, 90–91
"Million Reasons" (Lady Gaga), 94
minor key, 54, 60*f*, 85
minor scale, 53*f*, 53–54, 54*f*
minor triads, 56*f*, 56, 57*f*
mobile marketing, 157–58
momentum in rewriting songs, 107
motivation concerns, 12–13
musical integrity, 18, 86–87
music genres
   country, 70–71
   gospel, 73
   hip-hop, 70
   pop music, 69
   rhythm & blues, 69–70
   rock, 71
   understanding, 68–71
music theory
   chords in, 55–57
   chromatic scale, 49*f*, 49
   clefs in, 50–51
   grand staff, 51*f*, 51
   importance of, 4–5
   intervals in, 48–54
   key signature, 54, 55*f*
   lines and spaces, 50, 51*f*
   notes in, 48–54
   numbers in, 52
   octaves in, 51–52
   scales in, 48–54
   songwriting and, 47–48, 48*f*
   triads in, 56*f*, 56–57, 57*f*

negative traits, 7
NetRadio.com, 187

Index

networking opportunities, 133–34
networking skills, 9
nonessential elements in songs, 42
noninteractive streaming, 151
nonsense titles, 24–25
notes
   first position, 58, 59*f*
   in music theory, 48–54
   root position, 58*f*, 58
   second position, 58, 59*f*
   triads, 56*f*, 56–57, 57*f*
   use in melody, 78
numbers in music theory, 52

objects in room exercise, 24
octaves in music theory, 51–52
one-sheets, 173
online community-building, 140–42
opening lines, 97
opposite meanings in lyrics, 98
originality of songs, 43
overseeing logistics, 8

paid advertising, 157
passions, 7
pauses, in melody, 78
pay-per-click advertising, 157
perfect rhyme, 98–99
performance rights organizations (PROs), 124–25, 194, 215
performance royalties, 124–25, 130
Performing Rights Society (PRS), 194
Perry, Katy, 27–28, 29, 41–42, 96–97
personality traits, 5–7
Pessis, Andre, 132–33, 147*f*, 147–49
Phonographic Performance Limited (PPL), 194
photo shoots, 168
phrases
   collecting ideas for, 90
   the driver and, 34–35
   melody and, 67–68, 80
   in songwriting, 29
   transposing of, 78
   variation in, 77
pitch in music theory, 49
placement/recording of song, 127–28, 138
playing by ear, 4–5
pop music genre, 69
postproduction skills, 8
Powter, Daniel, 167–68
pre-chorus/B section, 21, 34–35, 36, 94, 109
preferred working conditions, 7

press releases, 172
production
   Asher on, 164–65
   DJ Toomp on, 104
   Glass on, 198
   Hadero on, 207–8
   Hayes on, 114, 117–18
   Kev Choice on, 217
   Lawrence on, 74
   music theory and, 4–5
   overseeing completion of, 9
   postproduction skills, 8
   Walden on, 87–88
professional organizations, 132
progressions, 4–5, 61–62, 62*b*, 62*f*, 71
Progressive Networks, 187
promotional tools. *See also* marketing
   electronic press kit, 171, 192
   email newsletters, 173–74, 179
   internet radio, 191–93, 195–96
   for live shows, 178–79
   one-sheets, 173
   overview, 171–75
   press releases, 172
   website, 174–76
pronoun usage in lyrics, 92–93
prosody, 65
Pro Tools, 117
publishing companies, 127–29
pulse, 63–65, 70, 107, 110

Quick Response (QR) code, 175*b*

Radio306.com, 188
Raitt, Bonnie, 92, 132–33
reading importance, 14, 90
RealAudio, 187
RealNetworks, 187
recording budget, 137–38, 200, 201
recoupable expenses, 201
refrain. *See* chorus/refrain
rejection, 139–40
relative keys, 54
release of digital music, 158–60
Remi, Salaam, 16*f*, 16–19
repetition in melody, 76–77
research skills, 10
rewriting songs
   finishing with, 110
   flexibility with, 106
   importance of, 105
   lyrics, 108–9
   melody, 109–10
   momentum in, 107

rewriting songs (*cont.*)
    rhythm in, 107
    tempo in, 108
rhyming lyrics, 98–99, 100*b*
rhythm
    accents, 5, 14, 41–42, 43, 63–65, 99
    contrast in, 65–66
    groove, 36, 45, 63–65, 65*f*, 69–70, 74, 84, 86, 114
    overview, 63–65
    pulse, 63–65, 70, 107, 110
    in rewriting songs, 107
    subdivision in, 63–65
    variation in, 77
    Walden on, 85
rhythm & blues (R&B) genre, 69–70
Robinson, Smokey, 98
rock music genre, 71
root position of note, 58*f*, 58
"Row, Row, Row Your Boat" (Lyte), 76–77
royalties, 123–26, 151, 152, 201

satellite radio, 190
scales
    major scale, 52*f*, 52–53, 53*f*
    minor scale, 53*f*, 53–54, 54*f*
    in music theory, 48–54
second position of note, 58, 59*f*
self-inventory exercise
    administrative skills, 10
    career-building skills, 5–6
    character traits, 5–7
    communication skills, 9
    determining short-and long-term goals, 10
    imagination, 14–15
    importance of listening to music, 3–4
    inspiration, 13–14
    leadership skills, 8
    literary skills, 9
    marketing skills, 9
    motivation concerns, 12–13
    negative traits, 7
    networking skills, 9
    overseeing logistics, 8
    overseeing production of songs, 9
    passions, 7
    personality traits, 5–7
    playing an instrument, 4
    playing by ear, 4–5
    postproduction skills, 8
    preferred working conditions, 7
    professional characteristics, 6
    research skills, 10

    skills, 8
    starting needs, 3
    transferable skills, 10–12
semi-rhyme, 99
"7 Years" (Graham), 97
"Shape of You" (Sheeran), 41, 107, 111
Sheeran, Ed, 38*b*, 41, 107, 111
"She's Always a Woman to Me" (Joel), 95–96
"She's Leaving Home" (Beatles), 81
Shopify, 181–82
short-term goals, 10
signature riff, 68
single-word titles, 23–24
skills in self-inventory, 8
SOCAN (Society of Composers, Authors, and Music Publishers of Canada), 123–24
social media, 156–57, 166–67, 169–70
songs
    demo songs, 135–37
    essential elements, 42
    middle eight section, 36, 37
    nonessential elements, 42
    originality of, 43
    sound recording *vs.*, 122–23
    structure of, 37–41, 38*b*–40*b*
    surprise elements in, 79–80, 108
song sections. *See also* chorus
    coda, 37
    ending, 36, 37, 79, 88
    introduction, 36, 94
    middle eight, 36, 37
    overview of, 35–37, 93–95
    pre-chorus/B section, 21, 34–35, 36, 94, 109
    tag, 37
    vamp, 36, 37, 41
    verse, 36, 94, 95
song sounds
    contrasts in, 65–67
    creation of, 58–60
    inversions, 58
    signature riff, 68
songwriting
    Asher on, 164
    beginnings, 34
    bonding, as concept, 26–27
    Carter on, 213, 215
    concept development, 25–29
    controversy, as concept, 27–29
    defined, xiii
    DJ Toomp on, 104
    Dozier on, 45
    drivers in, 34–35

fear of nonacceptance, xiii
friendship, as concept, 26–27
Glass on, 197–98
goal in writing songs, 20–21
good times, as concept, 27
Hadero on, 207, 210
Hayes on, 112, 113–14
importance of, xiii
journaling, 29
Kev Choice on, 217
key points, 43
keywords in, 29
Lawrence on, 74
love, as concept, 25–26
McKinney on, 185–86
music theory and, 47–48, 48f
Pessis on, 147–48
phrases in, 29
skills development, 3
tension and release effect, 36
Walden on, 85–86
songwriting career
attitude in, 142
bank account, 130
Carter on, 212–14
challenges with, 121–22
collaborations, 131
copyright, 122–23, 127–29
demo songs, 135–37
education for, 130, 143b
fictitious name statement, 129
film and television music, 126–27
first-year plan, 132–33
goal setting in, 130–31
Hadero on, 209–11
Kev Choice on, 218–20
networking opportunities, 133–34
online community-building, 140–42
placement/recording of song, 138
publishing companies, 127–29
recording budget, 137–38, 200, 201
rejection, 139–40
royalty payments, 123–26
song vs. sound recording, 122–23
SoundExchange, 125–26
synchronization license, 126
tax identification number, 129
teamwork in, 134–35
Sonicaves.com, 187–88
Sony Music, 199
SoundCloud, 170
SoundExchange, 125–26

sound recording vs. song, 122–23
Spotify, 170
statutory rate, 123
Sting, 39, 93, 101
story concept in lyrics, 91–92
streaming music, 150–51, 170–71
subdivision in rhythm, 63–65
subscriptions, 143b, 182–83, 189–90
surprise elements in songs, 79–80, 108
synchronization license, 126

tag section, 37
target market, 121, 169
tax identification number, 129
teamwork in songwriting career, 134–35
"Tears of a Clown" (Robinson), 98, 102
television music, 126–27
tempo in rewriting songs, 108
tension and release effect, 36
terrestrial radio, 124, 162, 187, 188, 190, 194
"That's What I Like" (Mars), 106, 111
thesaurus use, 89, 90, 91b
"This Is America" (Gambino), 27
TIDAL, 170
TikTok, 155, 171
Timberlake, Justin, 92
titles
adjective and noun exercise, 22–24
catchy title, 21
collecting ideas for, 90
Dozier on, 45
incorporated into song, 40b
inspiration for, 13–14, 21–25
nonsense titles, 24–25
objects in room exercise, 24
single-word titles, 23–24
transferable skills, 10–12
treble clef, 50f, 50–51
triads in music theory, 56f, 56–57, 57f
TuneCore, 153–54
twists on words, 98
Twitter, 170

"Un-break My Heart" (Braxton), 92
Universal Music Group, 199

vamp section, 36, 37, 41
variation in melody, 38b, 77–78
verse section, 36, 94, 95, 96–97
video marketing, 158
Virgin Radio, 187–88

Index

virtual audiences, 179–81
vocal range, 79

Walden, Narada Michael, 83*f*, 83–88
Warner Music Group, 199
website, 174–76

West Coast Songwriters Conference, 132–33
"What Goes Around" (Timberlake), 92
"Wide Awake" (Perry), 96–97
"Wind Beneath My Wings" (Midler), 90–91

YouTube, 170